Polish Customs,
Traditions
and Folklore

Polish Customs, Traditions and Folklore

Sophie Hodorowicz Knab

Foreword by
Rev. Czesław Michał Krysa, M.A., S.T.L.

Illustrations by

Mary Anne Knab

HIPPOCRENE BOOKS
New York

398
KNA

Third printing, 1994.

Copyright © 1993 by Sophie Hodorowicz Knab

For information, address:
HIPPOCRENE BOOKS, INC.
171 Madison Ave
New York, NY 10016

Library Cataloging-in-Publication Data
Knab, Sophie Hodorowicz.
  Polish customs, traditions, and folklore / Sophie Hodorowicz Knab
  foreword by Czesław Michał Krysa ; illustrations by Mary Anne
  Knab.
  Includes bibliographical references and index.
  ISBN 0-7818-0068-4 (cloth)
  1. folklore--Poland. 2. Poland--Social life and customs.
  I. Title.
  GR195.K53 1993
  398.09438--dc20   92-35389
                                                         CIP

Printed in the United States of America.

Dedicated to my mother
Józefa Zalewska Hodorowicz
and the memory of the late
Józef Hodorowicz,
Franciszek and Maria Dull Zalewski,
Andrzej and Zofia Gorczyczewska Hodorowicz.

Contents

Acknowledgments

I would like to thank the following individuals and institutions whose help and understanding have made this book possible:

The Polish Community Center of Buffalo, for all the workshops and programs that helped me to grow, to experiment and to meet the people who helped shape and create this book. My special thanks to Geraldine Berezuik, past program director, and Philip Lowrey, past executive director, and Annette Junciewicz, current executive director, for their support and commitment to the Polish community;

The *Polish American Journal*. My sincerest appreciation to Larry Wroblewski who first suggested that I write for the paper, and to Mark Kohan, Carol Szczepanski, Paulette Kulbacki, Dan Haskin and Christopher Misztal, who have worked with me over the years. I also wish to extend my deepest thanks to all the readers of the *PAJ* who read my monthly articles, wrote to express their appreciation, to ask questions, offer comments, and to ask when I was going to publish a book. Their feedback kept me researching, reading, and writing;

Villa Maria College and the members of the Villa Maria College Culture Circle, under the leadership of Judy and Frank Krauza with the support of Sr. Ellen Marie Kuznicki, for extending me the privilege of borrowing from the Polish collection, inviting me to guest lecture and present my findings and gauge interest in the subject of folklore and folk customs,

POLISH CUSTOMS, TRADITIONS AND FOLKLORE

The Polish Room at State University of New York at Buffalo and its curator, Jean Dickson, for helping me in my constant quest for material on Polish customs and traditions; Niagara County Community College and all the great reference librarians at the Library Learning Center, especially my sister-in-law Sheryl Knab, for their unfailing assistance. Many thanks to Kathleen Greenfield who processed all my interlibrary loan requests and worked so diligently to make sure I received the material without delay; a special thank you to Donald Topolski in Academic Computing for seeing me through the intricacies of converting my material to IBM and WordPerfect;

Michael Drabik, who gifted me with my first copies of the Kolberg and Gloger folklore books, searched through secondhand bookstores in Poland for me, and was never too busy to aid me in my constant search for material;

Bronislaus and Anne Trzyzewski, the entire Miecznikowski family, Frank and Judy Krauza, the Rev. Czesław Krysa for sharing dinners, books, information and entering into my numerous projects wholeheartedly;

My sister-in-law, Mary Anne Knab, who willingly shared her artistic talent to provide the illustrations for this book;

Most of all to my husband Ed, who has always valued my heritage and constantly encouraged me to try whatever it was I felt like trying without worrying about success or failure. This book certainly could not have been possible without him.

To all of you, *Bóg zapłać.*

Foreword

"What time is it?"

The answer to the question "What time is it?" is probably given on innumerable occasions daily. The response might sound like this, "It's seven minutes after five," or, "It's 5:07." Yes, it's "5," "0," "7." These three numbers, then, orient our actions. They may suggest it's dinner time, it's time to pick someone up from hockey practice, or it's time to leave the job for home. All this is contained in three numbers, 5, 0, and 7. At the same time, these numbers may elicit feelings of release, anxiety, happiness, or more often than not, another errand to complete. All this in digits which count away how much time is lost or what needs to be done next.

It was the Renaissance which fixed clocks on town halls and cathedrals assisting craftsmen and merchants to manage not only their profits, but also their time efficiency. The same period in human history placed such chronometers in pockets of city dwellers, as the hands of the clock began both to embrace as well as separate human relationships.

In 1890, in a village in central Poland, a poor peasant family bought its very first wind-up clock. After learning how to operate the apparatus, they called in their neighbors to look at this new invention. All present commented and even chuckled as the clock struck and the bells rang. After the visitors had gone, the family settled for the night under feather ticks, placed on straw mattresses along the walls of the single room cottage. Night progressed to morning and mother wakened, as the early morning glow illumined the eastern sky, to mix rye flour for fresh bread.

11

Father rose with the smell of rising loaves and the children to the scent of freshly cut bread and butter. Suddenly they heard a noise, a bell! It wasn't the sound of the parish toller or even the tinkling of the mass bell. The oldest daughter ran to the hutch and brought out the new alarm clock and placed it next to the steaming bread as everyone burst into laughter. The sun had just begun to peak over the pale green rye field on the horizon. They all sat down to an early breakfast and father asked, "Who will wake us up tomorrow, the clock or the sun?"

"What time is it?" one might ask in the nineteenth century village. The answers could be it's time to make bread, it's seed-time, it's Christmas time, it's time for the baby. Even though the clock was introduced some four hundred years earlier, the village had its own system, its own folk chronometer, whose hands embraced more than a circular disk and moments were separated by events rather than by the miniature black lines of minutes and seconds. Days were marked out by the sun, by the responsibilities of family members; weeks by the "un-work" (niedziela) day or Sunday. Months were mapped with milestones called holy days (święta) according to which one would either harvest the beets or sow the grain. Years were marked out by births and deaths and the wrinkles of time which fall between them.

Time meant season, and the seasons regulated human behavior. As the winter nights prolonged darkness, the people looked to the sky for a star which would signal the beginning of the Christmas feast. During these dark nights, they in turn fashioned other stars of wood and oiled paper which were carried from house to house in order to lighten the hearts of neighbors and friends. Later as nights grew shorter, daylight warmer, and the willow branch burst forth her catkins, the planting season drew near. These same branches were cut on "flower Sunday" (Niedziela Kwietna), ushering in the rebirth of Easter each year. The bark of the branches was used to make dyes which would mark lines of life, color and renewal on eggs given to godchildren and suitor.

Each season had its holy day. These days were awaited with expectation and preparation. They were marked not only by the passing of another phase of life, but more importantly summoned family and friends to seize the power of life in festival, song, food, drink, dance and custom. This was the reason for the feast: to enter into the dynamic exchange of life and draw from it not only strength but also purpose — meaning for the days to come. Days that followed major festivals had the potency to foretell the future and could even reveal climactic conditions. (The twelve days of Christmas would forecast the weather of the next twelve months). Hay pulled from under the tablecloth at the Christmas vigil foretold both the fortune and the harvest of the coming year. Wreaths that sank in the river on the Eve of St. John prophesied another unwedded year for the girl.

The cosmic cycle wove its strands into the tethers of the human cycle. Events and memorials marked special times for particular families. Celebrations of birth, death, and marriage were regulated by herbs, myrtle, song and the exchange of significant types of food and drink. Until this day, even in the United States, the term "Polish wedding" is synonymous with a real party. As joy is feted, so the ambiguity of death is memorialized in the hope of a flickering "Thunder candle" (*gromnica*), which is always lit when tragedy threatens a home or family member.

Rather than being understood as a measure of efficiency, a digital commodity or a product to be bought, sold, sectioned off and consumed, time is an event which invites its participants to jump from its heights and plunge into the vivifying waters of life. After such a leap, those who emerge from these depths rise to live time, no longer as a sequence of problems or a confluence of tensions. They emerge from the festival, the celebration, the holy day so transformed that a mere memory (*wspomnienie*) of the event can incite tears of joy. Time is not just "money" but

13

"meaning." The meaning is drawn from a custom, a practice, a tradition that was handed down by those who have long since died, but who have never been ultimately severed from our today. This is most eloquently captured in the words sung by a soldier who bids farewell to his beloved as he goes off to war. This World War II song makes an allusion to the Christmas custom of placing of a sheaf of wheat in the "holy corner" of the home as a memorial to the ancestors of a family. The soldier sings, "If I should not return, let my brother sow the seed next spring. As the moss shrouds my bones, so will I enrich the earth. One morning, go into the field and take a rye-stalk into your hand, kiss it as you would your beloved. I will live on in the sheaves of grain." Time here is timeless. It embraces lives, rather than separates minutes from hours.

It is to this memorial, this festival, this wedding of the enduring spirit of Poland with earth from which she drew nourishment and security that this book invites all readers. This union can engender not only a greater knowledge of the customs of the land of the Wisła, San, Odra and Warta rivers, but also may initiate a greater appreciation for the gifts of the earth, a respect to treat the environment not as another commodity to be consumed, but rather as a home which must be nurtured. Such respect for tradition and surroundings is closely related to the answer a person gives the question "What time is it?"

— Rev. Czesław Michał Krysa, M.A., S.T.L.
Associate Professor of Liturgical Studies
S.S. Cyril and Methodius Seminary, Orchard Lake, Michigan
1991 Recipient of the Oskar Kolberg Award in Ethnography

Gdy nie wrócę niechaj z wiosną, rolę mą zasieje brat, kości moje mchem zarosną i użyźnią ziemi szmat. W pole wyjdź pewnego ranka, na kłos żyta dłonie złóż i ucałuj jak kochanka, ja żyć będę w kłosach zbóż.

FROM THE SONG: *Dziś do Ciebie Przyjść nie Mogę*

Introduction

This book has its origins in my interest in herbs and folk medicine. Exposed to both areas while growing up in a Polish American neighborhood, the subject grew into an interest area while studying pharmacology in nursing school, and was further fueled while taking a cultural anthropology course in graduate school. Unable to locate anything substantial on the subject in the English language during the latter experience, I began searching for material written in Polish.

As happens in the course of research, other, unlooked for information, began to cross my path. The new material soon became as engrossing as my initial quest. Harvest customs, bridestealing, ancient forms of worship, and long forgotten folktales and legends, began to give shape and substance to a distant time and people whom I could claim as my ancestors. It was the lives of my parents, grandparents and great grandparents that I was reading about, detailed with a depth and richness that was certainly too fascinating to simply keep confined within the darkness of a closed notebook.

While there has always been a dedicated group of Polish Americans who actively lived and promoted the customs, traditions, arts and literature of Poland, the last ten years has seen a substantial escalation in heritage clubs, geneology groups, dance groups, as well as Polish folk arts and festivals. I believed that, given the paucity of information about Polish folk life in the English language, there were other individuals much like myself who had already exhausted what was available, were seeking more information and were perhaps experiencing the same frustrations as I had earlier. This belief was affirmed when I began receiving numerous letters from the readers of the *Polish American Journal* where my first articles began to appear. They not only enjoyed what they read but wanted to learn much, much more.

The readership fell into a variety of groups. The first group were individuals who practiced many of the Polish traditions, but wished to enlarge their fund of information on the lesser known customs and activities of their forefathers. The second group of readers were third and fourth generation Polish Americans who vaguely remembered "sharing a wafer at Christmas" but forgot why they had done it and how it was done. Could I send them some information? I also heard from a third group. These were not Polish Americans but various individuals from all walks of life — folklorists, historians, and educators — who would either write or call, asking for various specific information on the subject of Polish customs and traditions. Subsequently, in this book I have tried to be as specific and detailed as my findings allowed, trying to include the well known, the lesser known, and the more obscure, to meet the needs of anyone who might be interested enough to open its cover.

Many of the customs and traditions found herein are extinct even in today's Poland. World wars, massive immigration, the loss of the oral tradition, urbanization and politics have changed the face of a once agrarian people and their accompanying life style. In the U.S., the desire for membership within the "melting pot," marriages outside one's ethnic group, movements to the suburbs away from the "old" communities where customs and traditions were once strong, further weakened the link. Careful examination of old photographs, however, reveals a newly christened male infant being placed under a kitchen table as late as the early 1960's. Other photographs can trace the celebrations of Blessed Mother of the Herbs, Corpus Christi processions, the blessing of food on Easter Saturday and of throats on the feast of St. Blaze and the keeping of the thunder candle in the home through the generations. Although the purpose and meaning may have been lost and forgotten, the *oczepiny* ceremony (the unveiling) is still the mainstay of almost every wedding where the bride declares Polish heritage. Many Polish American communities still reenact the harvest celebrations, reminding themselves of their ancestor's reverence for the grains and gifts of bread. Eight million Americans still claim their ancestry as Polish, many still diligently practicing that which they learned at their parents' and grandparents' knees. Much has also been neglected or completely forgotten.

My hopes in writing this book are to educate and to celebrate, to act as a catalyst for the initiation of, or the revival of, various customs and traditions, to offer a sense of rootedness and belonging and lastly, to preserve a slice of what was the life of a people with whom many can claim, or someday may wish to reclaim, a kinship.

December

Advent

The word "advent" takes its meaning and origin from the Latin *Paratus sum ad Adventum Domini*. (I am ready for the coming of the Lord.) The Poles called Advent *czterdziestnica*, or 40 days, because a fasting of that length occurred during that period at one time, beginning the day after the Feast of St. Martin. The eating of roasted meats on this day was supposed to prepare everyone for the long, meatless days ahead. A strict fast almost as severe as that of Lent was observed, omitting meat, fats, and milk on Wednesdays, Fridays, and Saturdays.

On the first day of Advent, all merry activities and public gatherings ceased. All work in the fields ended. Marriages were not conducted during this period, and any necessary christenings were done quickly. Youngsters began the task of creating the masks and costumes that would be used for the rounds of caroling that took place during the Christmas season. They gathered together frequently at some person's house to learn and memorize the Christmas carols which were not written down, but rather passed on orally from father to son, from older generation to younger generation. It was also a time for everyone to prepare themselves spiritually for the coming of the Messiah.

In the Mazowsze and Podlasie area there was the custom of *otrąbywanie Adventu*, that is, to summon or signal Advent. Every morning and evening the *ligawka* was played. This was a long, wooden horn, usually two or three yards long, made of linden or willow wood, which was only played out-of-doors. One of the

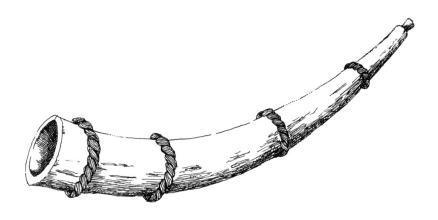

1 THE LIGAWKA

oldest musical instruments of Poland, its name comes from the word *legania*, which means to rest. It was generally placed atop something, usually a fence, when it was being played. Its sound called people to the early morning Mass during Advent, supposedly as a remembrance of the last Judgment Day, when horns were blown by the archangels. On a quiet winter morning or evening the sound of the ligawke could be heard for half a mile. In his memoirs as a pastor in the village of Zambrowie near Łomża, the Warsaw Archbishop Choromański indicated that during the time of the pasterka, the midnight Mass on Christmas Eve, all the young boys of the parish would stand by the church and play on large wooden horns.

The early morning Mass during Advent was called Roraty, derived from the Latin hymn "Rorate Coeli," which was sung at the Mass expressing the Chosen People's yearning for the coming of the Messiah. "Oh heavens, drop down your dew from on high, and may the Just One be rained by the clouds." No other country observed Roraty as solemnly as Poland. The ceremony was held before dawn, as a symbol that the world was in darkness until Jesus, the Light of the World, was born and also so that the faithful could prepare for the final Judgment Day, and be watchful in their preparation for the arrival of the Savior.

With this thought, seven candles, with the seventh placed in the middle, higher than the rest, symbolizing the Blessed Mary, were lit. This custom was begun during the reign of Bolesław Wstydliwy (1226-1279), by a man named Przemysław Pobożny of Poznań. It was taken up by the King at the Roraty Mass at the Royal Cathedral in Krakow. A seven flame candelabrum called *roratnica* was placed on the altar. Each candle symbolized one of the seven economic and social ranks of the county. A representative of each rank walked to the altar and lit a candle on the seven armed candelabrum. The King, as head of the nation, began the ceremony and on the highest sconce placed a lit candle, and stated "I am ready for the judgment day." He was followed by the archbishop and then by a senator, a nobleman, a soldier, a merchant and a peasant, each repeating "I am ready for the judgment day."

Three feast days broke up the rigid fasting and strict religious observances that generally occurred during the Advent period. The first was the Feast of St. Barbara (December 4).

According to legend, Barbara grew up in a pagan household, but secretly took religious instruction and was baptized. When her father found out about her conversion, she was forced to flee, but was captured and placed in a dungeon. To test her faith, her father had seven wise men argue her faith, but none could best her. Her father had her beheaded. When her head fell, it touched his foot, and lightning flashed from heaven and burned him completely. These particular circumstances surrounding the death of her father led St.Barbara to be a protectress against lightning and fire. She is the special patron saint of miners who work deep under the earth facing explosions and never-ending dangers, such as fire, water, and gas. A deep veneration for this saint developed among Polish miners. Each time a miner is to descend into the earth, he prays to St. Barbara, whose image is placed in every mine. In Poland, her feast day is celebrated with great pomp, beginning with a solemn Mass, followed by a torchlight procession, and ending with a party.

It is on her feast day that a branch of cherry called *gałązka Św.Barbary* was placed in water and then in a warm window. If the cherry branch blossomed on Christmas Eve, then the young girl who placed it there was sure to find a bachelor to marry during *zapusty*, carnival time.

The second feast day is that of St. Nicholas; it is known as *Św.Mikołaj* (Dec.6). The legends associated with St. Nicholas are numerous, but the one that associates him with the season of Christmas and gift giving is the legend of the three daughters.

An impoverished nobleman had three daughters who were unmarried because he could not provide them with a dowry. Upon hearing this, St. Nicholas, who at that time was a young man, took gold pieces from his own coffers, and on the night of December 5, threw them into the window of the house. Shortly thereafter, the eldest daughter was wed to a man of noble birth. He did this again twice, with the result that all of the daughters were wed. This legend was the basis for the foundation in Poland called the *skrzynka Świętego Mikołaja*, or the coffer of St.Nicholas. It was founded by a rich lady in Krakow named Magdalena Wonzamowa, who in 1588 donated 700 złoty to the Brothers of Mercy, which she designated as a dowry for poor girls who wished to marry. An official of Krakow named Mikołaj Zebrzydowski strengthened this foundation when he donated 3,000 *złoty* for the "coffer of St. Nicholas" as a perpetual fund "for those young girls, who, being well brought up but because of indigent and insufficient funds come by some misfortune to lose their virtue and innocence." In later years, this foundation had many supporters especially Father Andrew Łukomski, who donated three quarters of his own money to the fund. Father

Peter Skarga later wrote a statute that whatever candidate was chosen was to receive her dowry on the Feast Day of St. Nicholas. In 1786, the name was changed to "the dowry fund," which was dispensed by a religious group living near the church of St. Barbara in Krakow up until 1932.

In Poland, St. Nicholas is revered as the patron saint of cattle, horses, and sheep. His feast day falls during a time when wolves gathered together, attacking villages and generating great fear among those living in isolated areas. In the Kurpie region, the men fasted in order to beg St. Nicholas for protection against the wolves. People in the surrounding area brought linen, hemp, and poultry, and placed them on the altars as offerings.

In the Krakow area, the eve of the feast of St. Nicholas was awaited expectantly by the children. On this evening, a man dressed as a bishop in a mitre, a long coat, and holding a tall stick resembling a crozier, goes from house to house listening to the children recite their catechism and prayers. He praises obedient children, reminds the disobedient of their offenses, and threatens them with a stick, and in the end, distributes holy pictures, apples, and *pierniki*, cookies made from honey and spices.

Another custom called *Mikołaje* (Nicholases) was very alive in the villages of Jaworzynka, Istebna, and Koniaków in Cieszyn Silesia. This custom was not conducted on the sixth of December, but rather on the Sunday before or after the feast day. Preparation for the custom began two to three weeks ahead of time and included boys 18 to 25 years old. Those who participated in Mikołaje usually had participated the year before, but were generally picked for both their outward appearances and personalities to successfully carry out the roles.

The players in the Mikołaje were divided into two groups, known as the "whites" and the "blacks." The "whites" consisted of: (1) The bishop, who had to be tall and of a serious nature, carried a crozier and wooden cross, dressed in a paper chasuble or an old one borrowed from the rectory, and wore a colored paper mitre on his head. (2) The vicar had to be smaller than the bishop but had to be eloquent and be able to provide an interesting sermon; he was dressed in a sutan, wore a biretta and carried an old hymn book. (3) The soldier dressed in someone's full dress uniform, complete with medals, usually borrowed from someone who did active duty in a war; his outfit was completed with a wooden sword at his side and/or a pop-gun in his hand. (4) The best man was dressed in full górale (mountain) dress and carried a bottle of "liquor" usually consisting of fruit juice. (5) The bridegroom also wore full górale dress and carried "liquor." (6) The young woman dressed in full female górale dress; in her hand she carried a large basket with dried fruit, nuts, and carrots. (7) The doctor dressed in a dark suit, sometimes with a white apron over the front as if he were emerging from his pharmacy, had a stethoscope made of wood or wire around his neck; in his pocket he carried prescriptions, and in his bag, usually an old suitcase, he carried bottles of medicine made of cow or chicken dung, leaves, sticks, etc. (8) The forester usually wore dark green pants and jacket with trousers tucked into knee high boots.

The "blacks" consisted of: (1) Lucifer dressed in long underwear dyed red with a similar shirt and red mask with black horns. (2) Devils, often two or three of them, wore black shirts, pants, and boots; around their hips were skirts made of straw that hung down to their legs; bells were attached to the legs; they carried a large whip made of wire and leather. (3) The bear, in a sheepskin coat worn inside out, with a mask made in the guise of a bear, carried a rope with which to tie up the girls. (4) Medula (bear nanny or musician) wore very wide pants and a jacket that was stuffed with straw or rags; on his back he sometimes had a clock with the hands pointing to the left; he had a large hat with a wide brim and an umbrella with bells and fringe; he frequently had a harmonica hanging around his neck. (5) Jew wore a mask made of leather or paper mache that had a crooked nose and was painted in sharp yellow or red colors; he had a long black coat and carried an extremely long pair of scissors made of wood. (6) A gypsy dressed in regular mens' clothes with trousers tucked into knee high boots, and sometimes wore an old sheepskin coat and a half mask made of fabric or paper; he had a large hat with the brim turned down and under his nose sported a painted moustache. (7) Gypsy woman (a boy dressed as a girl) wore a long skirt, colored blouse and red beads around the neck with a half mask. (8) Death, made very tall with the addition of wooden extenders and long, wooden hands that moved with the help of rope, wore a mask made of wood or paper and was covered entirely in a white sheet. (9) Horse and rider was created with the use of two round sieves that were attached to the front and back of the individual by his belt, and then covered with a blanket; the head was made from a flat board and colored yellow, brown, and red; the tail, from woolen yarn. The rider or horseman was in the uniform of a cavalry man with shiny buttons; on his head he had a tall paper cap in the shape of a cone, with a large paper pompom attached to the tip. (10) Stork, also made to appear very tall with a head made of wood attached to a wooden pole or metal pipe, had a mouth of two pieces that moved with the aid of a rope, and was completely covered in white. (11) The chimney sweep smeared himself with soot or wore a black mask, then put on a tight jacket over tight black pants; he carried a long brush borrowed from a chimney sweep. (12) A potter dressed in pants and sweater over which he wore a long apron and carried a broken pot.

Each group of Mikołaje had their own areas in which they conducted their "show." They usually visited the more well-to-do landowners in the village and then their relatives and friends. The custom begins with the leader of the entire group, the soldier, going to the house of the people the Mikołaje are going to visit, and asking for permission for the Mikołaje to enter the house. If granted permission, the soldier pops his "gun" and the "blacks" burst into the house and start to dance and frolic. The devil tries to enter the house but each time his foot is about to enter he is pulled back by another devil, the bells tied to their legs making a great noise. When they have created enough mayhem with their pulling and noisemaking, the devils are sent out of the house by the soldier. He then calls in the bears. The bear and nanny initially dance together, but eventually grab someone from the household who is only standing and watching their performance. The bear dances with every girl present, even going so far as to tie the more reluctant girls together with the straw rope. When all the girls have been appropriately danced with, the soldier sends the "blacks" out and the "whites," preceded by the bishop, majestically enter. He gives his cross to be kissed by all present and never says a word. The vicar says a sermon using a chair or stove as his pulpit about the ungodliness of the home to which he has arrived and especially wants to hear the confessions of the girls. He reminds the young children to go to church, listens to them recite their catechism, and either praises them or warns them depending on their ability to recite their catechism. The vicar also takes up a collection.

As the vicar and bishop are about to leave, the bridegroom rushes in, runs after the girls, and gives them all kisses. The best man follows him in and offers the "guests" vodka from his bottle. The young woman comes in and begins distributing the candy and dried fruit which she has brought in her basket.

The forester makes his way into the house and tells the head of the house he must pay for the illegally obtained wood which he sees in the yard. The head of the house refuses to pay the fine, so the forester seeks the help of the military to arrest the man. The homeowner is forced to pay the military a higher fee as well as a fine for releasing him from jail. While the military man is unsure about what to do with the homeowner, the doctor arrives, pulling out his stethoscope and, of course, wants to "examine" the girls. The older folks present receive a bottle of his "medicine" and, fulfilling his professional responsibilities, he leaves.

Through the window, "death" is looking in, and upon his entrance, the head of the house says, "Mr. Death, how many years will I still live?" Death holds up two or three fingers. "Please! Be so kind as to let me live another two hundred years!" Death agrees and holds out his hand for remuneration, for these things aren't for free! The potter breaks pottery and then tries to repair it, and the chimney sweep sweeps all the dirt and rubbish into the middle of the room.

The last group to arrive are the rider with the horse and the gypsies. These are the most popular of all the figures because the horse is so spirited, and the gypsies because of the their fortune telling with cards. They try to sell the homeowners something taken from a previous house at twice the cost.

The last feast day in Advent was that of St. Thomas (Dec.-21). A custom that was practiced on this day was *winszowniki*, or well wishers. A young boy arrived at someone's home with a green branch from a fir tree. While offering the branch to the housewife, the boy stated, "*Winszujemy Świętego Tomy, żeby nie był żaden ślepy ani chromy.*" (Wishing you St.Thomas's Day, may no one be blind or ill.) The housewife took the fir branch in her hand through her apron and took it to the stable, lightly touching each animal with it. She then placed the evergreen in some crack in the wall to assure prosperity in the breeding and raising of the farm cattle. For his pains, the young child was treated to some kind of sweet or small change for it was generally believed that if the children did not arrive on St. Thomas with good wishes, there would be little luck that year.

Wigilia, wilia, or *dzien wigilijny* (Christmas Eve) comes from the Latin word *vigilare*, which means "to watch." This holiday was considered more important than Christmas Day itself. From very early on, everyone was careful of conduct and observed everything that occurred in the house, garden, and heavens. The rules were to rise early, say your prayers earnestly and carefully, wash thoroughly, dress cleanly, and then peacefully and patiently attend to your work. Whosoever argued on this day would be

29

arguing all year long and whosoever met misfortune on this day would meet misfortune all year long.

The first preparations for Christmas Eve began very early, right after midnight in the southern mountain regions of the Tatras. One of the young girls of the family went to the nearest stream and brought back pails of water. The water was used to sprinkle the cows in the byre and was also sprinkled on the family, awakening them in this manner:

Kto rano w Wigilje wstaje
Ten przez rok cały nie będzie ospały.

Who rises early on Christmas Eve
Will not be drowsy all year.

It was believed that water on this day had the power to heal and prevent illness. During the morning wash, the mother or father threw coins into the wash basin. The coins were supposed to be ones received from others, as from a wedding; this gave them more importance. The entire family washed themselves in this water in order to assure plenty of money for the rest of their lives.

The person who came first to the house on this day was very important. It was universally believed that if a man arrived first, then the cows which gave birth during the next year would bear bull calves; but if a woman were to come first, they would be heifers. Subsequently, women were much in favor and sometimes great lengths were undertaken to assure the arrival of a woman. Sometimes just the opposite was true. If on Christmas Eve a man arrived at the house first, this meant that there would be good luck in the home and if a woman, failure and misfortune.

Among the many things that had to be accomplished on this day was the necessity of the *gospodarz* to look over the house and inventory what he would need over the next three days when custom forbade engaging in any kind of serious work such as

30

chopping wood for the stove, cutting hay for the horses and cows, preparing straw for bedding, etc. It was also the responsibility of the males to go into the forest and bring back boughs of fir and spruce to decorate the house on this special day.

The oldest Christmas decoration in early Poland was called *podłaźnik, połaźnik,* or *sad.* The origins of the name are difficult to verify, but in the Podhale region of Poland it was known that *"podłazić kogo"* meant the same as going to someone's house on Christmas Eve with offerings of good wishes for the coming year. *"Dobrześ mnie podłaź"* meant "you brought me luck." A *podłaźnik* was someone that went from house to house with an evergreen branch and good wishes on Christmas Eve or New Year's Day. This custom was also known in Yugoslavia, where the podłaźnik was the first guest who entered the house on Christmas Day showering the inhabitants with grain, carrying the news that Christ is born. This guest offered wishes for plenty in the byre and garden. In Russia, the *podłaznyk* was any person who first entered the house on Christmas Day wishing good luck. Folklorists have surmised that if the podłaźnik was someone who brought blessings of good luck, good health, and plenty in the cupboard and cow shed, it can be conjectured that the same function was fulfilled by the evergreen bough which was hung in a corner of the main room of the house. This was not universal throughout Poland, but appeared mostly in the southeast of Poland in the Silesian Cieszyn area near Krakow, Nowy Sącz, Podhale, and those areas reaching towards the River San.

The podłaźnik was most often a spruce or fir, for both trees, like the oak, were believed to be inhabited by the gods. From the spruce, the mountain góral foretold on Christmas Eve the weather for each month of the coming year. The distribution of cones at the bottom, middle, and top of the tree foretold the frost for the beginning, middle, and end of winter. The fir tree was also believed to have secret magic by way of averting evil: a branch of fir thrown on the floor before the doors of the house and barn

31

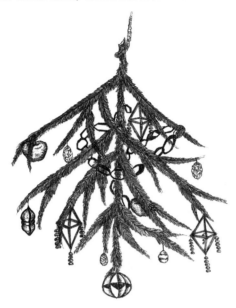

2 PODŁAŹNIK, OLDEST CHRISTMAS DECORATION IN EARLY POLAND

on Christmas Eve dispelled sickness, plague, and pestilence. In some districts, a branch of fir tucked on top of the dung heap and left till the Feast of Three Kings would prevent wolves from entering the cow barn.

The excursion into the forest for the evergreen boughs was very significant. Everyone hurried to be first to cut the top of a spruce or fir and other branches. The top of the spruce or pine was hung from a beam in the ceiling, with the tip facing down over the table where the wigilia (Christmas Eve supper) was to be held. Other branches were hung behind holy pictures, over the doorway of the entrance of the house, cow barn, and stable.

The bough was decorated with red apples, nuts, large circles cut from *opłatki* (colored bread wafers), *pająki* (spiders) made from wheat and paper, *łańcuchy* (chains), and at the very tip (that is, the bottom) hung a round *świat* (world) made from bread wafers. This early Christmas tree was decorated by the girls with some help from the boys, who were relegated to making the paper chains. The podłaźnik and all the various branches were left in place until the day after New Year or the Feast of Three Kings.

Another Christmas decoration which was retained for the longest time in the Krakow region was the hanging of a sheaf of grain, the tops pointed down, on the ceiling over the Christmas Eve supper. In some villages it was called *dziad* or *baba* or *chochoł*. In Wieliczka, near Krakow, the dziad was hung with the top of the grain pointing down and is believed to have preceded the podłaźnik. Straw was also used to decorate the main room of the house where the wigilia supper was held by tucking small bunches of wheat or rye behind holy pictures or in chinks in the walls. Sometimes these bundles of wheat were made into the shapes of crosses and stars called *krzyże wigilijne*, or Christmas Eve crosses. Two bunches of wheat were tied together in the middle with more straw and nailed to a beam in the ceiling or, as in some villages, placed on one end of the table together with a candle which was kept burning during the wigilia supper. On New Year's or during the Feast of Epiphany, the crosses were tied on the ends of sticks of hazelwood and stuck into the ground of a wheat field to ward off evil and to bring a bountiful harvest in the New Year. The *gwiazda wigilijna* was another decoration that was thought to provide the inhabitants of the house with plenty. This was nailed above the door of the main entrance of the house or to the ceiling or wall.

After making the gwiazda, any leftover straw was scattered on the floor as a remembrance that the Infant Jesus was born in a stable. In the Beskid Śląsk area, it was forbidden for anyone to touch the straw on the floor, i.e., sweep it up, before its time. To do so was considered a sin. It could only be swept up on St. Stephan's Day by the housewife or daughters. The swept-up straw was then taken to the fields, where next year's grains would be grown. Any wheat used in the house was always

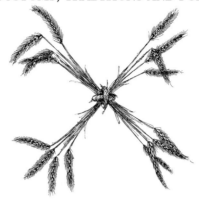

3 KRZYŻE WIGILIJNE, OR CHRISTMAS EVE CROSS

4 GWIAZDA WIGILIJNA

5 DZIAD

disposed of very carefully. If not taken out immediately to the fields, it was saved to be placed under cabbage seedlings in the spring to protect the plants from geese. In the Sandomierz and Tarnobrzeg region, it was burnt and used to incense the millet to protect it from blight. It was put in a child's pillow to protect the youngster against illnesses and/or given to cattle to protect them against illness and make them grow fat.

A very common practice throughout Poland was the placing of bundles of wheat, rye, or oats in one or in all the corners of the main room where the wigilia meal was to be eaten. In ancient, pre-Christian times Christmas Eve and the Christmas season were a celebration of the winter solstice and principal features were rituals that expressed reverence for the gift of bread and observances to assure the favor of the gods for a bountiful crop in the year to come. The presence and display of wheat and grains in the home, the baking of special breads, the performance of symbolic actions to ensure the fertility of the soil, and the honoring of the spirits of the ancestors were all part of the early ritualistic observances of that period.

In preparation for this most important meal of the year, the table was first covered with straw or hay, and then with a white linen tablecloth. On the best plate of the house, the blessed wafer or *opłatek* was placed. In some areas of Poland, a loaf of common, everyday bread was placed on top of it and then topped with more opłatek. This plate was left on the table until the Feast of the Three Kings. In other homes, a loaf of fresh bread and salt, covered with a white towel, was left on the table for all the twelve days of Christmas so that these gifts would not be absent during the 12 months of the upcoming year.

As the day began to darken and family members began to ready themselves for the evening meal, a child was sent out to look for the first star. At its appearance, the wigilia meal could begin. In and around Warsaw, the belief was that those sitting down to eat must add up to an even number. An odd number foretold that someone would not live to the next Christmas Eve supper. In Pomorze, if there was not an equal number of men and women, then the one left over would not marry. To make up for this, someone was always invited to make up the deficiency, be it honored guest or wandering beggar.

Before approaching the wigilia table, the family knelt down on the floor and prayed together out loud, grateful for all the blessings of the past year. At the conclusion of the prayer, the most important ceremony of the night, the sharing of the *opłatek*, was begun.

The opłatek is essentially unconsecrated bread wafer of the type used during holy communion in many different Christian religions. It has been suggested by Polish ethnographers that the sharing of this bread wafer at the wigilia table is a modification of what was once the sharing of a ritual bread called *podpłomyk*. This was a thin, flat bread traditionally baked before placing the loaves of bread dough in the oven. The baking of this first bread was not a chance happening, but an absolute responsibility. The housewife shaped this thin bread on a flat surface and, scraping aside the glowing embers of the fire, placed it right on the edge of the oven before the flames, giving its name — before the flames. To easily break this bread into parts after baking, the housewife made heavy marks of a checkerboard pattern across the top. This bread baked quickly, with bubbles forming on the top. It was eaten not only by the inhabitants of the house but was also sent to friendly neighbors as a goodwill gesture, with the knowledge that the neigbors would reciprocate in kind. The appearance of this bread in conjunction with the opłatek gave rise to the conjecture that it was an early form of the bread wafer. In Wieliczka, every individual in a household received a podpłomyk and on it an opłatek; in Kolbusz, they took the largest podpłomyk and shared it with their neighbors; in the middle of the 19th century, it was noted that immediately after the opłatek, podpłomyk with honey was shared. Hieronim Łopacinski, who traveled around Lublin in the 19th and early 20th century, wrote: "On Christmas Eve, even though I was a stranger, they gladly welcomed me and offered me a piece of podpłomyk and not accepting such was to offend."

The equivalent of the wafer as it is known today was baked by the Benedictines of Cluny in Burgundy, France. The flour for baking the wafers had to be ground in special mills and could not be used to bake regular bread. Special recipes held by the monastery were used to bake the wafers at Cluny and then taken up by other monasteries throughout Europe. In Poland, the bread wafer was known from the time of Christianity, but used only during Holy Mass. By the 15th century, the bread wafers were being made on a larger scale for popular use. The memoirs of Mikołaj Rej (1505-1569) indicate that the wafers were used as a snack with wine, as a seal for letters, and also for making Christmas decorations called *swiaty*. Developing simultaneously with the spread of wafers was the art of iron engraving. Rectangular shaped irons, the insides engraved with various religious motifs, were used to emboss scenes on the wafer. The dough was poured on one side, the other half closed over, and the iron held over a fire until the wafer was baked.

Over time, the responsibility of making and distributing the bread wafer was taken by the church organist, who received some small payment or accepted remuneration such as a few shocks of grain during harvest season. White bread wafers were made for human consumption and red, green, and gold for animals. The sharing of the bread wafer on Christmas Eve was not, however, universal throughout all of Poland. In many districts throughout the Pomorze area, the opłatek was unknown, but for the most part the mutual sharing and breaking of the bread wafer was, and still is, the very core and essence of Christmas Eve throughout Poland.

The male head of house began the solemn ceremony by taking the opłatek and turning to his wife, wished her good health for the upcoming year, success in her housekeeping, the fulfillment of her heart's desires and perhaps — if there was strain between them — to forgive him his faults and that the year ahead of them be a good one. At his conclusion, she expressed her thanks, broke off a piece of the wafer that was extended to her and consumed it. She then offered her husband a piece of her bread wafer, responding to him in kind: wishing good health and fortune, that they all be together at the next wigilia dinner and, because in the sharing of the opłatek one overlooks any ill-feeling, forgets hurts and ends any enmity or unfriendliness, she accepts his words of reconciliation and asks that he too, overlook her deficiencies. The husband would then break off a piece of the wafer extended to him, and eat it. The wafer was then shared with any older relatives present, honored guests, and then with the children, starting with the oldest and so on down the line. Everyone, down to the youngest child present, had the opportunity to say a few words and exchange good wishes. One of the wishes commonly offered was: *Życzę ci zdrowia, szczęscia i wielkiej fortuny a po śmierci w niebie koróny* (Wishing you health, good luck, and great fortune, and after death, a crown in heaven).

Sometimes the wishes were simple and to the point, i.e., that the next holiday be a better one, that there be no lack of food or shortage of heat. In the Podhale region, it was customary to spread honey on the opłatek in the form of a cross before it was shared; in other areas, it was shared plain. Remembering with whom you first shared the wafer on wigilia was extremely powerful when encountering a wolf and when drowning, for whoever in those moments does in fact remember is not harmed and will not drown.

After everyone had had an opportunity to share the wafer, the supper could begin. Tradition dictates that this be a meatless dinner, and up until the World Wars in some areas of Poland, this meal was eaten from a common bowl and in candlelight. Tradition also dictates that there should be an uneven number of dishes served. In the more well-to-do home this was 11 or 13, with 13 being the preferred number as it represented the number that sat down to the Last Supper. In more humble cottages, 5 or 7 different dishes appeared. For those of truly reduced circumstances, of which there were many throughout Poland, a dish often consisted of simply tasting a piece of food. People would share a piece of fruit, for example. Everyone received a slice, and this counted as one of the dishes.

Kucya or *kutia* was served in both the homes of the nobility and the serfs. No Christmas Eve was complete without it. Also known in Russia and Lithuania, the kucya was made from hulled barley or wheat, which was cooked until of thick consistency; it was then sweetened with honey. Milk and poppy seeds were sometimes added. The dish was set down in a place of honor on a bench near the wigilia table early in the morning of Christmas and it was the first dish to be eaten. The rest of the meal reflected the products of the family's labor, with dishes made from beets, cabbage, beans, various grains such as buckwheat and millet, potatoes, dried fruit, fresh apples, and nuts. Fish did not figure strongly at most Christmas Eve dinners unless it was plentiful in the area and/or a family could afford it. In smaller villages of Pomorze, the supper consisted of beet soup, sauerkraut with mushrooms, herring, noodles with poppy seeds, and a compote made with apples. Everyone was careful to eat a little bit of everything on the table so that next year they would not experience hunger. It was not permitted to eat everything that was placed on the table, including the bread and the opłatek, for something had to be left to be shared with the domestic animals. Since the purpose of the meal was to bring everyone together, portions of the food were also left on the table overnight for any departed souls who wished to share and partake of the meal.

In Beskid Śląski, tradition dictated that the meal be concluded with a prayer and the sharing of an apple in order to strengthen the bonds of the family, and so that each person present at the meal always safely found the way back home. The head of the house took food left from the wigilia supper, added bread and a piece of red opłatek, sprinkled it with a little salt, and fed it to the animals. In Bielsko Biała, a special bread with rose hips was baked for the cows. A piece of this bread was given to the cows every day until the Feast of Three Kings. In Upper Silesia, instead of rose hips, onions and oil were added. The bread assured a healthy cow that produced plenty of milk and was protected against spells and witchcraft. In some areas, the horses and sheep were also fed the opłatek, as was the dog.

Throughout all of Poland, the time after the supper was a time for the family to gather together to sing carols and to take part in making predictions and fortune telling. The smoke from a candle foretold life and death. Everyone blew out a candle three times. Smoke that traveled up evenly foretold health in the following year. Smoke that wandered around undecided or drifted towards the door announced illness or death. Bad or good luck could be forecast from the healthy or rotten state of the inside of a walnut. Girls listened for which direction a dog barked from for their future husbands would come from that direction.

The period approaching midnight was a magical time when animals talked and well water turned to wine. Sometimes the head of the house went out to the orchard to tie the trees with ropes of straw or hay made from that which had rested on the wigilia table. They "woke" the trees by knocking on them three times or shook them, saying "Do you not hear? The Son of God is born." Everyone readied themselves to attend the midnight Mass of the Shepherd or *Pasterka*.

In the Roman Catholic Church, the first mass of the Feast of Christmas takes place at midnight Christmas Eve, that traditionally being the time of Christ's birth. The Poles called it the Shepherds Mass, because the shepherds were the first to greet the new born Christ. Every able-bodied individual trudged through freezing weather in the dark of the night, or rode in sleighs to local churches by way of town streets or country roads. Their way was illuminated by lights falling from the windows of cottages and the whiteness of the snow. Only the very old, the sick, and the very young remained behind for this all-important greeting of the Infant Christ.

On their way to the Mass, the people carefully observed the heavens. If there were many stars, the people rejoiced, for as many stars as there were in the heavens, that many sheaves of grain would be harvested the next year. When the people of the villages between Krakow and Kielce traveled to the Shepherds Mass young teenagers brought *kowiorki* with them from home. These were small bundles of straw attached to poles which were set on fire and carried on the way to the Shepherds Mass. The people of this area interpreted these as a symbol of the fires burned by the shepherds on this night.

Christmas Day

Aside from Easter Sunday, Christmas Day was the most important holy day of the year, celebrated in an atmosphere of great solemnity and dignity. Everyone was careful not to do any work, such as sweeping the floor, peeling potatoes, splitting wood or even polishing one's boots. Cooking included only the heating of previously prepared food. Visiting was not allowed.

Everyone gathered before hearths and sang religious and secular Christmas songs.

Christmas Day began the twelve days from Christmas which was called *Gody*. These twelve days were observed very carefully, for it was believed among the Polish people that each of the consecutive days foretold the weather for the equivalent month of the year. Christmas Day foretold the weather conditions one could look forward to in January. The next day, St. Stephan's Day, foretold the weather for February and so forth. The nights were also part of the prognostication. If the day was fair but it rained or snowed during the night, then it foretold that the first half of the month would be fair but the second half would be damp.

The evenings of this twelve-day period were known as *świȩte wieczory*, or holy evenings. It was the custom not to engage in any significant work after sunset, for any work done at this time would bring misfortune of some kind. For instance, a spool of thread would reel in wolves to the village. Any work involved in shaking would cause anything that is born in the barn to also shake. To twist anything, for instance, as in making a whip, would cause twisting in birthing. These long winter evenings were spent with multiple generations gathered around the hearth, where elders recounted visits to distant cities, relived experiences with witchcraft where evil was bested, and retold ancient legends.

The second day of the Christmas season was St. Stephan's Day, a direct contrast to Christmas Day. It was the traditional day for visiting and wishing everyone the joy of the holiday season. Early in the morning in some parts of Poland, everyone awaited the arrival of the *połazniki* who made their appearance on this day. Similar to the custom called "first foot," known to people from China to Ireland, a child would cross over the threshold of the home, offer the inhabitants good wishes, and sing songs about the birth of the Infant Jesus. In Istebna, this was usually a young boy, while in other areas, it could be a child of either sex. Much the same as on the Feast of St. Thomas, the child left a small fir branch and received a baked treat or sweet of some kind in return.

Everyone attended Mass, bringing oats with them tied in a scarf or kerchief. The oats were usually taken from one of the bundles that had stood in the corner during the Christmas Eve meal. After the Mass was concluded, the kerchiefs were opened and received blessing by the priest. The people then threw the oats at the priest and at one another. Sometimes even before the blessing, the young boys in the choir dropped oats on those standing below — most often the girls. It sometimes happened that where the priest was unpopular, he received something harder from the parishioners. In some parishes, they threw not only oats, but also peas, and so plentifully that after the Mass, the priest gathered 50 kilograms of oats and peas. This throwing of oats and peas was to represent the stoning of St. Stephan.

The blessed oats were given by the handful to the horses or placed in their feed bags to protect them against illness and to give them strength. They were fed to the chickens in a hoop so that they wouldn't stray from home and also to the cows that would soon birth their calves. Another part of the oats were saved and mixed in with those used for sowing the following year to ensure a plentiful harvest. In some places, a small portion of the oats were placed in a cloth bag and hung in the room where all the grains were kept to protect them from hail and storms. Sometimes the oats were strewn over the farm animals and on fruit trees. In many areas St. Stephan's marked the end of work contracts for the year; new bargains were struck for the upcoming year. It was also the official day for carolling to begin.

The custom of caroling in Poland, or *chodzenie po kolędzie*, began on St. Stephan's Day and lasted until the Feast of the Purification on February 2. *Jasełki* is the general name given to two forms of Christmas caroling called *szopka* and *Herody*.

Szopka was a portable crib or manger scene carried by young boys from house to house. It has its origins in Grecchio, Italy, with a monk — later canonized as St. Francis of Assisi — who wanted to bring home to the people of his parish the humanity of the Christ Child. To recreate the setting of the first Christmas night, he constructed a life-size manger scene in a cave by borrowing some farm animals, collecting the trappings of a stable, and placing a statue of the infant Christ in a manger filled with hay. By special permission of the Pope, he was allowed to conduct a midnight Mass before his handiwork. The people were charmed and captivated by the sight, and the nativity scene immediately became a means of making the Christmas message more real. The custom spread throughout all the churches of Europe. In Italy the nativity scene was called *presepio*; in France, *creche*. In a letter dated May 1, 1207, Pope Innocent the III wrote to Archbishop Kietlicz and suggested that nativity scenes be displayed in Polish churches. The nativity scene was called a *jasełka*, from the ancient Polish word *żłobek*, or manger.

One of the oldest nativity scenes was exhibited at St. Anne's Church in Warsaw. It was shown not in the church, but near the gates of the monastery. The manger in which Jesus lay was lavishly decorated with flowers and rich fabrics, with the figures of Mary and Joseph standing on either side. It was exhibited once a year on the day of Christ's birth, during which time songs were sung and music played. Another very early jasełka was known in the 14th century. Three non-moving, non-speaking figures made of linden wood were sculpted by an unknown Krakow artist for the Church of St. Andrew in that city around 1370, and were supposedly commissioned by Elizabeth, sister of Casimir the Great.

When it first began to appear within Polish churches, the manger scene was displayed at a side nave from Christmas Day to Candlemas Day. It consisted of a thatched roof supported on four pillars, a back wall, and was open on three sides with non-movable figures made of wood or wax. These depicted Mary and Joseph seeking lodging, the Nativity, and the visit of the Three

Kings. The non-speaking, non-movable figures did not, however, draw great audiences.

In a continuous effort to do so, the religious orders of Bernadines, Capuchins, and Franciscan monks took advantage of the advent of the Italian and French marionette theaters and incorporated the concept into their manger scenes. Shown in one of the naves of the church from the time of the midday meal to evening devotions, the puppet theater attracted great crowds. Such a manger was set up in Wawel Cathedral in Krakow. Wood figures of the Virgin and St.Joseph were placed around the Infant Jesus. A multitude of other figures, also painted and dressed in very costly attire, were artistically distributed around the scene. With the exception of the Holy Family, all the figures were movable. The shepherds were mounted on small wheels and could be moved around; the Three Kings knelt down by means of springs; the angels moved their wings, Herod's head came off, Death swayed his scythe and the Devil his pitchfork.

Competition between churches to attract the populace became quite heated, with increasingly elaborate scenery, expensive dress, and theatrical effects. The singing of Christmas carols, especially the more secular, folk type that originated from local musicians and writers, did much to transform the original purpose of the early manger scenes. Sung in Polish rather than the mystifying Latin, with the birth of the Infant Jesus as a backdrop for the song, its action took place in a Polish village with a variety of inhabitants coming to pay homage. Soon, additional figures representing the general population were added to the scenes. Unable to handle the complicated changes in scenery and the numerous figures and puppets all alone, the clergy began taking on local, non-religious individuals to assist them in the productions. An even greater emphasis on the human rather than the divine began to creep into the performances, as did greater amounts of comedy and social and political satire. Little by little, the comic characters and scenes became more and more boisterous and outrageous, more of an entertainment than a religious performance. Besides depicting the birth of our Lord and the Three Kings, there were soldiers, girls milking cows, love scenes and dancing, and beggars and swindlers who were whisked away by the devil. The scenes and recitations were so amusing and generated so much laughter and racket that, at times, viewers began to climb on the pews and altars to better hear and see the action, requiring the church custodian to drum the boisterous crowd out of the church with a stick. In their haste to avoid the blows, those on the altars fell down on those below causing screams, raising bumps on heads and generated more laughter and entertainment than the production before them.

By the early part of the 18th century, the puppet shows began to pose a problem for church officials. Critics of the church claimed that the productions interrupted those who wished to pray and that the material, often rather scandalous and shocking, discredited the church and clergy. At about the same time, Martin Luther appeared on the scene and took advantage of the criticism to futher his stuggle against the Catholic Church. In 1711, Bishop Czartoryski forbade the presence of the puppet theaters in the churches of Warsaw. Following his example, other bishops issued similar orders. The manger scene inside the church returned to the original still figures. The puppet productions had gained such a popularity, however, that instead of disappearing, they moved out of the churches into public rooms, private homes, and city streets and took on a life of their own. Private individuals began to direct and manage the shows. There was one notable individual in Warsaw by the name of Zawadski who had a thousand holy and secular moving puppets in his collection, to which all of Warsaw hurried to see and be entertained.

The transformation of the manger from the church to public rooms, to a homemade one carried in the street, was believed to be helped along by a Frenchman named Brioche, a dentist from Paris. In 1680, finding himself in dire financial straits, he developed a portable creche with movable figures and traveled through France and surrounding countries, entertaining rich and poor alike and making himself a lot of money. His puppets were so cleverly presented and their performance so seemingly magical, that in Switzerland he was condemmed as a witch and taken to jail; he was not released until he explained the mechanisms for his movable figures. Brioche died in 1700, but his invention had already taken hold and continued to spread further, making an appearance in the streets of Warsaw for the first time in 1701, documented in the memoirs of a citizen of Warsaw by the name of Janicki. It was taken up by the churches and when banished from there returned once more to the street where Brioche had been earlier.

Making and carrying the *szopka kukiełkowa*, or puppet manger or crib as it came to be called, on the streets was readily taken up by children and students, apprentices, the poor, and individuals who found themselves without work over the winter. This traveling mode of entertainment provided a new and somewhat lucrative way of making money and/or receiving something to eat. The mangers underwent a few transformations in their settings. Whereas in the churches they had been fairly large, they soon became small enough to fit through the door of an ordinary house, a height sometimes 28 inches high by 16 inches wide and 8 or 12 inches deep. Rather than having three open sides, the scenes could only be watched from the front. Made of thin wood and sometimes of cardboard or an old box, the outer shape of the szopki were most often reminiscent of the homes of the carriers with a simple two-sided roof rather than appearing like a manger. The front was made of double doors that closed on a hook. The interior walls and doors were dependent on the imagination of the creator, and were sometimes pasted with colored paper — the bottom was green, the ceiling blue, to which were fastened angels and small stars. Grooves were cut into the floor for the entry and exit of the figures which were manipulated from below. In the larger szopkas the shepherds, King Herod, his Field Marshal, an angel, a devil, Death and a Jew figure were three-dimensional and made of wood, textiles, and colored paper. In the smaller, more humble szopki, the figures were made of paper cut-outs.

Three boys usually traveled with the szopka, staying within the confines of their neighborhood, but sometimes moving outside into other sections of town or even different villages. The show usually began by singing a religious carol such as *"Wsród nocnej ciszy," "Bóg się rodzi,"* or *"W żłobie leży"* when approaching a home. Sometimes the boys were invited in. Two boys stood on either side holding the szopka while the third boy hid behind it in such a way as to not be seen and operated the puppets and provided the speaking parts. The boys on either side sang and accompanied themselves on the harmonica. However humble or intricate, the portable crib always portrayed the mysteries of the birth of the Infant Jesus. The main figure in the performances was King Herod, who arranged for the murder of all male children under the age of two. Also included were songs and dances, monologues by local figures such as a shoemaker, chimney sweep, mountain góral or the shepherds who, according to the Polish texts, are always named Wojtek, Bartek, and Kuba.

In Krakow, the making of the portable manger scenes was influenced by Krakow's magnificent architecture, including the gothic Tower of St. Mary's Church, the Renaissance elements of the Cloth Hall and the Royal Castle. There were very big cribs as tall as three meters and 2 to 2.5 meters broad with elaborately cut and assembled pieces of colored tissue paper to imitate stained glass windows and gothic and baroque steeples. The individuals credited with originating the elaborate Krakow szopka were Michael and Leo Ezenekier, two Krakow masons who built the first elaborate szopka gilded with gold and silver.

The other form of Christmas caroling that was popular in Poland was *Herody*. This was a live production done by a group of individuals, usually older boys and young adults, about the last days of King Herod. The origins of Herody can be traced to the early church mystery plays, which were developed by the clergy

6 A SZOPKA

as a means of explaining and teaching the doctrines of the church to an unlettered and ignorant populace. Developed in the 13th century, and reaching its height in the 15th and 16th centuries, these mystery plays were simply dramatic religious performances acted out by monks or priests. The performances initially took place within a monastery, church, or cathedral and included singing and chanting. They became so popular that the interior of the churches became inadequate to accommodate the vast crowds that flocked to see the plays. The performances were moved from around an altar to the front entrance, then for similar reasons to the church courtyard, and then finally, to the open areas about town. The religious dramas continued to draw great crowds, but the further away from the church the performance took place, the more difficult it was for the clergy to retain the original nature of the performances. In larger towns, enriched by industry and divided into craft associations, the guilds began taking part in dramatizing various biblical episodes. Wandering minstrels, acting troupes, and self-made entertainers also took up the public performances and introduced some of their own material and characters and they began to move away from being strictly religious performances that educated to entertainments.

In its early form in Poland, the Herody were called "*Maryka*" or "Little Mary's," and was conducted by traveling acting groups. They consisted of a boy dressed as the Blessed Virgin with a white cloth and crown on "her" head, Herod in gold armor and cutlass, a bishop, field marshal, Jew, and Herod's minions. The acting troupe entered the house singing a carol. In the middle of the room, Mary sat down on a chair and everyone, with the exception of the Jew, surrounded her until the end of the song. Mary then gave up her place to Herod who boasted of being king of earth, sun, and moon. Then he called to the Jew, who is hidden in the corner and must be pulled forward, and they began a comical, satirical dialogue, which generated much laughter. The Jew was the character who, through his lines, had the task of entertaining the public.

When it was taken up by local folk, Herody was usually enacted by 6 to 10 young men within the ages of 16 to 20, who could take on and convincingly perform a certain role in front of an audience. The usual roles in this live performance were King Herod, his Field Marshal and other minions, a soldier or knight, an angel, Death, a devil, and a Wise Man or sage. Sometimes a Turk was present, or perhaps a Jew with a long beard, or the Three Kings, depending on personal preferences. Sometimes the group was accompanied by individuals playing the harmonica, drum, fiddle, or tambourine. Outfitted in appropriate dress for their various roles, they usually began their tours of homes at dusk and announced their arrival to a home by the sound of a bell after which they sang a Christmas carol. When the owner of the home answered the door, the marshal would come forward and say:

Jeżeli jest gospodarza zgoda proszę krzesło dla Heroda. (If the head of the house agrees we beg a chair for the king.)

If the head of the house was willing to host such entertainment, he placed a chair in the middle of the room and the individual playing Herod would sit down with the soldier and his sword standing behind him, followed by the angel and devil. The Wise Man or sage approached to tell Herod that Jesus Christ, King of the Jews, was born. This upset Herod, and here the play truly began in earnest. The entire performance concluded with another carol, *"Pójdźmy wszyscy do stajenki."* For their efforts, the carolers were given small money gifts as payment and offered some refreshment.

These two forms of Christmas caroling, the szopki and Herody, which visually reenacted the birth of the the Infant Jesus and all attendant circumstances surrounding His arrival, appeared full force among villages and towns on the second day of Christmas. A third form of caroling was the *gwiazdory* or caroling with a star.

In remembrance of the star of Bethlehem that hung over the manger the night of the birth of Christ and led the Three Kings to the newborn King, young boys dressed as the Three Kings in long, white shirts with chasubles of black paper and paper crowns on their heads. One of them carried a large homemade star on a long pole that was lit from within by a candle, so that it could be seen in the dark of night. Their particular repertoire was to walk throughout the village singing carols. One of the carolers played a musical instrument such as an accordian, fiddle, or a simple harmonica to accompany their songs. They usually began at the manor house or church rectory and then made stops at various homes. They stopped before a window and sang a carol. After obtaining permission to enter the house, the gwiazdory sang both religious and popular Christmas carols.

The oldest form of Christmas caroling in Poland, however, was caroling with the *turoń*. To go carolling with turoń required that at least one of the participants be dressed in some type of animal costume and mask.

The custom of people dressing up as animals is as old as mankind itself. It was known in ancient Greece and Rome and certainly among the pagan groups of Europe, including the Slavs. The oldest Polish documentation regarding turoń dates back to the 16th century. Most sources reveal that this particular form of caroling began on Christmas Eve and ended on the Feast of Three Kings. The custom was so powerful that neither time, Christianity, or the threat of excommunication could diminish its strength for hundreds of years.

7 TUROŃ

DECEMBER

According to primitive and pagan logic, animals were endowed with tremendous strength, great cunning, and courage, and were seen as being better than man himself. It was also believed that the animals had contact with spirits and had some power or authority over them. Early man thought that if he dressed as an animal he would become like the animal — strong, courageous, and fleet of foot. Besides disguising himself, he also employed special songs and dances and performed imitations of the beast to strengthen the magic. The time of the winter solstice when day began its triumph over the long winter nights was also a time when early man went around paying tribute to certain gods in the hope of receiving good crops, increased fertility among his farm animals, and whatever other favors were deemed necessary. Folk legends and customs have always ascribed magical properties to goats, storks, bears, wolves, and wild oxen. The custom of turoń is named after the wild ox or tur, the largest and foremost of the animals that were prolific at one time throughout Europe and caused great damage to the villages.

To enact this particular form of caroling, a group of older boys would get together and pick whoever was the most nimble and was also endowed with a sense of humor and fun. A homemade, wooden head of an ox, decorated with horns, was placed on his head. The jaws of the head were made in such a manner that they could be opened and closed with hands or by pulling on a string. In the mouth a red rag was the tongue. Underneath the jaw was a thick beard, and a bell was fastened around the neck. The boy covered himself with a sheepskin or a horse blanket so that the wooly, fuzzy side was to the exterior, in imitation of the beast itself. His hands and feet were also encased in sheepskin so that he was entirely covered and had the look of a wild beast. The turoń had to walk on all fours, hunched over. He was led on a rope or chain by another caroler, while the third usually carried a lantern to light their way.

In the Tarnów region of Poland, for instance, the carolers generally consisted of the turoń, and two other individuals dressed as a Turk or a Jew. In other instances, it was a *dziad* (a beggar) who led the the wooly beast. In some areas, specific dress was not required but had to be such that the individual within could not be recognized. Together they would go out into the night. Arriving at a particular home, they would sing a song and upon being invited inside, the turoń would go into his special act. The caroler leading him on the rope would instruct him to perform, to jump over someone, dance, or roar at the children. He plundered throughout the whole house, jumping on furniture and turning it over, looked for something to eat, pinched the girls and scared the children. The turoń was allowed much freedom and liberty in his carrying-on for "who would tell a wild ox what is the right thing to do?"

In some of the oldest enactments of this type of caroling, the turoń jumped, danced, and made noise, and then pretended to fall and lay dead on the floor. It was then the role of the dziad or one of his companions to lament, to try and pick him up, and to make attempts to break the spell that has killed the turoń. In the end, the turoń is saved. It rises, begins to dance again, and to incite the girls to hysterics. In this fashion, his death and ressurection imitated the death of nature in winter and its return to life in spring.

When the members of the household had enough of the group's animated activities, they in turn sang to the beast telling him to go home:

Idź, turonie, do domu
Nie zawadzaj nikomu
Nie tuś się ty wychował
Nie tu będziesz nocował.

Go home wild ox
Trouble no one
You were not raised here
You will not sleep here.

DECEMBER

The gospodyni or gospodarz then gave them a nominal money gift or something from the larder. The group, thanking their hosts for the gifts received then moved on to the next house. There were often so many groups caroling that the villagers would half-heartedly complain *"co patrzeć to kolędniki"* — wherever you look, more carolers.

January

January saw the continuation of much of the Christmas festivities of visiting friends and family, as well as the caroling that began the day after Christmas. The New Year was ushered in with a variety of activities, with the eve of this day, as on many other holidays, taking precedence over the actual day itself.

Much fortunetelling was done on this night. A tablespoon of oil was placed on a metal plate, held over a candle until warmed, and then poured into water. The shapes were studied to determine what one's future might be. Another method called for placing a variety of articles, such as a handful of earth, a ring, sprig of myrtle, water in a glass, keys, and rosary on a large plate. Those wishing to know their future were blindfolded and told to reach towards the plate. The handful of earth indicated a funeral; the ring, an engagement; myrtle, a wedding; water, a christening; the key, good husbandry; and a rosary, godliness. A marriageable girl, wanting to know her marriage prospects, would knock on the door of the henhouse long after dark. If a rooster woke and began crowing it was confirmation that the girl would marry within the next year. In some villages in Pomorze, the young men would draw birds, bears, a cat, or a dog on the window of a home where there lived a marriageable girl as a good luck token that she marry soon. When the girl noticed the drawing she was to wash it off, or a suitor would not be able to enter the home.

At twilight, the young boys went out into the orchard, circling around the trees banging pots and pans, ringing bells, and shooting off rifles in order to waken the trees from their winter's sleep and to cause them to be fruitful. In Śląsk and those areas of Poland which were influenced heavily by the Germans, "shooting parties" occurred on New Year's Eve. The custom was derived from old pagan beliefs that noise would drive away evil spirits. The tradition seemed very useful at mid-winter, when the forces of death and cold seemed to have such a strong grip on nature. Young men would travel from farm to farm filling the air with deafening noise. After they had properly scared off the evil spirits, the farmer invited the marksmen into the house to partake of refreshments.

At one time, almost universally throughout Poland, the New Year's greeting was "*Bóg cię stykaj,*" which simply translated offered "God's good graces touch you!"

Another popular greeting was:

Życzymy dostatków
Wyższych dostojeństw
Rodzicom pociechy z dziatek
Pannom i kawalerom dobrego
zamęsia lub ożenienia
A wszystkim błogosławieństwa
niebos i długiego wieku.

Wishing you plenty
Higher rewards
Parents joy of their children
Maids and bachelors good
husbands and wives
And everyone all of
heaven's blessings and a long life.

There was an approved method or hierarchy for the giving of this New Year's greeting. Nineteenth century folklorist Łukasz *Gołembiowski* indicates that the "lower positioned" individual was responsible for initiating the greetings. For instance, children

58

offered greetings first to parents and older adults; bachelors spoke first to young maidens and so forth.

Another popular New Year's greeting had its origins in the following story: Once, a very long time ago, there lived in Krakow a very worthy and religious woman by the name of Dosia. She lived to be over a hundred years old, and was always healthy, happy and charitable. It came to pass that she died exactly on Christmas Eve; tears and lamentations for her lasted till the end of the year. So strong was her influence that upon seeing one another on New Year's Eve, people would say "Życzę ci Dosiego roku," or "Wishing you a Dosia year," that is, live as long and successfully as Dosia.

Besides wishing each other well, people played various tricks or practical jokes on one another. One such trick was known as *podkradania*. This was a good-natured, playful kind of stealing usually done between neighbors and friends among the young Polish nobility and wealthier landowners. Young John would steal Mr. Wilinski's prize cow out of his barn. Upon discovering his cow missing, Mr. Wilinski would begin searching for her. Finding her contentedly munching hay in John's byre, Mr. Wilinski would have to pay a tidy sum to get her back. John and the friends that helped him successfully steal the cow away would treat themselves to a hearty feast with vodka toasts to Mr. Wilinski and his cow. Sometimes a homeowner would be missing his wagon or discover that his front gate was missing and nowhere to be found.

On New Year's Day, people often visited one another for the express purpose of offering good wishes. Those who earned their livelihood from the earth threw oats on one another as a symbol of plenty or, carrying oats in their sleeves, dropped a small amount on each corner of the table as a wish that their entire table be covered with bread in the new year. It was also felt that there should always be a loaf of bread covered with a white cloth on the table as a sign of God's gift. It was used to greet both honored guests and chance beggars.

New Year's Day was also a day on which it was customary for the local or parish priest and his vicars to travel through the village *po kolędzie*—going caroling. The priest usually announced which village or families he would be visiting. In more distant times, such a visit was done with the assistance of the organist and one or two of the students from the parish school. The organist and students would sing a song of the birth of Christ with the priest offering New Year's greetings. He asked after everyone's health, took a written account of everyone living within the home, and offered suggestions and reminders on various issues. He quizzed the children on their catechism, gave them holy pictures and his cross to kiss, and lastly, blessed the home. In rural villages, the priest was then gifted with a basket of mushrooms, a slab of bacon, a wheel of cheese, or dried nuts and fruit. In towns, the priest received money at the conclusion of his visit.

Proverbs for New Year's Day included:

Nowy Rok pogodny, zbiór będzie dorodny.
The New Year fair, harvest will be handsome.

Gdy w Nowy Rok jasno, w gumnach będzie ciasno.
When the New Year's bright, the barns will be tight.

New Year's Day and Twelfth Night were some of the most important days in the cycle of the winter solstice, and specially prepared breads were baked for the occasion. In Poland these breads were called *nowe latki*, which translates quite literally as "new year." In ancient times, the nowe latki were believed to have supernatural powers that could influence fertility and prosperity.

The constructing and baking of this ritual bread usually took place on the evening before New Year's and/or Three Kings, the work being done in a very serious manner. Rye or wheat flour was mixed with water in a dough bin, with salt sometimes being added. Wheat flour was preferred over rye, as it was felt to give a smoother consistency. The dough was kneaded for a very long time so that it would be dense and hard and not become misshapen while baking. A small clump of dough was torn off and figures of cows, sheep, chickens, goats, and geese, as well as fish and snakes, were formed by hand with the help of a knife. The figures were quite detailed; oftentimes the horns of a stag or the feet of a stork would be included. Figures of fruit trees, men on horses, hunters with game, or women with children in their arms were also formed and baked. In the heavily forested Kurpie area, where the tradition is still carried on to this day, figures of stags, rabbits, and squirrels were the preferred motifs.

After baking, the figures were hung from the rafters or on a high shelf above the fireplace or stove, where they remained until the following year. Sometimes they were tucked into a nest of herbs and hung in the window. If the farm animals were sick or were breeding, the dough figures were steeped in water and fed to the animals.

Besides single figures, another form of the nowe latki existed whereby the fully constructed animal and human shapes were placed on a circle of dough. According to primitive thinking, the round bread on which the figures rested was a magic ring and protected all who were brought within its circle.

The evening of the Feast of Three Kings was called *szczodry wieczór*, which means a bountiful or plentiful evening. The family usually spent the night around the fire singing carols, awaiting the arrival of carolers and gifting one another with tokens. A special wheat bread called *szczodraki* was baked in preparation for this night and either distributed among the poor, offered to visiting guests or to the poor children who came caroling on this night. It was tied so closely with the latter that carolers on this night began to be called szczodraki. The shape of the bread differed in various parts of Poland, being either crescent shaped or made into figures of a person, cat, goat, star, or cradle. Also very popular in the Ukraine, the origins of this particular bread are believed to be tied to ancient cults which originally fed the dead but later fed the poor and distributed food among children. Coming to the door to offer greetings and good wishes for a bountiful year, the children sang special songs about the baked goods:

> *Czy piekliście szczodraczki?*
> *Dajcież i nam!*
> *Nagrodzi wam Pan Jezus*
> *i Święty Jan.*

> Have you baked szczodraki?
> Give us some also!
> You will be rewarded by the Lord Jesus
> and St. John.

The housewife generously handed out the specially prepared bread with this particular proverb in mind: *Na szczodrych miara, na skąpych kara.* (For the generous, full measure; for the stingy, punishment.)

Homes were also visited by the *Gwiazdory*. These were carolers dressed in makeshift robes and crowns as if they were the Wise Men. One individual darkened his face in order to represent the Moor.

In many homes, especially the more well-to-do, another custom took place on the eve of Feast of Three Kings. After the evening meal was concluded, a cake or torte in which an almond had been added was brought forth. The cake was cut into as many portions as there were individuals present. Whoever received the piece with the almond became "the almond king" and had the right to pick himself an "almond queen" from the women present. In situations where it was an especially large gathering, two cakes were baked—one for the women and another for the men, with the pair finding the almond designated as Almond King and Queen. Within a family, becoming the Almond

King or Queen carried some measure of responsibility. During their reign, the monarchs were to uphold family tradition and honor, work towards the betterment of the family as a whole, and take special interest in each family member. It was also their responsibility to organize next year's gathering and to bake the cake.

Early the next day, the Feast of Three Kings, the gospodarz, or the male head of the family, removed the straw star which he had nailed over the main entry to the house and took it out to the fields and stuck into the ground to ward off evil and to bring a bountiful harvest in the New Year. He then hurried his entire family to church outside of which he bought a small painted box containing resin, juniper berries, a piece of chalk, and gold foil. This box was taken inside and blessed. On returning home, the gospodarz wrote the letters K + M + B, for the initials of the Three Wise Men (Kasper, Melchior and Baltazar), and then the year. This was done to provide protection for those within against illness and misfortune. The gold foil was rubbed against the neck to protect against sore throat and the juniper was used to incense the house and stables.

The Feast of Three Kings ended the święte wieczory — the twelve holy nights that began on Christmas Day and signaled the beginning of *zapusty*, or carnival time.

February

February brings the celebration of many important events in the Polish calendar year. One of the most interesting occurs at the very beginning of the month on February 2 and is known as *Oczyszczenie Matki Boskiej*, or The Feast of the Purification of the Blessed Mother.

In the Latin church calendar, the feast day recalls the ancient law of Moses that required every Jewish mother to be excluded from attendance at public worship for forty days after giving birth to a boy child. It also commemorates how Mary, after the birth of Jesus, fulfilled this command of the law by presenting two pigeons for sin offering, and through the prayers of a priest purified herself from ritual uncleanliness. Because it was the first introduction of Christ into the house of God, it was also called the Presentation of Christ in the Temple.

From Jerusalem, the feast of the fortieth day spread over the entire Church. In the eighth century (701), Pope Sergius introduced the celebration of the day with a procession but did not provide for any blessing of candles. It wasn't until the eleventh century that a blessing of candles made of beeswax and carrying them in solemn procession, entered into the ceremony. According to the Roman missal, the officiating priest or celebrant sang or recited five prayers of blessing, sprinkled and incensed the candles, and distributed them to the faithful who carried their lighted candles in a solemn procession within the church. During the Middle Ages, the clergy did not confine themselves to the inside of the church, but often proceeded into the open and walked through the churchyard, past the graves of departed parishioners. The procession symbolically represented the entry of Christ, as the Light of the World, into the Temple of Jerusalem.

The blessing of candles and the procession of lights came to be so strongly associated with the day there arose in many European languages a second name for the Feast of the Purification. The English called it Candlemas; the Germans, Maria Lichtmess; the Slovaks and Czechs called it Hromnice, and among the Poles, who revere the Blessed Mother before all others, the day came to be called *Matka Boska Gromniczna*, or Mother of God of the Blessed Thunder Candle.

On the day of the Purification, the people of Poland brought candles decorated with either ribbons or liturgical symbols to be blessed by the priest. They would then take the blessed candles, called *gromnice*, (from the word for thunder: *grom*) home. That night, the people would pay homage to the the Blessed Mother by burning one of the blessed candles before her picture until sunrise the following day. The other gromnice were kept in a safe place and used when needed at various times throughout the year.

One of the chief uses of the gromnice centered around the ritual cleansing of women following childbirth. In much the same manner as the ancients of Jerusalem, the Poles believed that a woman following the birth of a child was "unclean" and that her condition could spread to the fields where the grain would be ruined. During this period of being "unclean," the woman was temporarily shunned by the rest of the community and forbidden to mingle with them. The period of isolation ended with the ceremony of *wywód*, which cleansed her and released her and the child from the imposed isolation. Approximately six weeks or forty days after the birth of her child, the woman would leave her home, holding in her hand a *gromnica*. Kneeling at the door of the church, the priest would pray over her, sprinkle her with holy water, and then lead her into the church, which then brought her back into the fold of the community.

The blessed candles were also lit at the bed of the dying in order to protect the individual from Satan. It was believed that in that moment between life and death there was a contest for the soul of the dying individual between the angels, who were the deputies of heaven, and Satan, the king of darkness. So strong was this belief that there existed in Poland the custom of storing away a gromnica "for death," so that "their death would be easier and bad souls would not have access to them." Very devout and pious individuals often hung one of these blesssed candles over their beds as a reminder to be ready for death at every moment.

The most important function of the candle is evidenced by the special name of Matka Boska Gromniczna. It was an indisputable belief that the lighted candle protected the house and its environs against the ravages of lightning. When thunder rumbled and lightning flashed, our ancestors lit their blessed candle before holy pictures in the firm belief that the candle had the power to chase away the thunder and lightning, thereby protecting their property from being struck and ruined. Nineteenth century prayer books reveal special prayers which were said during times of storms and lightning; they entreated God not to thunder against His people and to turn the storm from their homes and property.

The gromnica was also used in a variety of other ways to ward off evil and bad happenings. Even at the beginning of the nineteenth century, it was noted that the country folk began the more important work of the fields, such as the throwing of the first seeds during sowing, the turning out of cattle to pasture in the spring, and the beginning and ending of harvest, with a blessed candle in their hands. Sometimes the farmer took the spilled wax of the candle and placed it among the seeds of the first row to be sown, and often enclosed a piece of the candle in the last bundle of wheat or straw stored in the granary after the harvest.

Even though the church condemned the use of the candles for casting spells or illnesses, the gromnica was used far and wide in superstitious practices and predictions. On the day of the Purification, the lit candle was carried around the house, outbuildings, and near cattle in order to safeguard all possessions. Often, the sign of the cross was burned on the backs of the animals for added protection. Towards the end of the nineteenth century, crosses were burnt on door frames and window sills with the gromnica, which also served to ward off evil spirits. The inhaling of its smoke after extinquishing the candle protected and prevented sore throats. Sometimes fingers were held over a burning gromnica as measures against soreness, inflammation, and splinters.

Numerous proverbs attest to the fact that the feast day itself was used to foresee and predict the future. The observation of the weather on this day foretold how long the winter would last, what the weather would be like during various times of the year, and what the harvest would be like.

> *Gdy na Gromniczną mróz, szykuj chłopie wóz; a jak lanie to sanie.*
> If there's frost on Candlemas, prepare the wagon; if rain, the sleigh.

> *Gdy słonce świeci jasno na Gromnicę, to przyjdą większe mrozy, śnieżyce.*
> If the sun shines bright on Candlemas, more frost and snow will come this way.

The Poles also examined the behavior of animals on the day as a method of predicting future weather. Whereas Americans use the ground hog to predict the weather for the following six weeks until the official spring in March, the Poles of the Tarnów-Rzeszow region used the bear. If, on the day of Matka Boska Gromniczna, the bear came out of his winter lair and found frost, he would knock down and pull apart his hiding place because he expected that winter would end shortly. However, if the day was a damp one, he came out and spent time mending it because winter would hang on for quite some time yet.

FEBRUARY

The last function of Matka Boska Gromniczna was that the day officially ended the celebration of the Christmas season. Decorations were taken down and carefully stored away for the next season. Carolers set aside their szopkas and costumes. Thoughts officially turned toward festive, pre-Lenten activities.

March

The period before the beginning of Lent in Poland was character-
ized by numerous parties and entertainments known as *karnawał*,
or carnival time. One such activity during this period was the
kulig, a sleigh ride party that was a favorite pastime of the minor
and major nobility. Where this custom began is unknown, but
there is no shortage of historical documentation to support that a
merry sleigh ride as a carnival pastime was enjoyed for over
three hundred years. The name is supposedly derived from the
word *kula*, a cane that was passed from house to house and
village to village, the bearer usually bringing some type of
announcement or official news. The sleigh parties usually began
the week before Ash Wednesday and continued right up until
midnight of Ash Wednesday, at which time all manner of good
times ceased.

The lead actor or organizer of the kulig was a young nobleman who secretly conferred with the girls or young married
women as to where and how to conduct the kulig. Snow conditions permitting, they would make a list as to where the party
should begin, the route to various residences, how to gather
everybody along the way, and where it was to end. It was an
unwritten law that it was to be done as a surprise. They did not
wait for an invitation.

Under the young nobleman's command, unmarried daughters,
wives, and in-laws all gathered together, dressed in their finery
and furs. Climbing into horse-drawn sleighs or on horseback,
everyone rode to the first home on their list. The sleighs of the
very wealthy were often in fantastic shapes of dragons or pagodas
and were pulled by richly appointed horses, complete with

71

expensive harnesses, with ribbons and tufts of feathers braided into their manes. Accompanying the crowd would be a group of musicians hired by the organizer of the kulig, who generally headed the entourage.

As dusk approached, the entire retinue would ride through the villages. The ringing of sleigh bells, the playing music and the shouting and singing of the sleigh party would draw people from the warmth of their homes unto the street to witness the merry spectacle.

The secrecy in planning the kulig was critical, for it was believed that half the fun was arriving unannounced so that the neighbor could not hide or go away from his residence. On the other hand, notifying anyone ahead of time of their arrival was practically unknown in Poland. Whatever time of day or night, visitors would always be offered something to eat or drink. As soon as the cavalcade entered the courtyard, the horsemen and drivers of the sleighs would begin cracking their whips with all their strength and make a great deal of noise singing to announce their arrival. The gospodarz would hurry to the porch, as always, to greet his guests while the matron began lighting the house and bringing food to the table. The guests and their animals were given the best food and drink that the house had to offer. When they had eaten their fill, the house party began in full swing with music and dancing. The singing and dancing were interspersed with innumerable vodka toasts and glasses of wine. Such carryings-on led moralists, who viewed such surfeit with a jaundiced eye, to write:

Kulig, ta zabawa jeszcze od Popiela
Ma za cel, by każdemu zalała gardziela.

Kulig, that entertainment from the time of Popiel,
has as its purpose, to drench everyone's throat.

In the more well-to-do residences, the kulig lasted for days with dancing, singing, playing group games, performing wild feats on horseback, and sometimes even getting up a spontaneous hunting party to the nearest forest. Some of the revelers would dress up in costumes as gypsies, chimney sweeps, and beggars, or as Turks or Cossacks.

On the last Tuesday, someone in the group, usually the wittiest, would dress as a priest, donning a shirt rather than a surplice, and instead of a stole, hanging a long scarf around the neck. The "priest" then stood in the corner of the room on a stool with a rug tacked to the walls in front of him, as if in a pulpit, and delivered a hilarious sermon on the bidding of farewell to carnival time.

When the revelers had eaten and drunk their host dry, they bundled their host and hostess up, packed them into the sleighs, moved on to the next person on their list, and so on. They continued on in this way until they finished their round of merrymaking at the home of the person who initiated the merriment in the first place.

Of kulig festivities, folklorist Łukasz Gołębiowski wrote: "During these times quite a few neighborly feuds or conflicts were mended. Overflowing with merriment and old-fashioned sincerity, it was unknown to see sneers or jibes, arguments or challenges to duels. Age-old misunderstandings became drowned in brotherly handclasps and embraces."

The last days of carnival were ushered in with *comber* or *babski comber*. This custom occurred on the last Thursday of carnival called *Tlusty Czwartek* or Fat Thursday. The flower vendors and tradeswomen of Krakow dressed in various outlandish costumes on this day and, accompanied by a hired musician, visited taverns and coffee houses, dragging along a straw figure named *combra*. Imbibing generously at each stop, the women slowly wound their way towards the Cloth Hall in the center of Krakow's Rynek (Square). Any male, be he common or high born, who happened to cross their path, was accosted, forced to dance with them, and not freed until he bought his freedom with a round of drinks. No one was safe from assault. Members of the King's court were halted in their conveyances, made to alight, were hugged, kissed, and made to dance all the while hollering "comber! comber!" The poorer males had their caps whisked off their heads, their hair touseled, and their faces kissed by one and all.

Once they reached the front of the Cloth Hall, the straw figure was then torn apart. Documented evidence of this custom can be traced back to 1600, and it is believed to have been brought to Krakow by German settlers and to have spread out far beyond the city to the surrounding towns and villages. Polish legends and beliefs, however, give a different origin for comber: There once lived in Krakow an unscrupulous mayor by the name of Comber who had the gardeners and tradeswomen of Krakow under his jurisdiction. He baited them mercilessly, fining them for the least offense, and squeezing exorbitant taxes from them so that he beggared many a vendor. It seems that the curses placed on Comber finally reached him, for on Fat Thursday he died a very sudden death. The news was met with such happiness and jubilation that the women left their stalls and merchandise unattended and ran through the streets singing and dancing.

The last three days before Ash Wednesday and the beginning of Lent are called by a variety of names including *kuse dni*, *mięsopust*, *ostatki*, and sometimes *podkoziołek*. The last name generally refers to a type of entertainment that took place on Shrove Tuesday. While carnival celebration took place throughout the season, the most concentrated burst of merriment took place during the last three days, which is why the Mazowsze called them *bachusy* (Bacchus) or *dnie szalone* (crazed days).

Young men dressed up in animal costume were generally seen throughout the Christmas and pre-Lenten season, but their appearance intensified during these last three days. The main animal disguises were a goat, a bear being led on a straw rope, a horse, or a stork. All figured as principal fertility figures in days of old. The goat was typically seen in Pomorze and Krakow; the bear was more indigenous in the Śląsk and Kurpie region, which was at one time a very heavily forested area. The horse was also part of the Kurpie tradition, while the stork appeared throughout Krakow and the surrounding countryside.

On Shrove Tuesday, the individuals dressed up either one or more animals, accompanied by a variety of other masqueraders such as an old man and old woman, chimney sweep, gypsy, policeman and a Jew, and began their journey through the village. Accompanied by music, the procession was led by an individual cleverly disguised on a wooden horse. It was he who asked the homeowner if the group could enter. If the head of the house agreed, everyone entered. The musicians began to play a tune and the head of the house was required to dance with the masqueraders. The chimney sweep, if he could manage it, scraped out some ashes from the stove and smeared them on the girls, while the stork jabbed at those present with his long jaw. The goat, dressed in a hairy blanket with a head fashioned from wood, and carrying a mobile jaw that opened and closed at the pull of a string, behaved boisterously, jumping, making bleating sounds, calling for food, and chasing the girls around the house.

The homeowner generally offered the masqueraders something to drink and eat and/or provided something for them to take away such as eggs, sausage, bread, or money. Before they left, the masqueraders wished the gospodarz success in his home and husbandry and, again accompanied by music, went on to the next farm or croft. They made a lot of noise, grabbed passers-by and dirtied them with soot, blocked everyone's way and demanded that they pay their way out. Old customs dictated that the animals walk the entire borders of the village, touching everything in order to ensure prosperity. Old Polish songs best describe the beliefs:

Gdzie koza stąpnie nogą
Tam żyto wyrośnie kopą.

Where the goat stomps his foot
There the rye grows abundantly.

Gdzie nasz konik pochodzi
Tam się żytko urodzi

Where our horse walks
There the rye grows.

After the masqueraders made their rounds through the village, they went to the local tavern or someone's house to eat the food that had been given them and to have some fun and dancing. At 11 o'clock in the evening, the custom of *podkoziołek* began. This was a dance between single men and women and was a remnant of the ancient custom of buying a bride.

The main figure of this custom was in the shape of a goat called a *koziołek*, i.e., billy goat. Sometimes the figure was that of a naked boy or that of a doll dressed in pants, coat, and hat. This figure was prepared ahead of time by the men and was usually cut from a turnip, beet, potato, apple, or piece of wood. The figure was placed on a plate and was propped up on the plate with the help of three sticks placed in the shape of a triangle. The plate with the figure was placed on a table or a barrel turned upside down in front of the musician, usually a fiddler. When midnight approached, the musician, who had been keeping everyone dancing merrily up until this time, announced that it was time to go home, for soon the church bells would ring announcing the beginning of Lent. This meant that marriages, which popularly occurred during carnival, would no longer be taking place. At the fiddler's announcement, the young women present who had failed to marry during carnival became targets for teasing, ridicule, and laughter by the bachelors. The fiddler also took his turn verbally abusing them saying no one wanted them, calling them fickle, etc. Suddenly the young men would change their tone and side with the girls, saying to the fiddler, "Don't be angry with the girls, for we'll take them." Taking a young girl by the hand, one of the bachelors approached the fiddler and begain a dialogue with the fiddler: "What do you want for this piece of livestock?" asks the bachelor.

"Five ducats," says the fiddler " for it is pleasant, efficient, and prone to work."

"But it is crooked and lame and look at those teeth!" the male replies.

"Well, then give me four ducats," is the the loud retort.

"I won't give you that much for I'll get no return on this one. "I'll give you one ducat."

The haggling continues with the fiddler praising the virtues of the "animal" with the bachelor pointing out the faults until such time as an agreement is reached. The ducats are paid in pennies and the money is placed under the billy goat, hence the name *podkoziołek*. The fiddler begins an *oberek* and all the unmarried men and women dance and sing:

> *Trzeba dać pod koziołka, trzeba dać*
> *Jeźli która ma się jeszcze z nas wydać.*

> One must give under the billy goat, one must give
> If one of us is still to marry.

When the song finishes another bachelor approaches with another unmarried female and another version of the same dialogue begins until all the unmarried girls have been "paid for" and danced with.

There were variations on this custom. When the musician announced it was time to leave, one of the bachelors approached the figure with his female partner and had to sing a song about the figure, the *podkoziołek*. It was the female who was obligated to throw some money on the plate as if buying herself a husband.

In both instances, however, the musician usually received the monies on the plate as payment for his services.

When all of the young girls had been danced with, all the older married men and women, who up until this time had only been observers, joined in, for dancing before the billy goat was the privilege of the unmarried men and women. The next dance, was called "*na wytrzymanego*," the endurance dance, and whoever lasted the longest, outdancing everyone else, would have the best crop in the upcoming year. In some villages, this last dance was called "*na wysoki len*," for tall flax, where all the women jumped over the tree stump believing that as high as they jumped, their flax would grow. In more ancient times, before it was curtailed by the church, everyone danced until the light of new day. Under later influence, when midnight and Ash Wednesday loomed closer, someone brought out a large herring and sang a song of goodbye to meat and carnival time.

Until it was strictly forbidden by the church and priests, Ash Wednesday had been another day of celebrations and carryings-on, especially for the married women of the villages. In the Poznań area, this custom was also called comber, a variation on the babski comber from Krakow which took place on Fat Thursday. In the morning all of the women went to church to receive ashes and from church went straight from church to the local tavern where they drank vodka, sang, and danced.

Around noon, the women dressed themselves up as tinkers, gypsies, and beggars, and carried a bag of ashes on a stick. If it happened that a man ventured across their path, he was assaulted on the head and shoulders with the bag of ashes or his hat was taken away; he was forced to buy it back with a round of drinks. When they'd had enough of these antics, the women took an old sleigh (if it was snowing), a wagon, a two wheeled cart or, short of finding something larger, a wheelbarrow, and placed a canopy over their vehicle made from four sticks and a large scarf or old sheet. If they had a wagon, the women hired a fiddler, placed him in the wagon, and, pulled by four women, the entire entourage headed for the home of the most newly married woman. The rest of the party, meanwhile, sang and danced around the wagon, hitting each other and anyone else who came along with the bags of ashes until those ashes floated across the entire village. When they arrived at the home of the newly married woman, they forced her into the vehicle (tumbling her out of the wheelbarrow a few times along the way, if that's what they were using) and returned to the tavern, where the new bride had to stand a round of drinks. When all of the newly married women had been brought to the tavern, the fun began in earnest, with the men joining in. They also danced *"na wytrzymanego"*- (for endurance) or *"na wysoki len"* (for tall flax). On Ash Wednesday, everyone attended morning services to have the priest make the sign of the cross on their foreheads with ashes obtained from the burning of last year's palms. During the reign of August III (1733-1763), it was customary that, for the sick and infirm who could not come to church, the priest visited the home to dispense the ashes.

For forty days, rich and poor alike renounced wordly things, abstained from every pleasure of the senses, as well as from food. To understand the Lenten fasts of Poland, it is necessary to go back to the times of the Apostles, when the days of Wednesday through Saturday were singled out as days in which to commemorate the Passion of Christ and the actions that led up to it. In memory of the Lord's suffering, Christians observed a strict fast on Friday as the day of Christ's death, and on Wednesday because Judas made his contract of betrayal on that day. In the fourth century, Saturday was added as one of the weekly fast days, because according to scriptures, on the day that Christ rested in the tomb, the Apostles had spent the day in sadness and fasting. Eventually a longer period of fasting was introduced by Christian churches. A fast of forty days was adopted in imitation of Christ who fasted forty days in the desert. The form of fast and abstinence for the entire Christian Church was announced by Pope Saint Gregory as far back as 604 AD. It stated: "We abstain from flesh meat and from all things that come from flesh, as milk, cheese, eggs, and butter." For almost a thousand years, this remained the norm of abstinence for all except those who were excused for reasons of ill health.

The Poles observed the imposed fast with a vigilance and strictness that makes the excessiveness of the pre-Lenten festivities understandable. The forty days of Lent was called the *Wielki Post*, or "Great Lent," or "Great Fast," differentiating it from other, less rigid fasts such as that of Advent.

In his normal, day-to-day existence, the Polish peasant did not, as a rule, enjoy an abundance of meat. His usual diet was fairly meager, with meat available only on special occasions. Beef was rarely eaten because cows were killed only when they went dry. Calves were always sold at the local *jarmark* or marketplace to buy other necessary essentials. Fresh milk was also sold, but the dairy by-products obtained from milk were often the saving grace of many a meal. Buttermilk and cream were valuable accessories to the otherwise plain flour, potato, and grain dishes that were the usual fare of the peasant. Sour cream was also used in just about everything, as were a variety of cheeses. Pork, another Polish favorite, also was rare on the table except for holiday splurges. In its place, salt pork, lard, and suet gave a "meat effect" to a host of grain dishes. The removal of all of these basic food enhancers from their meals created an extremely plain and unvaried diet.

Many individuals observed an even stricter fast and abstinence, eating only once a day, often breaking their fast late in the evening after devotions. On Saturday, the more pious limited themselves to eating bread only, washing it down with a few gulps of weak beer. The drinking of vodka and wine was strictly curtailed throughout the Lenten season but totally abstained from on Fridays. Water was the common everyday drink for Lent. Where it was available, fish and fish soups were common Lenten fare. Herring was the most popular fish and it wasn't unusual for families to order an entire barrel of herrings for Lent. Carp, pike, perch, cod, catfish, salmon, and even eel were brought to table in those areas where it was plentiful. Because of the lack of fats or dairy products to make sauces for the fish, it was often wrapped in a plant leaf with herbs and wine and baked on hot coals in the fire.

Other basic foods during Lent consisted of black bread, plain vegetables, and a soup called *żur*. In essence, żur was a sour soup made from fermented, raw bread dough, much like the starter dough for today's sourbread. The *gospodyni*, or housewife, would mix coarsely ground rye and water in a stoneware crock to which she would add some sugar and salt and, if she wished, some garlic. On top of this, she would place a piece of rye bread which would assist in the fermenting process. Covered with a piece of cloth it was then placed in a warm area and allowed to work. When it came time to make the soup, she would boil a pot of water, add a cup of the fermented żur and whatever else was available, such as mushrooms, chopped onions, and a pinch of flavorful herbs. This sour soup was then poured over plain, boiled potatoes, either whole or mashed.

In the Krakow area, the żur was made from water in which beets had been cooked and instead of rye, oat flour was used. The żur was so much the main meal of Lent that it was inevitable for it to become the subject of village customs and songs. As Lent drew near around the village, under the loosening influence of the vodka that was common during carnival, the people kicked up their heels to dance and sing to "Pan Żurowski":

> *Wstępna środa następuje*
> *Pani matka żur gotuje*
> *A pan młody siedzi w dziurze*
> *Witaj, witaj, panie Żurze*
> *Wiwat! Wiwat! Wiwat!*

> Draws near Ash Wednesday
> Mother-in-law is cooking żur

And the young groom sits in a hovel
Welcome, welcome Mr. Żur
Hurrah! Hurrah! Hurrah!

In another custom, the peasant would tie a herring and a bag of ashes to a long stick on Ash Wednesday. With his wife following behind him, carrying a bowl of żur, the peasant would walk around his house shaking the stick. This apparently served to drive out any lingering remnants of carnival. They would then enter the house which had been thoroughly cleaned of any traces of meat and dairy products in the preceding days, and ritually place the żur on the table. Everyone in attendance at the ceremony had to at least take a taste of it.

By the end of Lent, the villagers were so sick of eating żur that they made much of ending its "reign." On Holy Saturday, housewives and farmhands, happy that soon they would be able to feast on blessed eggs and juicy sausage, made an elaborate ritual of burying the remaining żur and then breaking the pot by flinging rocks at it from a distance. Whoever first broke the pot had the right to go from home to home on Easter Sunday and be warmly received and treated to holiday food and drink. Over time, the church lessened its Lenten restrictions and granted many dispensations in the matter of Lenten fasting to all countries of Europe. People who did break the fast could make amends by giving donations for the building of churches, or by giving alms to the poor. However, many people, especially the Poles, retained the old and strict routine, refusing to take advantage of any leniency. For instance, in the 16th century when Erazm Ciołek, Bishop of Płock, brought from Rome a papal dispensation stating that it was permissible to eat meat on Wednesday, he could not find a single soul throughout his diocese who would avail themselves of the dispensation.

Besides being a time for the atonement of sins committed during the year through fasting, Lent was also a time of reflection and contemplation through prayer. For the Catholic Pole, this was essentially a preparation for reliving one of the most dramatic episodes in the history of mankind — the story of the birth, life, and death of a man called Jesus of Nazareth. From the ancient times of Christ, down through the centuries, the Catholic Church has striven to interpret the story of a humble carpenter who was condemned to death because He was guilty of doing good and asked people to follow His teachings.

One of the very early methods utilized by the Church to teach the moving accounts of the suffering, death, and Resurrection of Christ was the use of a theatrical drama known as a passion play, complete with action and music, which was incorporated right into the Mass itself. The average citizen of Poland in the Middle ages, illiterate and without the means of schooling, would be drawn to a living, talking drama which would teach the lessons of the Church. So popular were the plays, particularly during Lent and Holy Week, that large audiences would crowd the nave and isles of churches eager to witness the story of Christ's last days on earth.

Over time, the Church realized that the passion plays and hymns, especially the the custom of chanting a long lyrical *planctus*, or lament, of the Blessed Virgin, which became attached to the Good Friday veneration of the cross in the twelfth century, were not well understood by the people. Originally written and produced in Latin, the language of learned monks and priests, the dramas and accompanying hymns were not always completely or well understood by the majority of Polish people, who had little or no schooling in Latin. Subsequently, both the plays and hymns were translated into the language and dialects of the people. One of the best loved hymns that evolved during this transition was the *Gorzkie Żale*. It is not known exactly who was the author of Gorzkie Żale, the plaintive lamentations of the Passion of Jesus Christ and the sorrows of His Mother that have no equal in Polish Lenten hymn books. It is known, however, that it was first heard at the Vincentian Holy Cross Church in Warsaw. Near this church there existed at the time the Order of the Brothers of St. Roch, which was headed by Father Wawrzy-niec Stanisław Benik. It was under his aegis that the Gorzkie Żale, as it is known today, was first printed in 1707. At that time they were called *Snopek Mirry*. The present name was taken from the first words of the first of the hymns which are arranged on the pattern of a priest's breviary. Each of the three sections unfolds in a hymn which ponders a particular moment of the Passion of our Lord and ends with the invocation of *"Któryś cierpiał za nas rany, Jezu Chryste, zmiłuj się nad nami."* (You who have suffered for us, Jesus Christ, have mercy on us).

The first Gorzkie Żale was said before an audience of the faithful by Father Szczepan Wierzkowski at Holy Cross Church. The souls and hearts of the Polish people responded to these beautiful lamentations until it was being sung in even the smallest of hamlets throughout the country. Throngs of faithful gathered every Sunday afternoon in Lent to recall Christ's passion. In some places, the lamentations were sung on Fridays, and were an integral part of Good Friday services. Sung with deepest feelings and often committed to memory in entirety, Gorzkie Żale was sung by Poles in exile during two World Wars. Immigration saw the establishment of Gorzkie Żale in the newly formed churches in both North and South America and the passing on of it from generation to generation of Polish Americans.

The long fasting period of Lent was not without some festivities. In the northeast of Poland, during the early spring, a figure representing death was braided from sheaves of grain or straw into the shape of a human, and was thrown into a river or pond. This was called the drowning of *Marzanna*.

The oldest writings about Marzanna in Poland come from Jan Długosz (1415-1480), who wrote: "In some Polish villages on the 4th Sunday (*Laetare*) in Lent, the people place an effigy of Marzanna on long poles and then throw it into the nearest bog." Marcin Bielski, in his *Kronika Wszystkiego Świata*, published first in 1551 and then again in 1564, wrote: "There was a custom among us in the villages that on the fourth Sunday during Lent

8 THE DROWNING OF MARZANNA

they drowned an effigy that was made of straw or hemp and dressed in the clothes of a person. This effigy they called Marzanna. The whole village took it to the nearest body of water, removed the clothes and threw it in singing sadly:

Śmierć wije się po płotu
Szukająca kłopotu.

Death is hanging around
Looking for trouble.

Then, everyone quickly ran home. It was believed that whoever fell on this run home would die in that year. Death, seeking retribution, would grab those who fell and cause their death."

The drowning of Death in effigy was done with the understanding that Death would not visit the village that year. It was also believed to purify the village and protect the inhabitants from sickness and plague.

In the Śląsk area, this Sunday was called *Biała Niedziela*, or White Sunday, and the figure was also called *marzanna* or *marzanka*. A figure was made of straw and dressed in local girls' costume. This custom was originally done by the women, but was gradually transferred to the young girls.

After drowning the figure, the girls returned to the village with a *gaik*, a long green branch or small tree decorated with ribbons, feathers, and colored egg shells. They made a walking tour of the village singing:

Wyniosłymy marzaneczkę ze wsi
Przyniosłymy zielony gaj do wsi.

We have taken death from the village
And brought the green branch to the village.

9 GIRLS WITH GAIK

The girls visited various homes with their gaily decorated tree and received eggs in return which they decorated during Holy Week. This custom was also known in Great Poland, but it was called *śmiercicha*, (death), and the green branch was known as *nowe latko* (New Year). The girls paraded from house to house singing:

> *Pani gospodyni*
> *nowe latko w sini*
> *Zeli chcecie oglądować*
> *to musicie coś darować*
> *Zielony gaj*
> *Koszyczek jaj.*

> Lady housewives,
> The green branch is in the maypole,
> If you'd like to look at it
> You must give
> A basket of eggs.

Another later account of this custom from the hamlet of Jaworzynki-Zapasiek in the Beskid Śląsk area recalls: Long ago during the Great Fast, the marzanny paraded through the village. This was two twelve year old girls who carried a doll as large as an infant made from rags and decorated with ribbons. With the doll, the girls visited homes singing Lenten songs, and in exchange received eggs and money. The doll was not destroyed, but put away for the following year.

In some parts of Upper Silesia, the effigy, representing an old woman, was made in the house where the last death occurred and was carried on a pole to the boundary of the village, where it was either thrown into a pond or burnt. Sometimes the figure was dressed in a white shirt and carried a broom and a sickle. The entire group then returned to the village with an evergreen decorated with ribbons and colored egg shells. The group sang the following:

> *Do tego domu wstępujemy*
> *Szczęścia, zdrowia winszujemy*
> *Nasz gaik zielony*
> *Pięknie przystrojony*
> *Wszędzie sobie chodzi*
> *Bo mu się tak godzi*
> *Dajcież, dajcie, macie nam co dać.*

> Into this home we enter
> Good fortune, good health we wish.
> Our green branch
> Decorated beautifully
> Travels everywhere
> Because it pleases to do so.
> Give, give, you are to give us something.

After receiving eggs, bread, and other gifts, the group offered thanks and more well wishes for success and good luck.

In the Podhale area, the girls paraded a doll throughout the village dressed in white and adorned with ribbons and called *śmierzteczka,* and also received eggs or small change. In some parts of Poland, the custom of drowning *marzanna* underwent a transformation under the influence of the church and was called the drowning of *Judasz* and *Popielec.*

The other small festivity that occurred during Lent was a custom associated with school age children called *gregorjanek* or *chodzenie po gregórkach,* known in English as "going a-gregoring." Celebrated by children in elementary school, this custom harked back to the times when Pope Gregory IV established March 12th as a holy day commemorating Pope Gregory the Great.

Elected Pope in 590 A.D., Pope Gregory the Great made numerous reforms within the church, including revising the liturgy and church calendar, encouraging the growth of monasticism, as well as making tremendous contributions to the establishment of schools and the spread of education. On his orders, children who were brought to the marketplace seeking work were bought up and taken to school and given an education instead. Pope Gregory died on March 12, 604 AD, and upon his elevation to sainthood, became the Patron Saint of elementary school children.

The custom of celebrating the Feast of St. Gregory by elementary school children began in Italy and spread to France, Belgium, Germany, and finally to Poland, where it survived the longest in western Poland. It was on this day that parents took their children to school for the first time. Long ago, this feast day was associated with the older boys of the area carrying banners of the likeness of St. Gregory. They frequently dressed up in costume as bishops, priests, schoolteachers, and church deacons. Carrying a long branch of birch covered with ribbons and crepe paper streamers, the boys visited all the homes of the village with the express purpose of amusing the inhabitants with poems and songs that they may have learned in school. As a reward, the villagers would treat them with small gifts of eggs, dried fruit, or sometimes butter and cheese. The children would then return to the school where the teacher would distribute their "earnings" among all the school children present.

In some districts of Poland, the parents dressed their children up in their Sunday best and took them to the local school where various games and entertainments for the children were held. For instance, a rope on which *obwarzanki* (pretzels) were strung, was tied around a teacher's waist. The teacher then tried to evade the children, running here and there, while the children tried to catch him and pull the treats off the rope. The chodzenie po gregórkach had a hidden purpose behind its fun and games. At a time when sending children was not a mandatory affair, it was the hope of local officials to try and get parents to send their children to school; chodzenie po gregórkach was a method of publicizing the school and a way of getting both parents and children to enter the school building itself. The rhyme was used to encourage attendance at school and began like this:

Dziś mamy święto Św. Gregorza
Sławnego patrona,
już idzie śnieg do morza
Szkoły, klasztory, on wszystkie założył
Aby te wiarę po świecie rozmnożył.
Ojcowie, matki!
Swoje miłe dziatki
Do szkoły dajcie — a nie odbierajci
Nauka klejnot, nauka skarb drogi
Tego nie wydrze nieprzyjaciel srogi
Nie spali ogień, nie zabierze woda.

Today we celebrate the Feast of St.Gregory
Illustrious patron,
the snow is melting back to the sea.
Schools, monasteries he established
In order to propagate the faith.
Fathers, mothers!
Your loving children
Send to school—and don't remove.
Education is a jewel, education is a priceless treasure.
No fierce enemy can take it away,
It will not burn in a fire nor be taken away by flood.

The month of March ends with the return of the *bocian*, or stork, to the trees and chimneys of rural Poland. Old Polish folk legends say that once upon a time, frogs, snakes, lizards and others of their ilk were multiplying excessively on earth. Because they were making a nuisance of themselves, God gathered them up into a sack and, calling man, told him to empty the sack into the sea. Man—feeble and weak creature that he is—was unable to contain his curiosity and untied the sack along the way to see what it was he was carrying. All of the creatures slipped out and scattered, hiding themselves lest they be gathered up again. As punishment God turned man into a stork, a bocian, and condemned him to hunt the creatures for the rest of his life.

All other Polish legends and beliefs surrounding the stork repeat the same theme—that man and stork are kindred spirits endowed with human qualities and virtues, capable of both helping and harming, but above all, to be made welcome to nest on the chimneys or to take up residence high on top of the poplar trees. No other bird or beast was more esteemed or more closely connected with Polish home life than the European white stork. To have them anywhere on your property was to bring good fortune. Happy was the farmer whose roof gable was chosen! He could look forward to a heavy harvest, healthy livestock, and much joy in his family life. If, by chance, the paired storks nested on some public building such as the church steeple, they then became community property, and the whole village could feel free to feel blessed and draw on their good luck powers.

Now on the decline, the European white stork once resided in great numbers in rural Poland; their close proximity to man made it possible to observe and carefully scrutinize their behavior. The nesting and migratory patterns of the storks were consistent and unfluctuating. They returned to the same village, often to the same rooftop year after year. Their arrival could be timed almost to the day. "On the Feast of the Annunciation (March 25), the storks come." Or, "The stork is here, then St. Joseph's Day (March 19th) is not far off." Their comings and goings became the yardstick by which the Polish farmer could measure the change of seasons. Their arrival told him that the grass would soon be green and that the plowing of the fields must begin. Their departure indicated that cold weather was at hand and that the chinks in the house ought to be filled.

MARCH

Probably no bird is more devoted to its mate or takes better care of its young than the stork. Mating at the age of three or four, the storks often live to the age of seventy and, once mated, are mated for life. For centuries all over Poland, people watched the storks working in teams, skillfully building and adding to their nests and returning to them year after year to mate and lay their eggs. Because of the exceptional care they took of their young and their faithfulness to one another, they became the source of numerous folk songs and poetry. The loud and rapid "kle-kle-kle" clattering noises made by the storks when one mate returns from a feeding trip or gathering nest material became incorporated into the Polish vocabulary. To "*klekotać*" or to be a "*klekotka*" is to make rattling, clattering noises, to be a prattler or to chatter noisily—usually said by a husband to his wife in a less than supportive manner. Children and adults, dressed as storks during the pre-Lenten carnival, along with those disguised as the bear or wild ox, were believed to have magical powers. The influence of storks also extended into the school, where their unmistakable white plummage, jet black wing feathers, bright red bills, and long, stalk-like legs became the subject matter for children's first readers.

Birds and birdwatching have always absorbed the interest of agricultural peoples, and the conspicuously tall storks were no exception. The much-loved, snowy white storks always brought the last of winter's snow on their wingtips in early spring and disappeared when cold winds blew, wandering around in warmer climates and having interesting adventures, marking time until they could return to Poland.

April

The last week of Lent was ushered in by Palm Sunday. On this day, long before the first rays of dawn brightened the horizon, the village girls and boys gathered together in groups to go to the stables and barns where the young stablehands and servants slept, to wake them by hitting them with branches of willow, saying:

> *Nie ja biję, wierzba bije*
> *za tydzień, wielki dzień*
> *Za sześć noc, Wielkanoc.*

I don't strike, the willow strikes
In one week, the great day
In six nights, the great night, Easter.

Added to this were wishes for health, happiness, success, and enjoyment of the upcoming Easter holiday.

Palm Sunday was more likely to be called *Niedziela Męki Pańskiej* (The Sunday of the Lord's Passion), *Niedziela Wierzbowa* (Willow Sunday), or *Niedziela Kwietnia*. The latter name April Sunday stems from the fact that it falls frequently in the month of April; Blossom Sunday comes from the custom of bringing to church a figure of Christ riding on a donkey while spectators throw flowers and pussy willow branches.

Lacking the "palms" indigenous to Jerusalem, the Polish people simply cut whatever greenery they found in the fields to use as palms. In the northern Mazowsze area, the "palms" brought to church were willow branches on which pussy willows had bloomed. If Palm Sunday fell early in the year while the earth was still covered with snow, the people would cut branches of birch, raspberry, or wild currant and place them in water in a warm room in order to force them to bud green. In close keeping with the scriptures, the people in the Mazowsze region placed their palms on the floor of the church so that the priest walked on them on the way to the altar during Palm Sunday procession.

As people came out of church following the Mass, many individuals hit each other other again with the same exclamations of *"Nie ja biję, wierzba bije,"* etc., and good wishes. Everyone took their palms home to place high in the rafters of the barns to protect the building against lightning, and to encourage the cattle to grow strong. They were tucked into beehives so that the bees would produce a lot of honey, or under the nest of a goose to protect the future goslings from harm. Within the house they were also placed behind holy pictures in the belief that the palm would protect the house and its environment from lightning, fire and other misfortunes. Sometimes the blessed palms were walked around the house three times, the house touched by the palm each time around. Three of the catkins of the pussy willows were swallowed by every member of the family in order to protect or prevent problems of the throat, teeth, or stomach.

When the farmer drove his cattle out to pasture for the first time in spring, he used a palm, making the sign of the cross across the animal. He then stuck the plant into the earth to protect the fields against hail. A branch was fastened to the plow when it went out for the first plowing in spring. Dipped in holy water, it was used to sprinkle the house and outbuildings during a storm. A cross made from the palm was nailed over the main entry of the house to protect it against lightning. Burnt over hot coals, it acted as incense to drive away evil spirits. From year to year, the pussy willow branches were always appropriately taken care of. Old branches were burnt and the ashes distributed over the ground or chopped finely and mixed with the first sowing.

In other parts of Poland, the palms took on still other forms. In the heavily forested Kurpie region, the people made their palms of forest plants, such as club moss, that remained green through the winter. This greenery was attached to a stout pole or branch in order to be carried to church. Some individuals simply cut branches off a pine or juniper tree. Both these methods caused their palms to be unusually tall, sometimes ranging from one to seven meters high. Lacking real flowers because the earth still had not warmed, the older women of the villages fashioned artificial ones from the white interior of the bulrush. Much later, following the emergence of colored paper, the women switched to making paper flowers in hues of gold and orange or violet and yellow and braided these flowers between the tall, green branches.

Another custom on Palm Sunday which can be dated back to the Middle Ages was *puchery*, from the Latin word *puer* for "boy." Documentation in *The Kurjer Warszawski* in 1822 indicates that after Mass on Palm Sunday the schoolboys organized themselves in two rows and recited speeches about herring, the Lenten fast, the hardships of school, and the baked goods they looked forward to on Easter. On their conclusion, the local boys, dressed as shepherds, pilgrims, hussars, and other soldiers, pushed themselves forward. The soldier uniforms had braided rope across the chests and the boys wore mitered hats made of gold paper from which hung paper streamers and mustaches and beards made from hemp. The small soldiers carried a hammer on a long wooden stick, as if it were a battle ax, which was used to pound on the floor after every third verse. Like the schoolboys, they also recited in verse, but took on a more wordly and amusing tone than was proper. This eventually caused the priest of Holy Cross Church in Warsaw to forbid the orations in the church, with other priests quickly following his example. The end result was that the singing and orations were then moved from within the church to the homes. Wandering from house to house, carrying a basket for the expected eggs or baked goods they were to receive, the children called on the inhabitants of the house by knocking on doors with their long hammers and then reciting amusing verse. They offered good wishes for the Resurrection of Christ, for which they usually received their edible rewards.

Similar to puchery was the *koniarz* whose place of origin, like puchery, was Krakow. A boy smeared soot on his face and dressed in a sheepskin coat, with the sheepskin facing out. A straw rope crossed his chest and he wore a long tail made of straw. In one hand, the young boy carried a wooden sword while in the other, he held a basket for receiving gifts for his orations.

Palm Sunday marked the beginning of intensive preparations for Easter. On Holy Thursday some individuals began an even more intensive fast by not eating anything from that day until the morning meal on Easter Sunday. If anything, they drank holy water, which was blessed on Holy Thursday.

In some regions of Poland, Holy Thursday spurred the organization of what was called *pogrzeb żuru*, or the burial of żur. A group of boys got together, with at least one among them who was uninitiated or easily gulled. They talked the individual into gathering the glazed, clay pots in which the żur was fermented, and tied it to his back or instructed him to carry it on his head. The unsuspecting individual was then walked to the boundaries of the village, where the żur was supposed to be buried, followed by a small entourage of the village children. One of the rascals who had set him up carried a shovel with which to dig a hole to bury the żur. Just as the group was about to dig the hole, however, the pot was hit with the shovel and the contents spilled all over the carrier, causing great mirth.

In some villages in Pomorze, there was a custom that on Holy Thursday and every afternoon until Easter Sunday when the church bells were silent, the boys walked around the entire village creating a dreadful noise with a *klekotki* or *grzechotki*, a wooden clapper. About fifty of them would gather together and walk around the church three times, making a racket with their instruments, calling everyone to pray and remember their

10 WOODEN CLAPPERS CALLED KLEKOTKI OR GRZECHOTKI

responsibilities to attend church. The clappers were either homemade or bought during the year at one of the church fairs.

On Holy Thursday or Good Friday, eggs were first colored. The coloring of eggs was chiefly the province of young girls and women, and was done in great secrecy with the room considered "off limits" to males. If through some misfortune a man happened to enter the room, not only was he chased away, but the women had to throw a pinch of salt over their shoulders to cleanse themselves.

The different colored eggs were called by a variety of names: *malowane* or *malowanki*, when a colorful design was painted on top; or *kraszone* or *kraszanki*, when a single color made from a dye using herbs and roots was used. In some areas these were called *byczki*. *Pisanki* were batik style eggs on which wax was carefully applied in patterns with a stylus before they were placed in colored dyes. Other styles were known as *oklejane* and *nalepianki*, when the outside of the egg was decorated with a variety of materials such as colored paper or straw.

On Good Friday in the Pomorze area, the boys and girls hit each other with branches of the willow tree, calling out "*Boże rany, Boże rany, Chrystus był ukrzyzowany,*" i.e., "God's wounds, God's wounds, Christ was crucified." In Kaszuby, Good Friday was called *Płaczebóg* or God crying. Being awakened in the morning, individuals are hit with a green branch and told to cry, for God is crying today.

Good Friday was devoted to the memory of the Passion of Christ. The people spent the day fasting and praying in church. Beginning at 3 P.M., people began visiting the church to pray before an altar where a figure of the crucified Christ in an open tomb, surrounded by burning lamps, candles, and flowers was displayed. These tombs or sepulchers, popular throughout all of Poland, were called *Boże groby.* Their origin can also be attributed to the early mystery plays, which began in Italy and spread slowly throughout Europe, and were especially popular in Poland during the time of Zygmunt III (1566-1632). Acting troupes consisting of monks and their students came to the small villages and put on performances about various aspects of the life of Christ. Boże groby were one of the remaining remnants of the dramas that were enacted during the Easter season. Sepulchers, similar to that used by actors and religious folk, continued to be erected even after the decline of the passion plays.

In the village of Radomyśl on the Lower San River, they mounted a guard at the Easter sepulcher called "Turks." On Good Friday, next to the grave of Christ, stood a sentry who kept a vigil throughout the night, as well as through the next day and night until the Resurrection Mass on Sunday. During this entire time, the church was open for those individuals who wished to come and pray. The sentry changed every hour and was dressed in costume to represent these Eastern peoples. Each one wore a high hat with a crimson top. Instead of the wool that usually covered their hats, there were wide strips of ribbon, usually red and gold, that were tied in large bows on the right side, the ends hanging all the way down to the hip. On top of the ribbons were ropes of coral beads. From the left shoulder there was a wide blue or red ribbon that tied with a bow beneath the right hand. On his left side the sentry carried a sword or an old Polish cutlass, along with an accompanying sheath. There was usually someone older in charge of changing the sentries who was differentiated from the others in that he had the reddest of ribbons and a red or white feather in his cap. The uniform consisted of the old-fashioned crimson frockcoat called *żupan*.

The oldest inhabitants of the town indicate that after the expedition of King John III Sobieski to Vienna, the inhabitants of Radomyśl who had followed their King returned to their native town during Easter week. Dressed in Turkish attire taken from the enemy, with battle axes in hand, the men went directly to church on Holy Friday to thank the Lord for safely bringing them home. They stood on guard in front of the Easter Sepulcher until Resurrection on Easter Sunday morning.

In larger cities such as Krakow, which boasted many churches, the visits to the sepulchers at the various churches were done with the greatest solemnity and considered to be a type of pilgrimage. Even the poorest and most humble churches were visited and an offering for the poor was made.

On Good Friday, the boys made an effigy of Judas from tattered clothing and stuffed it with straw. In a pocket or a cloth bag, thirty pieces of broken glass, representing the 30 pieces of silver accepted by Judas for his betrayal, were placed. This was dragged through the streets by a rope around its neck, and then taken to a church, where it was thrown from the belfry. From there, followed by local children who futher beat the figure with sticks while calling "Judas," "Judas," they dragged the battered effigy down to the river where it was drowned, or if there was no body of water at hand, burnt.

Early on Holy Saturday, the young boys went to church with a bunch of long twigs and, assisted with the blessing of fire, lit their sticks and brought them home. From this, the housewife lit a new fire and tried to keep that "new" fire burning for as long as possible. What was left of the long sticks was burned in the field or saved for various purposes. With the new fire, the women began preparing food that was to be taken to the church to be blessed in a specially decorated basket called *święconka*. What was placed in the basket depended entirely on the finances of the family, but usually it contained a loaf of bread, a few eggs, horseradish, a piece of pork, a length of sausage, cheese, and fresh churned butter. Tucked in among the foodstuffs was boxwood.

If the village was so small as to not have a church of its own, everyone gathered at some agreed-upon spot and a priest would come in from a neighboring village to bless the food. If the village was so remote as to preclude a visit by a priest, the people brought their baskets with them when they either walked or rode to the church for Resurrection Mass. Their baskets were blessed by the priest at its conclusion.

APRIL

At midnight on Holy Saturday, water was believed to have miraculous powers. At first light people flocked to rivers and streams to bathe, for doing so would help mend slow healing wounds as well as prevent skin disorders. It brought health and strength to the eyes. Young women went to bathe in the water in order to assure a beautiful complexion as well as happiness and good luck. The hands and face were not wiped dry but allowed to dry naturally. To complete this ritual successfully a young maiden was reminded not to talk to anyone or look around her while en route to the stream or river. If a cat or rabbit crossed her path, she had to return home or some misfortune would occur. If she met a bachelor, he would surely become her husband. If a member of the family was sick and unable to make the trek to the water, it was possible to bring it to the house, but after the washing, it was necessary to return the water from where it was obtained.

In some villages in Pomorze in the predawn hours between 3 and 5 A.M., the hours just before the expected Resurrection of Christ, a drum, kept especially for this occasion, was beaten by two boys who walked through the darkened village waking everyone and calling them to Mass. The purpose of the drum was to recall the shaking of the earth that took place during the crucifixion and when Christ rose from the dead. The only people excused from attending the early morning Mass were children who still didn't know their prayers and the very infirm.

The Resurrection Mass began with the rising of the sun. As the vigil of Easter, the *Wielka Noc* or Great Night, passed into the dawn of Easter Sunday with the jubilant words of *"Chrystus Zmartwychwstał"* (Christ is Risen), rifles and guns were shot into the air during the Mass to announce that the season of Easter, the *Wielkanocne Święta*, had begun. In a small village called Chełmzy in Pomorze, each child was given a bell to carry to the Resurrection Mass and during the procession that usually circled the church, the children would ring their bells in response to those rung by the priest and altar boys, as if an echo.

If someone happened to oversleep and not get to the Resurrection Mass, that individual could forfeit the right to eat *swięconka*, the blessed food of Easter breakfast.

Following the Mass, it was the custom in many areas of Poland for the males to race home on their horses and wagons. Whoever reached home first was supposed to be the first to harvest his crops. On return from church, the family and any hired help or servants sat down to partake of the blessed food. The long period of fasting had ended. Following the actions of his ancestors before him, the Catholic Pole broke his long Lenten fast with the eating of a blessed egg. In this simple but almost sacred act, the blessed egg was cut into quarters and then again into eighths. Each of the family members and guests present at the table partook of a slice of the egg, while wishing each other joy of the Easter Day and blessings for long life and happiness.

The origin of the presence of eggs in Easter customs dates back to ancient pagan nature rites that celebrated the beginning of spring. Living in a world over which man had no control and where nature was often unpredictable, hostile, and destructive, the changing seasons were regarded with a mixture of fear and awe. The earth, lying lifeless and dormant through winter, suddenly began bursting with new life. Subsequently, objects such as trees and stones were invested with magical powers. The simple, seemingly lifeless household egg, suddenly breaking and revealing a young creature, became an object of wonder and amazement.

Unfamiliar with the complex workings of creation, ancient man engaged in activities and celebrations that would ensure that the earth grow green and once again give birth to the crops so vital to his existence. The egg became a symbol of life, for it contained new life in an embryo, the seed of the future, and was a vitally important part of these ancient spring fertility rites.

With the advent of Christianity, however, the egg took on a religious meaning during Easter, but in Poland, as well as many other Indo-European countries, the egg as part of the ancient fertility rites continued in various shapes and forms for many centuries after conversion to Christianity. One important folk belief that persisted among Poles over the years was that the egg brought life to the fields and assisted in the growth process. The Polish farmer took an egg with him out to the fields when sowing grain in the hope that the grain would "grow as large as the eggs." Or, they would place an egg between the vegetable rows in order to protect the garden against insects and to drive away geese, mice, and moles. Some felt that burying the egg in the earth near fruit trees would increase their yield of fruit. The shells were thrown on the fields in order to increase the yield of rye and to protect the wheat against any blight. Cattle, as important to the livelihood of the Polish peasant as the crops, were anxiously guarded. Small portions of the Easter eggs were given to the livestock for their health and also given by the shepherds when they first drove the animals out to pasture in the spring for that very same purpose. The yolk was fed to the chickens so that they would lay well.

The power of eggs extended even to things with which they came in contact. The water used for boiling them was supposed to possess magical powers. It was felt that washing in the water used to cook eggs bestowed health and beauty. Farmers in Poland poured the water along the byre. It protected against the evil eye, fire, and lightning, and, when placed in the beehive, it increased the swarms of bees. It was also employed as an effective medicine in various illnesses such as fevers, jaundice, and erysipelas, an inflammation and redness of the skin which in Polish is called *róża*. In the area of Zakliczyna, the women of the village buried the shells of colored eggs in the garden with the belief that from them grew madder, which was used as medication for colic.

As a symbol of fertility, the egg played a critical role in almost all customs and traditions throughout the year. Up until the middle 1800s the elaborately decorated and ornamental eggs called *pisanki* served as gifts in the Polish wooing and courtship

105

process. In the districts of Łańcut and Lisk, the girls would wear eggs concealed in their bosom in hopes that the boys would reach for them. A girl would allow herself to be caught, searched, and dispossessed of the egg by the one she hoped to marry. Force was not uncommon and more than one ancestor caught himself a wife in this manner. In the Radom area of Poland, this giving of Easter eggs by the girl was seen as a symbol of her interest and permission for matchmakers to call. In a ceremony of girl auctioning, which existed during the last days before Lent, a young man bargained for his sweetheart much as one might haggle over the purchase of a cow or horse. The successful bidder (and future husband) was rewarded at Easter with a gift of exquisitely decorated pisanki. The receiving of pisanki was so special that village girls without a special boyfriend would promise the boys pisanki as a way of securing a dance partner during the Zapusty celebrations. On Easter Monday, when the boys would pour water on the girls in the *dyngus*, the girls would have to offer the boys eggs to get them to stop, thus giving meaning to the translation of dyngus as "ransom." The girls would literally buy their freedom from being doused with water by paying a ransom of pisanki. The following day, on Easter Tuesday, when the girls would go around with a branch striking the boys, they often received pisanki in return.

Following courtship, eggs continued to figure strongly in marriage rites, only this time as a symbol of future fertility. Eggs were utilized as a decoration for the wedding bread, which the newly married ate as a means of ensuring fertility and the continuation of the reproductive cycle. The wedding bread called *kołacz* or *korowaj* had to be made of numerous eggs, and the surface of it made bright and glossy by the application of a beaten egg before baking. Eggs were almost always included in the dishes served to guests during the wedding festivities.

Lastly, eggs played a critical role in customs and rites honoring the dead. To primitive man, life and death were not separate entities, but rather a continuous cycle of existence that was closely linked with the agricultural year. The dead were believed to lie in the earth guarding the seeds, enabling them to germinate, helping the crops to grow. Twice a year, during the spring and fall, ancient Poles honored and appeased their dead by bringing food and drink to their graves. If they failed to do this, the dead would grow angry and cause the earth to be barren and unfertile. Although changed in character over the years, the Poles still honor their dead every fall in the *Zaduszki* ceremonies of November. The oldest written knowledge of pisanki at the graveside was documented in the life of St. Hedwig, which was penned after her canonization in 1267. The many miraculous healings attributed to this saint were documented by the wife of King Henryk Brodaty, who told the following story: When the son of a prominent judge was still unable to walk at eight years of age, his mother brought the boy to the grave of St. Hedwig in her arms and was praying to St. Hedwig to heal him when, lo!, a miracle happened. In the presence of the priest who baptized him and the abbess of the monastery, the boy suddenly stood up, took an egg that lay before him and walked around the saint's grave. The abbess took other decorated eggs and threw them at the feet of the young boy, compelling him to walk further from the tomb. This miracle is said to have happened near Easter between 1274 and 1287.

Writings of the 15th century indicate that the priests urged their faithful to stop the pagan custom of "feeding" the dead, but remnants of bringing food could still be found in Śląsk until the 19th century. Usually on the third day of Easter, on Easter Tuesday, the village folk throughout Poland would carry eggs, bread, apples, and something to drink to the cemetery. After placing a clean white cloth on the grave, the food was set out. Candles would be lit and prayers for the souls of the departed were said by the priest and people present. The food would then be distributed to the poor or divided among the priest and church attendants. Games played with eggs can be documented to the beginning of the 13th century. In *wybitki*, two boys or a boy and a girl take one colored egg in their right hands and hit one against the other, and whoever's egg does not break wins the other individual's egg.

Besides the all-important egg, the rest of the Easter breakfast very often consisted of a long string of sausage coiled in a circle on a platter, with sprigs of boxwood tucked here and there. In the more well-to-do homes, a large ham dominated the table with home grown horseradish as the chief condiment. A butter lamb stood off to one side. On the corner of the tables were braided breads with hard boiled eggs on top, tall *babas* in the shape of a hat and *placki*—a long, narrow bread made with cheese and herbs. Everyone ate and drank their fill on this joyous morning. The rest of the day was spent quietly at home with family or with a special guest invited to share an egg and slice of ham. It wasn't until the next day that celebrations and merriment began.

There have been various names given to the ancient Polish Easter Monday custom of dyngus. These include *śmigus, dzień świętego Lejka, oblej,* or *lany poniedziałek.* They all refer to a ritual dousing with water. Chroniclers say that dyngus dates back to the time of Jerusalem when the Jews used water to disperse the Christians who had gathered together to talk of the risen Christ. Others claim it is a remnant of the times when Christians were immersed in water as a means of baptism. This custom is not limited to the Polish culture alone. It was known in many countries and historians claim that the custom is really German in origin.

The first known Polish writings on dyngus date back to the Middle Ages. A Polish historian wrote of what he called the *oblewania.* "It is the universal custom, among the common masses as well as among the distinguished, for the men to soak the women on Easter Monday. On Tuesday, and every day thereafter until the time of the Green Holidays (Pentecost), the women doused the men."

Those who saw themselves as too refined and above pouring water on some unsuspecting friend or lover would lightly pour rose water on their hands from a small bottle or flask. Those who did not subscribe to delicacy and refinement approached it with gusto, dashing water from cups, glasses, and buckets right into an individual's face. Very often men, women, nobles and peasants alike, didn't necessarily wait for their appointed day but grabbed whatever vessel was at hand and began throwing water at whomever was close at hand.

Dyngus began somewhere around five in the morning, and the custom demanded that the house where the women slept be secretly invaded. The men crept through a window or through a chimney. Sometimes the male head of the house, in collusion with the perpetrators, let the men into the house himself to have his womenfolk abruptly awakened and doused liberally with water. The spirit of dyngus is best described in this lively description from the Poznań region during the 1800s: "Barely had the day dawned on Easter Monday when I woke the boys and gathered some water to start throwing it on the girls. Up with the *pierzynas*! (eiderdowns) There was screaming, shouting, confusion. The girls are shrieking and hollering, but in their hearts they're glad because they know that she who isn't gotten wet will not be married that year. And the more they are annoyed, the more we dump water on them calling, "dyngus!" "dyngus!" I'm telling you we didn't begrudge them any water, dumping it on them from pots and pans, glasses, watering cans, and buckets, so that in the house the ducks could have swam. Then we had to change our clothes because there wasn't a dry thread on the girls and we boys were no better off."

It is inevitable that sometimes the merriment of dyngus got carried away to the point where someone got hurt. Eyewitnesses recount how in a certain village, a hired hand climbed on the roof of a house after vespers on Easter Sunday, and shouted loudly that Magda would get five pails of water, Barbara would get eight pails of water, and so on, naming each girl in the village. The next day, no matter whether it was cold or warm, he dragged each girl, one after another, out of their homes and amongst hollering and resistance took her to the well and drawing water, poured it on the girl until she received her number of dousings. Sometimes if a girl was caught near a pond, she was thrown into the ice cold water without mercy. It happened more than once that the girl caught a cold or chest condition and died. This kind of carrying things too far led the bishop of Poznań in 1420 to issue a "Dingus Prohibetur," when it was "forbidden on the second (Monday) and third (Tuesday) days of Easter to pester or plague others in what is universally called Dingus."

In some regions, dyngus took place as lashing or striking someone with a green branch. In Pomorze, the boys ran all over the village striking girls and young women with pussy willow branches or those of birch, gooseberry or juniper, on the legs until the woman cried for mercy, at which time she had to buy her way out, usually with a few colored eggs. Sometimes it was just the opposite, with the girls striking the boys on the first day. The branches for dyngus were prepared as far back as New Year when they cut branches, placed them in water, and set them in a warm place to bloom, because the branch for dyngus had to be green.

Another aspect of dyngus was similar in manner to the caroling or masquerade that occurred at Christmas. After Easter, it was called *po dyngusie, po święconem* or *po wykupie.* The individuals involved received eggs, baked goods, ham, and other gifts in exchange for causing amusement and entertainment through clever recitations or songs. Sometimes they dressed as gypsies or old men and women and were called *dziady śmigust-ne.* In the Poznań area, a bear in a costume made from the dry stalks of beans and peas visited from house to house with this particular recitation:

Ja mała dziecina
Nie wiem po Łacina
Nie wiele wiem, nie wiele powiem
Powiem wam nowinę

Że będziemy dziś jedli jajko i słoninę
I jajka farbowane
I ser przekładany
I święcone prosie
I chrzan gorzkawy, co kręci w nosie.

I am only a small boy
Who knows no Latin
Who knows little, will tell you little.
I will tell you news
That today we will eat eggs and salt pork
And colored eggs
And cheesecake
and blessed pork
And bitter horseradish which will curl your nose.

In Wieliczka, near Krakow, the Easter masqueraders were known as *siuda baba*. The *siudy* usually went in pairs. The face of one of the boys was smeared with soot and he was dressed as a woman holding a child made of rags. The other, also darkened with soot, was decorated with a rosary made of rope strung with chestnuts and a cross made of nails. The masqueraders prowled along the streets, making a general nuisance of themselves, until their victims gave them a treat of some kind.

Another activity on this day was called *kogutek*, centering on the rooster or cockerel which in more ancient times was part of the rituals to symbolize the onset of spring and assure fertility. In the Łęczyca region north of Łódź, the custom was called *kurcorze*. This called for 10 to 15 youngsters who divided themselves up into two groups: younger and older. Everyone wore caps decorated with red or pink ribbons and carried a long pole painted red or black. Sometimes the boys dressed themselves as Polish cavalrymen, and made themselves a wooden saber, paper epaulettes and belt, a cap in the shape of a shako, and wore a white shirt and black pants tucked into their boots.

11 DZIADY ŚMIGUSTNE

APRIL

The most important requirement in the hands of the older kurcorze was a two-wheeled cart with a shaft and a rooster in the middle. The wagon was painted red or green and sometimes silver. It was decorated with flowers and ribbons. The rooster figure itself was made of wood, cloth, dough, or clay. It was decorated with rooster feathers, or perhaps the feathers of a pheasant or turkey—the turkey feathers generally served to decorate the tail. The beak and neck of the rooster were made of red paper and the eyes from glass beads.

The rooster was fastened to the center of the cart and surrounding him were wooden dancing figures. The figures, representing a bride and her bridesmaids, had dresses made of tissue paper and hair from flax. Another figure, representing a blacksmith, was dressed in black, with a hammer in his hand. On the pull of a string, everything on the cart moved: the rooster began to nod, the girls jumped up and down and the blacksmith, as in a smithy, hit a metal anvil with his hammer.

The younger group carried banners, that is, pictures of saints fastened to a stick or pole. The kurcorze began going around with the rooster on Holy Monday after the morning dyngus. They arrived single file into a yard. First, one of them stepped into the house, stood at attention, raised his saber, and said: We're here with the rooster for dyngus!" Behind him two other kurcorze entered and crossed their swords over his head. Next came another three kurcorze, one rolling in the cart with the rooster and the other two crossing their swords over the cart. After this, the remainder of the revelers arrived and then sang songs of the death and Resurrection of Christ with resounding "alleluias" added at the end of each stanza.

In other villages, entering with the rooster was less ceremonial. If the head of the house allowed them to enter, all the kurcorze entered together after the youngster with the cart. Upon entering, they sang, gave orations on either a religious or wordly theme, and received eggs for their performance. If there was a young, marriageable girl in the house, the boys were sometimes asked to sit and have refreshments.

Another variation on this occurred in the Krakow area, and was called *chodzenia z traczykiem*, i.e, going with the sawer. Three boys dressed themselves up as *uhlans* with red badges on their chests, a paper cap on their heads, and a wooden sword at their sides. Behind them, two boys pulled a wagon on which there was a wooden lamb, that held in its hoof a saw as a reminder that Jesus, as a child and innocent lamb, helped St. Joseph in his carpentry, cutting wood with a saw. With each revolution of the wheel, bells rang, and the lamb moved up and down as if he were cutting wood.

Another Krakow custom on Easter Monday was called *Emaus*, in memory of the meeting of the Risen Christ with the apostles bound for the city of Emmaus (Gospel of St. Luke 24: 13-26). In the Middle Ages, Emaus was the name given to pilgrimages to the church or chapel beyond the town which held a Mass and *odpust* (church fair) during the Easter period. Each year, even to this date, in the suburb of Zwierzyniec near the Church of St. Salvator, booths are set up and a church fair is held. The stalls are heavily laden with candy, *pierniki* (honey and spice cookies), trumpets, rattles, pipe reeds and harmonicas, providing the children with a veritable paradise of sweets and toys. It was the most beautiful fair in Krakow and was famous for centuries throughout Poland. The oldest reference to Emaus was written by an Italian, Giovanni Paolo Mucanti, who was enjoying himself in Krakow in the year 1586-7. "On Easter Monday," he wrote, "the entire young population of schoolboys in Krakow observe the ancient custom of carrying a willow branch on which were blooming catkins and on the way to Emaus hit the girls, saying, "You're lagging behind getting to Emaus. Why aren't you eager to get to Emaus?"

A custom for greeting spring was *gaik, gaj, gajik* or *maik* or *nowe latko*. This was done primarily by the girls in the village and sometimes by the boys anytime from Easter Monday until what were called the Green holidays in June. In the Łęczyck region near Łódź, the gaik was a branch of spruce, sometimes pine, about 100 to 150 centimeters long, that was decorated with white or red-dyed goose feathers, paper streamers, colored egg shells, and holy pictures of the saints or the Blessed Mother. A doll decorated with rue or myrtle was sometimes fastened to the top branches. Girls in ages ranging from ten to fifteen traveled around the village with this branch on Easter Monday, entering the houses and singing of the onset of spring. One of the girls carried a basket to receive the eggs, nuts, and fruits which they received. Another girl carried the gaik and the third carried a cane, which she used to beat out the rhythm of the songs.

On Easter Tuesday, the third day of Easter, the people of Krakow also celebrated *rękawka*, which means "sleeve." On the bank of the Vistula, a mound near a rocky cliff called the Krzemionek is supposedly the burial ground of the legendary "Krak" who slayed the dragon of that city. He was much loved by his subjects and when he died, thousands of his subjects carried a handful of dirt tied into a sleeve of a dress or shirt to create his burial mound.

In ancient times, the people of that city gathered on the mound to throw down eggs, nuts, and other foodstuffs left over from their own Easter feast to the poor schoolboys waiting below at the foot of the mound as part of the rituals of feeding the dead. Even after embracing Christianity the people continued to honor their dead by bringing food to burial sites in the spring and distributed it to the poor in memory and honor of the dead. Polish priests of the fifteenth century kept chastising their faithful to stop the pagan custom of "feeding" the dead, yet the people of the city of Krakow continued to gather on the mound and enact their familiar customs. Towards the end of the nineteenth century, the day became a church fair where one could buy pisanki, sweets, and more, and enjoy meeting friends and acquaintances.

May

The gradual victory of spring over winter, with its promise of new life, was celebrated in a multitude of ways among the Polish people. One of these springtime festivities was the celebrating of May Day with a maypole. Singing and dancing were conducted around a gaily decorated green tree that was cleared of all its branches except on its top. In such countries as England, Germany, and Czechoslovakia, the custom was much more widespread than it was in Poland. Maypoles were found most frequently in western Poland (Great Poland, Silesia), where they were called by a variety of names including *maj, moj, majka,* and *majów*. They were also known in the southern parts of Little Poland as well as the Kaszuby region. In the Rzeszow and Łancut region the maypoles were called *wicha*.

There were two approaches to putting up the maypole. In the Lower Silesia and Poznań areas, the erecting of the maypole was a community affair. The men setting out to the woods for the tree were dressed in their best, most festive apparel, and their wagon was similarly decked out in boughs and branches of greenery. This going out and picking of flowers and branches and bringing them home was the symbolic act of bringing home the May, i.e, bringing new life into the village. The tallest tree to be found was chopped down and brought back from the woods, stripped of its bark and trimmed of its lower branches, leaving only a green top. The maypole was placed on the village green, or sometimes a little bit beyond the village at a crossroads. In some cases, the maypole was erected in front of the homes of individuals who were especially respected or esteemed in the community, such as the parish priest or an official. These preliminaries were accompanied by much singing.

Sometimes there existed in the village a tall post that had been hewn from a tree and put up in previous years. In this case, a juniper bush or some type of evergreen picked in the woods was fastened to the top of the existing post. Another approach was to form a large green wreath from the branches, which was then hung at the top of the post. Sometimes clusters of flowers, herbs, or green branches from a birch, gooseberry, or linden tree were fastened to the top. Whatever method was used—the tree top or tree branches or wreath—the greenery was then decorated with ribbons, strips of colored tissue paper, silk kerchiefs, and sometimes with blown out colored eggs. It also sometimes sported a banner, flag, or roosters, cut from tin or whittled from wood. In the Poznań area, something good to eat or drink was added, and young men would each take turns trying to climb to the top (getting scraped and scratched in the process if the bark had been left on) to retrieve the delicacies. It was the victor's privilege to retire to the village tavern, share his spoils with his friends, and choose the prettiest girl present to dance with him.

In the remaining parts of Poland, the maypole was not a joint community affair, but more of a courtship event with young men erecting maypoles for their chosen loves. This custom was still alive in Poland between the world wars, and even after WW II. In this case, the tree for the maypole was cut down in the woods at night. It was better still if the tree was one that was stolen from a wood in the dead of the night. The young man chose the tallest spruce in the wood—the taller the better. Once the besotted young man had dragged the tree home, he would trim off the limbs, strip it of its bark and paint it in stripes in numerous colors. If the boy couldn't afford to buy paint, he embellished it with colored paper, and failing that, put it up plain. At the top of this tall, painted post, a small fir tree was fastened and decorated with ribbons and colored paper. Such a completed maypole was set into the earth near a fence, or in front of the home of a loved one on the night of April 30th for May 1st. The girl, awakened by the noise of the young man and his helpers putting up the maypole, would invite the young people inside "after which they made merry with singing and dancing until dawn."

Sometimes, when a young maiden had many swains vying for her attention, competition was so keen that preparation for the maj began two weeks ahead of time. Each young man strove to erect the highest, most beautiful maj of them all and, as often happens in these cases, their struggles resulted in numerous fights between rivals, each one trying to sabotage and ruin the other trees. If a village maiden was especially comely, it wasn't unusual for her to discover a few maje erected in her front yard.

In the Zywiec area, there also existed the custom of "refurbishing" the maypole. In the event that rain spoiled the decorations located at the top of the tree (especially the tissue paper), a repairing or freshening up of the maypole took place a few weeks later. This was usually done on the 15th of May, again during the night and again accompanied with much music, laughing, and dancing.

In the instances where there were hurt and angry feelings towards a girl, a rejected suitor was known to take his revenge by putting up a *dziad* in her front yard. This was a large stick to which he would attach an effigy made of straw. Sometimes it was a worn out old broom or simply a dried tree without any life left in it. Fathers and brothers stayed up on the night of the 30th to drive away any such attempts.

Over time, the custom of erecting maypoles in Poland declined. Polish folklorists attribute this to the fact that, while popular in some regions, the tradition was not as widespread as it was in places like Czechoslovakia, nor was it associated with as many spheres of life as in Germany. There, erecting a maypole wasn't limited to May Day, but existed as an expression of good wishes for the birth of a child, the moving of a young couple into their new home, or the transition of a worker from

119

apprentice to craftsman. Among Poles it was limited to May Day and tied more closely to the rites of courtship.

The beginning of spring meant that thoughts turned to the task of plowing. A variety of magical beliefs and practices were carried out to ensure that every phase of plowing, sowing, and reaping was successful. In the Podhale, Spisz, and Orawy regions in the Carpathian Mountains, the first day of plowing was begun with great solemnity and ceremony. The farmer first prepared the plow, and placed it with the other implements necessary for plowing in his wagon. When the horse was hitched to the wagon, the housewife came out of the house carrying a bowl containing holy water and a few pussy willow branches that had been blessed on Palm Sunday. She dipped the branches in the holy water and walked around the horse and wagon three times, sprinking and blessing the ensemble, which also included her husband. The rest she poured on the plow near the wheel. She then tucked one of the pussy willow branches into the collar of the horse and another one on her husband's cap. The rest of the branches, along with the heel of a loaf of bread saved from the Christmas meal, she bundled into a scarf and placed in the wagon. After the blessing was completed, the farmer himself made the sign of the cross before the horse and began moving out. When he arrived at the first field, he hitched the plow to the horse and plowed the field. Before going on to the next field, he took off his cap and unwrapped the bundle prepared by his wife. He divided the bread into parts, placing a piece under the plow. He then gave one to the horse and ate a piece himself. The last piece he wrapped back up into the scarf and would, upon his return home, give it back to his wife, saying, "This bread was plowed."

After concluding the sharing of the bread, the farmer took earth from beneath the plow and spread it on the chest of the horse murmuring, "May you be as hard as this earth," so that the horse would not be hurt during the plowing. The farmer then knelt and prayed the Our Father, Hail Mary, and Angelus. When the plowing was completed and it was time for the sowing, the farmer first mixed oats that came from the Christmas Eve table and had been blessed on St. Stephan's (December 26) with his seed oats. Taking the oats in his hand, he made the sign of the cross on the earth with the oats and only then began his sowing.

In some villages, it was the custom to shower the horse with oats or to incense the plow with blessed herbs that had been spilled on hot coals. In the Kujawy region of Poland, when the farmer arrived at the field and before he sank the plow into earth, he would take a small cross made of blessed palms and place it before the first row to be ploughed. In like manner, the seeds to be sown were first placed in a sack that contained blessed herbs. The peasant sprinkled his hand with holy water and threw the first handful of seeds at the cross, saying, "In the name of Jesus."

In Western Galicia if, because of some oversight, a field was not sown, it meant that someone in the house of the farmer would die. If strong winds toppled the trees in the forest, careful inspection was made of the trees. If they were young trees, then the young in the village would die; if they were old trees, then the elderly would begin dying. If an apple tree blossomed and bore fruit while it was still cold, then whoever owned the apple tree would certainly die. When a young tree bore fruit for the first time, it was not be eaten because first fruits belong to God, not man.

Monday and Friday were considered unlucky days, days on which one shouldn't start any new work. Friday, commemorated as the day of the Lord's death, was considered an unlucky day. The best day for beginning any new tasks, such as plowing and sowing as well as reaping the harvest, was a Saturday, as the day was under the protection of the Blessed Mother. Saturday has traditionally belonged to the Blessed Mother since the very first days of the existence of the Catholic Church. St. Thomas Aquinas arrived at the conclusion that its roots hearken back to the first Holy Saturday when, grief-stricken and disheartened after the events of Good Friday, the Apostles and followers of Christ returned to Mary to seek comfort for themselves and to console her in her sorrow and travail. As soon as Christ was no longer available to them, the Apostles turned and clung to His mother with their entire hearts. Artists in the first centuries of Christianity also contributed to the tradition of Saturday belonging to the Blessed Virgin Mary. They often painted the Mother of God at the entrance of the tomb where her Son lay buried. Similar paintings became deeply etched in the consciousness of believers and followers of Mary. Saturday became a day of special veneration to Our Lady in order to commemorate her extreme desolation on the day following her Son's burial.

In those early centuries of the Catholic faith, individuals who found themselves in grave danger or distress took their troubles to Mary and put themselves under her protection. The prayer *Pod Twoją Obronę* (under Your protection) became established somewhere in the third or fourth century and was soon one of the most universal prayers to the Blessed Virgin. As early as the beginning of the eleventh century, St. Peter Damian mentioned the custom of celebrating a Mass in honor of the Blessed Virgin every Saturday except on feast days and during Lent. His contemporary, Bernold of Constance, testified the same thing, making special mention that the practice was introduced, not because of ecclesiastical authority, but to satisfy the devotion of the people.

Devotion to Mary grew significantly during the Middle Ages when poets, musicians, and writers wrote hymns, songs, and poems dedicated to the Blessed Mother. At about this time, the church incorporated liturgical rites and celebrations to the Blessed Mother, particularly the Little Office of the Blessed Virgin which was to be recited on Saturdays. The Benedictine Monks of Monte Cassino and Cluny were among the first to adopt this method of sanctifying Our Lady's day. In 1095, at the Council of Clermont, Pope Urban II recommended the continuation of this devotion to ensure the success of the First Crusade. From the Benedictines, the practice soon spread to other religious orders whose members were eager to pay devotion to Mary. The song *"Witaj Królowo (Hail to the Queen)"* became one of the most popular songs to sing on Saturday in homage to Mary. The Cistercian nuns of Poland were chiefly responsible for spreading the custom of singing *"Witaj Królowo"* as the last prayer of the day.

Other beliefs centering around work include:

> Do not begin any work that involves cutting on Friday for that is the day of the Lord's death.
>
> On Friday one should never take out manure. Whosoever does, will be punished with hail.
>
> Whosoever violates the holy day of Sunday with work in the field will be punished by God with an unfruitful yield.
>
> Wheat will grow best if sown on St. Valentine's Day before the sun goes down.
>
> To sow on the Eve of St. John (Midsummer's Eve, June 20th) is to protect the crop against hail.
>
> To sow on the new moon is good.
>
> On the first day of planting or sowing of the wheat, do not lend anything from the home, otherwise the wheat crop will be a poor one.
>
> Seeds which have been set aside for planting should never be placed on the table because they will not grow.
>
> Two spikes of wheat on the same stalk is a sign of good luck for the owner. (This was proudly displayed on the peasant's cap.)

The Polish holiday of *Zielone Świątki*, or Green Holidays (Pentecost), brought the folk customs that were associated with spring to a close. In its truest sense the holiday was another celebration of the blossoming and greening of nature. Churches, homes and yards were decorated with branches of birch and ash, on altars, porches, and gates. The doors and window sills of homes were decorated with branches of pine, spruce, cedar, or yew.

In the north of Poland, the people carried herbs and flowers to church to decorate the altars, holy pictures, and statues. They decorated their doorways with branches of the beech tree and took branches of the maple and stuck it in the middle of their fields so that hail would not damage the crops. The people didn't stop at just decorating their homes and church but also adorned their horses and wagons. If a young man had a sweetheart, he would plant a small birch as a symbol of his affection. The women also spread *tartarek* (calamus) on the roads. Calamus, also called sweet flag, was especially looked for and used during this holiday, particularly for decorating around the windows and for strewing on the floors and at the entrance to the house. This herb was introduced into Poland by the Tartars in the thirteenth century.

In Little Poland, on the upper Vistula, it was customary to build bonfires on the eve of the Green Holiday, rather than the actual day itself. Throughout the whole year the people in this region saved their worn out brooms, which they called *skrabaki*, to nail to a long pole. They also took bunches of straw, wrapped it in an old rag, and fastened this to another long pole or stick. Both of these were dipped in resin extracted from the pine trees. On the eve of the Green Holiday, the young men would find a clearing and build a great bonfire made from the dry branches of pine and juniper. With music playing, they jumped over the fires and danced around it. The men would then light their homemade torches and walk between the fields of rye.

On the second day, the actual holiday itself, the same events were repeated except that the torches were used to walk around the fields of wheat. The custom was called *opalenie zboża*, or the firing or singeing of the grain. Up until the time of World War II, on the Saturday before or the Monday after Pentecost, the farmers of the villages in the Beskid Śląsk area of Poland would herd their cattle out into the fields after the morning Mass with the help of the rest of their household. The housewife would follow along, having taken from the house a large frying pan, a dozen eggs, and a slab of bacon. In an age-old custom associated with ancient rites of vegetation and new birth, the group would construct a bonfire. Over this open fire, the housewife would fry the simple meal and divide it up amongst the people present. Another custom in this Pomorze region was called *fryce*, when the younger farm hands gathered together in a field and baked potatoes over an open fire and drank some beer.

The Zielone Świątki was also a special day of recognition for shepherds who spent long and lonely days and nights grazing cattle and sheep in foothills and mountains. On this holiday, the shepherds decorated the horns of the cattle with flowers or greenery and placed a wreath around their necks. Once in a while a wreath was even placed around the neck of a goose or two.

In the Kujawy region, on the day after Pentecost, the shepherds placed horns of cows and oxen on their own head and held a race. The shepherd who was the first to drive his cattle to pasturing grounds was crowned "king." The last one out had to tend everyone's animals for three days, while the rest of the shepherds made merry. The first and last shepherdess were also given the same treatment. The "king" and "queen" were presented with a small gift: a ring, a peacock feather, or a wreath of flowers. The king "appointed" a king's court—a field marshal, a head cook, and cup bearer. A bonfire was built somewhere in a clearing and the cook prepared a tasty meal, the makings brought by those participating in the celebration. The field marshal placed a cloth upon the grass, set out bowls, and, when the meal was ready, sat the royal pair and the rest of his entourage down in their appointed places, with the come-lately shepherd, wearing a wreath of straw on his head, seated last. After the meal, an ox was chosen, decorated in greenery and ribbons, and with the royal couple leading, the road before them strewn with flowers, everyone circled the village amidst singing

12 COW DECORATED FOR ZIELONE ŚWIĄTKI

and the cracking of whips. Finally, the ox was taken to its owner who had to "buy" it back with the standard round of drinks. Dancing and revelry continued long into the night.

The customary races on this particular holiday are also held by two other groups. In the villages closer to Wrocław, horse races were held and the winner was also proclaimed "king." In the Wielkopolska area, where there were plenty of marksmen or sharpshooters, a competition was held that gathered riflemen from miles around. Whoever had the most bull's eyes was named king and given a crown.

In some areas of Poland a group of girls secretly chose a queen along with six other girls to act as her escorts. The queen was dressed in a rose-colored dress tied with a red or blue sash, her head decorated with a crown of rue and periwinkle, and her face covered with a scarf so that no one recognized her. Her honor guard was dressed in white skirts, dark men's cloaks, and caps decorated with rue, periwinkle and ribbons. The queen and her guard circled the borders of the village singing: *Gdzie królewna chodzi, tam pszeniczka rodzi* (Where the queen walks, there the wheat grows). All the young adults of the village came out of their homes to greet the queen and followed behind with music as the group made its way to the outer limits of the village, and around the fields of growing crops.

On their return home the entire procession headed towards the home of the richest landowner in the village where they were greeted and invited in. A large table was brought forth, the queen sat down on a pillow and here finally uncovered her face and revealed her identity. The host distributed refreshments, and the men and women brought out mead and foodstuffs. A merry time ensued with much dance and song.

June

The feast of Corpus Christi, or *Boże Ciało*, the day on which the Catholic Church commemorates the institution of the Holy Eucharist, was celebrated with both pomp and great solemnity throughout all of Poland.

There were three important rituals associated with the celebration of this special holy day. The first of these was the erection of special, portable altars away from the confines of the church building. A small tent or pavilion-like structure made of cloth was set up. An altar was placed within and decorated with various statues and figurines of the saints. On the side and back cloth walls, numerous holy pictures were hung, usually of the Blessed Mother and St. Joseph. The final product resembled a small chapel.

The people of the Pomorze area called this small chapel *Boży Domek* (Little House of God). Usually four different altars were erected at various points in the towns and villages by the more affluent or well-to-do. Writings in 1824 indicate that in the Mazowsze area, four special altars were set up in the square or market place at the time of the celebration of Corpus Christi, each one beautifully decorated with the special skills of the different guilds of tradesmen and artisans. In some communities, the altars were erected at the four corners of the cemetery.

The second custom associated with the celebration of Corpus Christi was the decorating of the altars with greenery. Branches of birch were usually used to decorate the Boże domki. Wreaths as small as the palm of the hand, made from various herbs and flowers, were blessed in church by the priest. The blessing ceremony begged the Lord to accept the fragrance of the offered herbs and to bless those who offered Him the wreaths. The wreaths were hung on the monstrance where they stayed for a week following Corpus Christi. The wreaths were then taken home and hung on the wall behind holy pictures and preserved until such time as needed.

In the Podlasie area near the muddy waters of the Narew River, the people maintained a custom of weaving nine small wreaths, each wreath made from a different herb. These herbs were: thyme (*macierzanka*), hazel wort (*kopytnik*), stonecrop (*rozchodnik*), lady's mantle (*nawrotek*), sundew (*rosiczka*), mint (*mięta*), rue (*ruta*), daisy (*stokroć*) and periwinkle (*barwinek*). In some parts of Poland the herbs and flowers were formed into a wreath and attached to strips of paper on which were written exerpts of the gospel of St. John: *A słowo ciałem się stało i mieszkało między nami*. (And the word was made flesh and and dwelt among us.)

Another variation was to write the beginnings of four different gospels on separate sheets of paper, which were then rolled up and tucked in among the herbs and flowers of the wreath. These small wreaths were hung on the altar or, as was done in some districts, hung directly on the monstrance. The wreaths were usually blessed by the priest on the eve of the feast day.

Once the little chapels were built and decorated with holy pictures, greenery, and herbal wreaths, it soon neared time for the third and most important ritual associated with Corpus Christi — that of the Corpus Christi procession. For this event the entire village assembled before the church dressed in their Sunday finest. Individuals or special groups were singled out to act as an honor guard around the Blessed Sacrament at the head of the procession. They were followed by trade and craft guilds, magistrates and town officials, religious organizations and individuals and family groups. Publicly proclaiming and reaffirming their devotion to the Holy Eucharist, the entire congregation walked around the church and its grounds to the sound of bells ringing and voices lifted in sacred hymns. The procession then walked and sang their way to the first of the four altars. There the Blessed Sacrament would rest while the assembled faithful kneeled to pray and sing in adoration of the Holy Eucharist. The procession would then continue on in the same manner to the other altars until finished.

After the last evening of devotions (it was usually an eight day observance), the rolls on which the gospels were written were removed and placed into bottles. They were buried in the four corners of the village early before sunrise the next day. This ensured protection against hail, plague, and other unforseen disasters. The branches of birch were placed among the growing field crops with the belief that this would serve to protect the crops against hail. At harvest time, when bringing in the first wagonload of grain to the barn, the farmer would place the first sheaves on the clean floor in the form of the cross. On top of this he placed a wreath that had been blessed on Corpus Christi. Everyone who had helped bring in the grain would then make the sign of the cross, and the farmer would say the gospel according to John:

Na początku było słowo
A Bogiem było ono Słowo
A ono Słowo było u Boga

In the Beginning was the Word
And the Word was with God
And the Word was God.

This religious ceremony granted safety for the harvest crops and protection against disease and lightning. It was also believed to scare away troublesome pests such as mice and rats.

The wreaths also served in various capacities around the home. They were placed under the foundation of a newly built house. In the Pomorze area, the blessed wreaths were an important health measure used to prevent sore throats. For this it was necessary to crumble some of the herbs from the wreath, mix them with warm bran, and apply liberally to the neck. In a similar function, some of the herbs were crumbled and burnt as a form of incense for those suffering from dropsy. The smoke from thyme and stonecrop were believed to be able to disperse hail clouds and lightning, thereby saving grain crops from destruction.

In Poland there was a proverb or saying for just about every situation, every type of weather, incident, or event. The Feast of Corpus Christi was no exception. The proverbs focus, as is often the case, on the weather and planting of crops. For example:

Na Boże Ciało, siej proso śmiało.
On Corpus Christi, sow millet confidently.

Jaki dzień jest w Boże Ciało
Takich dni potem niemało.
Whatever day is on Corpus Christi
Such days later will be many.

And lastly we are warned:

W Boże Ciało—z boską chwałą
Słowo nam się Chlebem stało
Więc w oktawę puść obawę
Nie tknij zboża, ni kapusty
Bo znajdziesz dzień pusty.
On Corpus Christi—with God's glory
The Word was made flesh
So on the eighth day release your worries
Neither touch the grain nor the cabbage
Or you'll find the day empty.

The other major holiday that occurred in the month of June involved the midsummer celebrations. It was Shakespeare who forever immortalized this holiday in his *Midsummer Night's Dream*, and such sayings as "midsummer folly," and "midsummer madness," are still frequently used. The Mazovians gave it the name *kupalnocka* in honor of the ancient god Kupala. In other parts of Poland it was called *sobótka* or *świętojańska*. All refer to the night of June 23rd, the night of the summer solstice, when the position of the sun gives the earth its longest day and shortest night of the year. Since time immemorial, it has been a night fraught with magic and superstition, when witches and devils roam freely looking to do mischief, where dancing and revelry are believed to change the course of the sun, where homage is paid to the ancient gods of fire, water, and vegetation, lest they be angered.

The Polish custom of celebrating St. John's Eve can be traced back to before the spread of Christianity. From earliest times man seemed aware that life on earth somehow depended on the sun and constantly watched its orderly progress across the heavens. Its great importance gave birth to a sun god who was the source of all light, heat and fire. As an agricultural people, they rejoiced each day as the sun climbed higher and higher, once again moving in its cycle of prolonging the daylight hours. When the time of the solstice came, when the sun hardly seemed to leave the sky, man fearing that it had lost its way, built huge fires, believing that he could influence the continued movement of the sun. The influence of the church and the opinions and writings of the clergy had an effect on curtailing the midsummer celebrations. The custom was practically lost without trace throughout the western part of Poland and where it wasn't entirely eradicated, a Christianized version took its place among the church calendar customs.

The rituals for midsummer which had been celebrated in pre-Christian times were in some cases taken up by cults separately. Among these rituals were the water rite and the fire rite. St. John the Baptist, who had baptized Christ in the Jordan, became the patron saint of all customs associated with water. The first of these rites survived in the form of the wreaths released on water. Young unmarried girls wove wreaths of flowers and herbs, each girl trying to make her wreath as distinctive as possible. Lining the sides of the river bank or pond, the girls would attach lighted candles to their wreaths and then cast them into the water. So plentiful were the wreaths and flowers on the waters that the saying arose that "on St. John's the water blossoms."

In pagan times, the throwing of flowers on the waters had as its purpose the gaining of the good intentions of the water spirits, of asking protection against thunderstorms and deluge, but this changed over time and became associated with marriage predictions. If the wreath thrown by the girl went around in circles for a long time, she would remain a maiden a while longer; if the wreath flowed downriver quickly it augured matrimony within the year. As the girls watched their wreaths, they sang songs to the boys who either jumped directly into the water or skimmed over it in small boats to retrieve the wreaths of their choice. For some, marriage matches were made on this night and if not, young maids went to sleep thinking of the man they would like to marry, for it was believed that dreams dreamed on midsummer night were likely to come true. The celebration of the water rite was even more important along the Polish seashore. There, where people made their living from the sea, the fishermen sprinkled their boats with holy water, strewed branches of the plane tree on the bottoms of their boat, and wove blessed herbs and grasses into their nets in an attempt to appease the evil gods that would raise the winds and churn the sea against them.

The most outstanding feature of the summer solstice festival, however, were the midsummer fires. People would travel up into nearby hills and mountaintops, or to large clearings in the forests. Once there, they would ignite huge bonfires by the traditional, primitive method of rubbing two sticks together, or by striking flint in order that the fire be "live" or "new." The darkening horizon would be fiery with hundreds of bonfires while young and old sang and danced around the flames, teasing each other with riddles, suggesting improbable matches between toothless old crones and handsome young men, as well as joining together the names of boys and girls who were known to be interested in each other. When the flames of the bonfire had subsided, young men and women would leap over the fire in pairs and, if they managed to jump over the fire with their hands still clasped together, it was said that they would soon marry.

In other parts of Europe, it was believed that as high as individuals jumped over the fire, so the flax would grow that year. Like the wreaths, the fires had similar characteristics of providing protection against calamities. It was believed that as far as the smoke from a midsummer fire reached, the fields would be protected from the destructive forces of hail. Very often the ashes from the fires would then be sprinkled over the fields to ensure fertility of the crops. It was also believed that cattle would be protected against sickness if they were driven over the places where the fires had burned.

Eventually the church gave new meaning to the bonfires. Jesus had once called John the Baptist "a burning and shining light" (John 5:35), and so it was declared that the fires were to be symbolic for St. John, and not the sun god that had been previously worshipped. Of considerable importance in the Sobótki celebrations were various plants and herbs. All magic, both good and bad, was said to be released on this night. Certain plants had the power of both creating happiness and warding off evil spirits. No other plant played as important a role in these festivities as mugwort, so much so that the midsummer bonfires were also called mugwort fires. A garland of the herb thrown on a midsummer fire would render the thrower safe from all ill fortune for the next twelve months, and if one held the garland up and peered through it at the bonfire, it would prevent headache and smarting eyes. Once known as the Mother of Herbs, mugwort was one of the nine herbs employed to repel demons in pre-Christian times.

Over time, it came to be called St. John's plant, in honor of St. John the Baptist, who supposedly wore it for protection while traveling through the wilderness. It was believed to have the special ability of foiling witches, who were out on their broomsticks looking to make trouble for man and beast. Branches of it were hung under the eaves of barns and stables to keep witches from coming in at night and milking the cows.

Numerous other herbs were also credited with protective powers against evil spirits and witches. Sprays of St. John's Wort were hung above the doors of houses and churches. Those said to be possessed or insane could rid themselves of their madness if they inhaled the odor of the crushed leaves and flowers or drank a potion of it. Because the Crusaders brought back the story that it sprang up on Calvary, when the nails were driven into Christ's hands, vervain is called herb-of-the-Cross. As a holy herb, it is thought by many to be proof against enchantment and charms. Vervain, along with burdock, hazel, and wormwood were hung above the entrances of many a Polish cottage as protection against evil forces. Medicinally, herbs gathered on the summer solstice were thought to possess more than their usual powers for cures. Aged men, women, and children headed for the fields and woods in search of chamomile, white clover, and coltsfoot. If gathered before sunset, these herbs were thought to be especially curative for such illnesses as rheumatism, arthritis and lung disorders. Of special importance was the search for the male fern flower. It was believed that somewhere in a wild ravine the barren male fern bloomed at midnight with a flaming flower. This magical flower was very small, difficult to see, and unlikely to be found, because the devil himself was said to watch over it. The plucked flower was said to give the owner the power to see beneath the earth, where secret treasures were hidden. Whoever found it would be sure to have good fortune and happiness.

Over the centuries, the beauty and mysticism of the midsummer celebrations was perceived by such Polish literary figures as Jan Kochanowski, the outstanding Polish poet who wrote the

Song of St. John's Eve, as well as S. Goszczynski, who used the Midsummer celebrations in the Tatra Mountains as the theme for his unfinished epic poem.

July

The month of July, Lipiec, derives its name from one of Poland's most loved and respected trees, the *lipa*. In America, the tree is called basswood. In Europe it carries the name of linden tree. Sometimes it's called a lime tree. Oftentimes it is affectionately called *lipka*. The tree held special meaning for the Polish people.

The lipas, especially those that were very old, were considered sacred trees in Poland. "Whosoever should cut such an old linden down, let them expect that in a short time someone will die." A peasant, living in the village of Borowie, supports this belief with this story which was chronicled by a folklorist: "In the year 1897, a man near us cut down a linden which had stood for over a century. The next year the man's wife died after a short illness." According to Polish folklore, the lipa or linden tree was sacred and blessed because it was considered the tree of the Blessed Mother. It was believed that the Blessed Mother often hid herself among its branches, revealing herself to children. One particular folktale reads: "There was a poor girl who tended cows. She wore a coat of pigskin because her stepmother was evil and didn't want to give her any other clothing. The poor girl had the habit of always praying under a linden tree. One time the Blessed Mother emerged and said to her, "My dear, what is your coat made of?" The girl answered her. The Blessed Mother took pity on her and took from herself a beautiful dress, gave it to the girl, and took the pigskin coat."

This belief gave rise to the placing of small wayside shrines under a linden as a place for the villagers to pray. Since the tree was under the protection of the Blessed Mother herself, it was also believed that lightning would never strike a linden.

There are other very significant reasons why the linden rose to such importance in everyday Polish life. In July, the linden tree, laden with creamy white to light yellow flowers, exudes the sweetest fragrance imaginable that perfumes great distances. Sensing the nectar, bees come from far and wide to gather it, so that there is a constant buzzing and humming around the blossoming branches. The linden was therefore an important chain in nature's cycle to provide the country folk with honey for use as a sweetner, and for making mead, as well as for the beeswax necessary for the making of candles. Numerous accounts can be found regarding the tremendous wealth of beehives in the woods and wild, primitive forests scattered throughout Poland. It was the Mazowsze area, however, that was most celebrated for its production of honey. Among its immense tracts of wilderness with herbs, wildflowers, streams, and meandering brooks, there existed countless linden trees, where colonies of bees multiplied by the thousands. The ancient trees, often with hollowed out areas in their trunks, provided prime places for the colonization of bees. The people of the Mazowsze were the first to pass laws regarding the protection of bees and beekeeping in 1401. Anyone caught damaging beehives or stealing honey was brought publicly to the site of the damage, disemboweled, and left to die. On the gentler side, however, it was these same people who preserved their love of the linden tree through countless songs, one of which follows:

Lipka, lipka zielona
Lipka, lipka zielona
a pod tą lipką
a pod tą zieloną
trzej ptaszkowie śpiewało

Linden, linden green
Linden, linden green
under this linden

under this green
three little birds sang.

Over time, when the forests were cut, cleared, and plowed, beekeeping became domesticated, with apiaries becoming common sights in the villages and towns. The various aspects of beekeeping were divided into guilds, and became associated with churches and monasteries. Each guild had its parish and priest, who carried the title of "promotor" of the guild and who was obligated to say a special Mass on day of the patron saint, St. Bartholomew, on August 24th.

Because their flowers were so attractive to bees, rings of linden trees were usually planted around the perimeter of church grounds with beehives standing nearby along the length of the cemetery wall. This close connection to the church eventually evoked a special respect and reverence for the bee, since it was felt that the bee was working for the glory of God by providing wax for the candles that illuminated His church.

There is one final gift which the linden so graciously provided. Few things were more precious to the Pole than his physical health. Each peasant knew that unless he was hale and hearty to rise each day with the dawn to till the soil, the future was unthinkable. Since doctors almost never came to the small, rural villages, it was up to individuals to treat themselves as best they could with what nature provided. When plagued with a bad cough or feverish cold that was accompanied by much sneezing, the Polish peasant would reach up into the perfumed branches of the ever faithful linden, pinch off a few clusters of blooms and carry them home. Placing them in a cup, covering them with boiling water, and perhaps sweetening the mixture with a small amount of honey, he would slowly sip the liquid. This linden tea induced sweating and the breaking of the fever, much to the joy and satisfaction of the individual.

There are no important customs associated with the month of July, except for July 2nd which was called *Matka Boska*

Jagodna, or Blessed Virgin of the Berries. On this day, the first fruits and wild berries would have ripened. The period between the sowing of the grain and first harvest was a difficult one for those who depended entirely on the land for sustenance. Larders were often nearly empty and nothing was to be had from the earth. The collection of wild strawberries and blackberries often marked the end of the scarcity of food that was so common among rural, peasant Poland in late spring.

According to an old Polish custom, mothers who lost a child through death refrained from eating berries before that day, based on the legend that on this day the Heavenly Mother of the little ones gathers them around her in Paradise and distributes sweet berries among them. However, those children whose mothers have eaten berries before that day have to go without.

The middle of the month saw the first gathering of honey from beehives. In villages surrounding Krakow, it was gathered twice a year—the middle of July and the latter half of September. Those who maintained an apiary and could afford to do so held a small celebration on this day. Inviting neighbors and relatives, the host offered bread, cheese and a vodka drink made with honey called *krupnik*. The drink was heated and placed in a bowl on the table and glasses filled from a ladle.

On July 13th, St. Margaret's, the rutabaga was planted and the first pears ripened, thereby giving the name *Małgorzatki* or Little Margaret's. The middle of the month also saw the beginning of the much awaited harvest. In the Kaszuby area, where the wheat was ripened by this time and the first cut made, at least one sheaf was left to be cut after the festival of Our Lady of the Scapular, which is on the Sunday after July 16th. The grains were quickly ground and new bread baked so that by Św. Jakób, the Feast of St. Jacob (July 25th), the proverbs declare:

Po Świętym Jakubie w swoim garnku każdy dłubie
After the Feast of St.Jacob in their own pots everyone digs

Jaki Jakób do południa taka zima aż do Grudnia.
As Jacob does in the morning, so does the winter til December.

Jaki Jakób po południu taka zima też po Grudniu.
As Jacob does in the afternoon, so does the winter after December as well.

July 26 was the Feast of St. Anne. In the Tarnów-Rzeszow area, whoever lit a candle every Tuesday and let it burn all night while praying to St. Anne would never be visited by poverty. The proverb of the day was: *od Św. Hanki—chłodne wieczory i ranki.*(From St. Anne's—cool evenings and mornings.)

August

The beginning of the harvest was met with a mixture of feelings by the Polish peasant, for it signaled the crowning event of an entire year's work—that which had been planned for, anticipated, and brought to fruition, often against tremendous odds. It also heralded the beginning of a great deal of back-breaking work.

A few days before the beginning of the harvest, the women began getting ready for this important event by baking more bread so that their sons, daughters and husbands could be properly fed through the upcoming weeks of exertion. Light-weight, clean clothes were prepared. Shirts were washed and whitened so that they glistened in the sun as a man bowed over his scythe. The girls prepared white scarfs to protect them against the burning rays of the sun and clean, white aprons to protect the grain. Meals of eggs and cheese were prepared to be taken to the fields.

The harvesting usually began on the Feast of St. Jacob (July 25). This was usually "prime time" as noted by the saying:

Na Święty Jakób, już chleba nie kup,
A od Świętej Marty ze żniwami nie żarty.
On St. Jacob you need not buy bread
But from St. Martha (July 29) harvesting is no joke.

If one wanted the harvest to go well, an intricate set of rituals had to be performed. There were lucky and unlucky days to begin such important work as this. It was unheard of, for example, to begin on a Monday or Friday. The first cut was always done on a Saturday, a day blessed by the Blessed Mother.

Before the beginning of work in the fields, at about 4 A.M., a Mass was said. Everyone would arrive, leave their scythes outside the church, and start the day with prayer and the song *"Kto się w opiekę podda Panu swemu."* (He who commends himself to the protection of the Lord.)

A universal custom called for all the reapers to bless themselves before beginning. In some villages, it was customary to have scythes blessed before the beginning of the harvest and the field blessed before the first cut. On this first, celebratory day, it wasn't unusual for the the workers to wear their special holiday clothes with the girls decorating their hair with flowers. In Grębosz, in western Galicia, the harvesters rode out to the fields on the first day of harvest dressed as if going to a wedding.

The first cut stalks of grain were placed in the shape of a cross, and it was customary that the first stalks be cut by the person who owned the field or, in his absence, a family member, usually a daughter. If both these people were unavailable, the first stalks were cut by the *przodownica* — the forewoman — the woman who was the designated leader among the harvesters. These first stalks were very important. In the Śląsk area, whoever tucked three stalks of the first grain behind a mirror in the the name of God would have good luck in harvesting all year long. They were used as protection against pain of the spine; the reapers would tie the first stalks around their waist. In some areas the first sheaf was brought home and placed in the corner of a room under a crucifix and was ground separately. Sometimes the first grains were taken home and saved to be placed in the corner of the room on Christmas Eve, and later perhaps for mixing with next year's seed bag for the first sowing.

In Wielkopolska there existed the custom of *wilk*, or wolf, which was the initiation given to a young farm hand who wanted to participate in the reaping but had yet to qualify as a reaper. The older, more experienced reapers would give him a hard time by placing him in an area that was hard to mow, or they would have him lead. Being more efficient in their movements, they would catch up to him, nearly cutting off his heels with their razor sharp scythes. If the "wolf" somehow managed to keep up, as well as tolerate their pranks and teasing, the lead harvester would place a wreath of flowers on his head and the initiate was then led or carried on someone's shoulders to the the manor house, accompanied by the other reapers. The village would be alive with the sound of bagpipes, fiddles, bass, harmonica, and the ringing of scythes. The lord of the manor would come to the door in order to greet the "wolf." He would hit him with a strickle on his back and give him a small money gift. Expressing thanks, the "wolf" was led away by the reapers and the rest of the harvesters to a nearby barn, where they placed him on a bench. Each of the reapers in turn hit him with a staff until one of the girls involved threw a scarf on him. This was a sign that she wanted to "buy him out," i.e, stand the group to a round of drinks. After the refreshment, the lead reaper, a trifle merry by this time, perhaps would make a speech full of jokes and jests, testifying that the "wolf" had qualified.

During harvest, everyone worked from first light to sundown, regardless of the heat, for *"kto w żniwa patrzy chłodu, nacierpi w zimie głodu,"* i.e., "who looks for coolness during harvest, will suffer hunger during winter." At dusk, sometimes by the light of the moon, everyone returned home, cracking their whips to urge on their tired horses, the girls carrying long, wooden rakes on their shoulders, with everyone offering the day's work to God by singing the song:

> *Wszystkie nasze dzienne sprawy*
> *Przyjm litośnie, Boże prawy*
> *A gdy będziem zasypiali*
> *Niech Cię jeszcze sen nasz chwali*

> All of our daily happenings
> I accept, dear God
> And when I fall asleep

Let our dreams praise you further.

The last stalks of grain to be harvested were critically important and filled with many customs. These last stalks were given different names in different regions, but the most universal were *przepiórki* (quail), used by the Mazowians and *kozy* (goat), used in the south of Poland in Lublin, Krakow, and the area known as Galicia. No matter how humble the landowner or how small the field, it was considered a sacred obligation to leave a handful of uncut stalks standing in the field.

On the day when the last wheat field was to be cut, the lead woman harvester, the *przodownica*, picked out a spot on the field, usually near the road, where the przepiórka could be seen. This area was left standing and the reapers continued on, mowing around this designated spot. Towards evening, when the entire field was cut, everyone returned to the stand of wheat, cutting a little from each side until only a few were left. These remaining stalks were divided into three parts. Each part was then braided, and all three braids were tied together at the top near the ears of grain. Beneath this dome a smooth rock was placed, as if in imitation of a table. It was covered with a piece of white fabric as if it were a tablecloth, and on this were placed a piece of bread, some salt, and money. This marker was left standing in the field.

After this was completed, *oborywanie przepiórki*, i.e, ploughing the quail, took place, whereby a young girl, helping with the harvesting for the very first time, was dragged around the przepiórka by the leg three times, supposedly so that the custom would be forever etched in her memory.

Two other names for these last stalks were *broda* (beard) and *pępek* (navel), the latter name used in western Poland. Here the last handful of rye or wheat was cut, and flowers were added and tied together with a straw band or ribbon put into a bouquet. This pępek was then attached to the scythe of the man who was considered the most senior reaper and taken to the home of the

13 SCYTHE WITH FLOWERS

man whose fields they had just completed. In some villages, a pępek was made after the harvesting of each particular grain such as oats, barley, or buckwheat. In Podlasie, after each particular grain was gathered, a *równiak* was made and presented at the manor house.

Sometimes the last ears or sheaves were made into the shape of a person and called *baba* (old woman), or *pszenna baba* (wheat woman), or *dziad* (old man). The reapers would tie the last bundle into the shape of a female person, dressing it in a blouse, skirt, and scarf. In some regions, the baba was made especially heavy from eight or more bundles weighted down with a rock. This custom of making the last sheaf unusually large or heavy was a charm to ensure a large and heavy crop during the following harvest. In the region of Więcków, when it was time for the wagon to go out to the field for the very last sheaves, it was called "going for the old man." When the wagon reached the field, they placed a stick through the top part of the last sheaf in

14 THE PRZEPIÓRKA

order to suggest arms, and then dressed it in the clothes and hat of a male.

This last trip from the field to the barn was also considered very important. The wagon was often decorated with greenery, such as in Śląsk Cieszyński, where on the top of the last wagon, a small pine or spruce tree decorated with ribbons and flowers was fastened. Another custom was the placing of a stick into the spokes of the wagon in such a fashion that when the wagon moved, it made a great, rattling noise. On its return trip, the wagon circled around the perimeter of the house and was drenched with water by the hired hands. The gaily decorated tree was placed by the fence leading to the house and the last sheaves of grain were taken into the threshing barn.

The end of the harvest was a satisfying and triumphant accomplishment for the Polish farmer. After planning and working the land against numerous odds and much difficulty, he could breathe easily knowing that the very last grains were safely

15 A RÓWNIAK WAS MADE OF EACH GRAIN

stored away. It was time to celebrate.

The harvest celebrations of Poland also had a variety of names. It was called *okrężny* by the Mazowians, *obżynek* in Galicia, *wyżynek* in Krakow and *wieniec* in Poznań. The most common name for it, however, was *dożynki*. There were some locations where this festival was unknown, such as among the Górale, the mountain folk, where there was an absence of large tracts of land suitable for growing grain, and in the Beskidy Śląskie, where the end of the harvest was simply concluded with a celebratory shot of whiskey. Among the Kaszuby, however, even the smallest landowner who could complete his harvest in one day celebrated by placing a small wreath of whatever grain he had harvested on his scythe and then went home to his wife who solemnly accepted it and prepared a special supper. Most of the dożynki celebrations were held by the nobility and larger landowners — those owning huge tracts of land that required hiring individuals from all around the countryside who had to be rewarded for their hard labor. This was especially so in Mazowsze and Podlasie.

The absolute zenith of the dożynki was the presention of the all-important wreath, or *wieniec*, to the landowner. This large wreath was made of a mixture of wheat and rye, sometimes one or the other, since of all those harvested, these grains were considered the most important. Crafted from the most beautiful ears of grain, the dożynki wreath was made in the shape of a dome-shaped crown. It was decorated with flowers, ribbons, hazelnuts, and the fruit of the mountain ash tree. The conclusion of the harvest and the making of the wreath generally fell around the Feast of the Assumption of the Blessed Virgin (August 15) so that it was taken to church to be blessed.

Wearing the wreath was considered an honor. Generally, it was worn by a young girl involved in the harvesting, someone who was considered a very good worker. In Krakow districts, the chosen girl went to church in great pomp and ceremony, wearing the wreath on her head while sitting in a wagon pulled by four

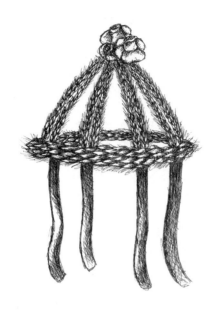

16 DOŻYNKI WREATHS

horses decorated in greenery and surrounded by other young maidens wearing flowers in their hair. The group was followed by all those involved in the harvest. After the wreath was blessed, the entire procession made for the manor house, singing quite loudly. The songs that accompanied the event were usually those that were indigenous to the area, perhaps unknown in other villages. If the landowner was a very religious individual, songs such as "*Kto się w opiekę podda Panu swemu* (He who commends himself to the protection of the Lord)," "*Czego chcesz od nas Panie* (What do you wish of us, Lord?)," or "*Pola już białe, kłosy się kłaniają* (The fields are white; the ears of grain are bowing)" were sung.

In the Kalisz area, the dożynki began with the words:

Otwórz panie swój dziedziniec
Bo niesiemy z pola wieniec

Open, sir, your manor
For we carry a wreath from the field

One song that was universal throughout Poland had the refrain of:

Plon, niesiemy plon
ze wszystkich stron.

We carry the harvest
From all directions.

The entire procession stopped at the gate leading to the manor house, its members continuing to sing until the owner emerged. The girl wearing the wreath approached, removed it from her head, and either handed it over to the owner or placed it on his head. Sometimes the owner removed the wreath from the girl himself and placed it to the side on a large plate. She was often given a handsome reward consisting of either money or some gift.

In the Poznań region, the presenting of the wreath was done a little differently. On the last day of the harvest, two girls remained behind in the threshing barn making small bouquets of wheat or rye, enough for all the workers involved in the harvesting. Two other girls were entrusted with making two other wreaths: a large one of all the different types of grain harvested in the shape of an arched crown, and a smaller one of nuts gathered from the forest, also made in the same shape, with every nut covered in blue or red paper. The wreath of nuts was placed on a plate and was carried by the girl who wove it. The large wreath was placed on the head of the foreman, the *przodownik*, who in this area was usually put in charge of the harvesters. There was also a female lead harvester, the *przodownica*, in this area, but she did not take on the role of wearing the wreath.

All the harvesters gathered at the barn. Everyone lined up in two rows carrying their bouquets. Ahead of them were two young men on horses, dressed in their best red coats carrying a cloth banner of half red and half white. Behind the two rows was a wagon hitched up to a pair of oxen whose horns were also decorated with clumps of grain. In the wagon were a fiddle and bass player, both wearing wreaths of grain (the circular type), and the przodownik wearing the special arched wreath with the przodownica next to him. Walking next to the wagon, if one could be found, was a clarinet player. The entire group headed towards the manor house, circling around the house three times before coming to stand in front of the gate, singing songs. After the singing was concluded, the przodownik entered the house, removed the wreath from his head, and humbly offered it to the lord of the manor. The girl carrying the wreath of nuts entered and placed the platter on the table and then sprinkled another bag of nuts on top. Both wreaths were accepted, and the individuals rewarded.

155

There were, of course, many variations on how the wreath was handed over, but the very act of handing it over was the high point of the festivities. After rewarding those that offered the wreaths, the owner signaled to the musicians to start playing again. Taking the young girl in his arms, the lord of the manor started dancing, and the part of the festivities that everyone had been waiting for, the dancing and refreshments, began in earnest.

The wreath, arriving only once a year, was cherished and given much care. It was hung in a prominent place, such as in an entrance hall, above a chest of drawers, or above the door of the main living room as a symbol of prosperity.

The people of Poland have the "Legend of the Spike of Grain," that recounts how it was that grains only grow on the tip of the stalk rather than along its full length. The tale runs something like this:

It was long ago, when Jesus Christ and His Holy Mother lived on earth. One fine and sunny day Jesus was walking with His mother on a road that ran between large fields of grain.

From afar they caught sight of a crowd of people beneath the shade of a wild pear tree holding each other by the hand and dancing while others were playing on bagpipes and fiddle. Jesus was amazed to see the idleness of the people because it was a common work day and this was the time of the reaping of the grain. So He stopped and asked the first person He ran into: "Why do you play and remain idle instead of taking quickly to your scythes and sickles?" But this person was preoccupied with throwing clumps of earth at a flock of birds that were twittering in the roadside thicket, and so did not respond to Jesus. In vain Jesus repeated his questions. No one took heed of the two wanderers. Finally, someone growled out a reply as if granting a favor. "And why should we hurry to work?" "Don't you see," said Our Lord, "that the grain all around you has ripened? That it is heavy? If you don't gather it soon it will fall from the stalk and be ruined." Loudly everyone laughed. "And so what of it?" they asked, not stopping their laughter. "Let the grain spill if it

156

wants. Even if half of it is ruined, there's so much that we always have enough for bread to the point where we're sick of it. Nobody wants to gather such enormous amounts of grain from the field, haul it to the barn, and then grind and grind at the flour mill."

In those times the stalks of rye were covered with grain from the base where it emerged out of the earth to its very tip. Listening to what the people said, Our Lord knit His brow and looking severely at the people pronounced: "When you do not value the gifts of God and know not how to cherish them, then be left without them." Hardly had Jesus spoken the words when the golden grain began rustling and shaking and falling down to the earth, revealing a pale, empty, straw-colored stalk. Every single grain would have fallen off if Blessed Mother had not extended a loving hand. She quickly grasped the tip of the nearest spike of grain and squeezing it in her hand she called to her Son. "My Son, have mercy. Leave at least this much grain on the stalk as I have in my hand." Jesus looked at the His Most Holy Mother. His severe look receded, His eyes brightened. "It is always so that the Mother of God intercedes on behalf of the people to me," he said sincerely. "For they are like children," whispered Holy Mother. "They sin, then later regret that they sin. Allow them to improve themselves and improve they surely will." "Then let it be as you wish it, Mother dear," Jesus said. "I'll not take away their daily bread, but from this time forward, the grain will only have spikes as much as you have in your hand."

The other major event that took place during the month of August was the celebration of the Feast of the Assumption of the Blessed Virgin Mary, which falls on August 15th. In Poland, it is also called Blessed Mother of the Herbs or Our Lady of the Herbs, i.e, Matka Boska Zielna. There were many other feast days on which herbs were gathered, such as for Corpus Christi, the Eve of St. John the Baptist, and Palm Sunday but the main, most important date for gathering of garden, field, and forest

157

herbs and flowers occurred on this special day. Bound to the land as serfs and peasants for thousands of years, the Pole was in such close communion with the earth that every tree, every flower and herb took on special meaning, playing an important role in both private lives and in public rituals. The plants were so important and so well loved they often became the subject matter for songs, legends, beliefs, and superstitions that were handed down from generation to generation.

On this special feast day, every village housewife brought a bouquet of herbs specially collected from the fields and forests to church in order to be blessed by the priest, believing that this heightened the powers of the plants. In some areas of Poland, the women gathered the herbs and plants in the afternoon, the day before the Blessed Mother of the Herbs, and gathered only until sunset. This was because it was believed that only witches gathered herbs after dark. During the time of the gathering, the women also watched to see if any woman stole herbs from another. Such a woman was also thought to be a witch. The plants and herbs were gathered only within their immediate vicinity. If a strange and unfamiliar girl was seen on their property, she was also perceived as a witch and was driven away and sometimes taken a stick to.

The women gathered whatever plants and greenery grew in their area, or the herbs and flowers they especially loved, or for which they had a fondness. In the Mazowsze and Podlasie areas, the people took hyssop, southernwood, lavender, mullein, and chamomile. They also took lovage and branches of the hazel tree, hemp, and mint. Both garden herbs and herbs growing in the wild were gathered. These included poppy (*mak*), peony (*piwonia*), sage (*szałwia*), thyme (*macierzanka*), tansy (*wrotycz*), dill (*koper*), caraway (*kminek*), mugwort (*bylica*), melissa (*mellisy*) and henbane (*lulek*). On this day in the Pomorze area, the northwest section of Poland, they have the saying, "*Każdy kwiat woła—weź mnie do kościoła.*" (Every plant calls, "Take me to church.")

The blessing of herbs on the Feast of the Assumption of the Blessed Mother was, and still is, strictly a Slavic custom and not universally incorporated in church rituals. Since it coincided with the time of the harvest, it was also the custom throughout Poland to take at least a few handsome spikes of the various grains that gave them their livelihood. This included millet (*proso*), poppy (*mak*), rye (*żyto*), wheat (*pszenica*), barley (*jęczmień*), oats (*owies*) and flax (*len*).

In the Pomorze area, because August 15th falls at the end of the harvest season, they have this particular proverb:

> *Do Maryi Wniebowstąpienia, miej w stodole połowę mienia.*
> On the Ascension of Mary have in your barn half of your property(harvest).

Another proverb deals with the production of fruit products:

> *W Wniebowzięcie Panny Marji słońce jasne*
> *Będzie wino godnie kwaśne.*
> On the Assumption of Blessed Mary the sun is bright
> The grapes will be suitably sour.

The gathered and blessed herbs were used in endless ways. The housewife would crumble some of the herbs and flowers into the seed mixture when going out to the fields for the first sowing. Boiled in water and allowed to cool, it was fed to cows for a few days after dropping a calf to aid the healing process. In Pomorze area, in the northwest of Poland, where the people drew their livelihood from the lakes and rivers, the herbs were taken along in their fishing boats to ensure good catches of fish.

Sometimes the herbs and plants were woven into a wreath and hung near or over holy pictures on the wall. Some of the herbs were tucked under the eaves to protect the house from lightning, communicable diseases, and other forms of disasters. But most importantly, the housewife had gathered and blessed specific plants that she used for healing purposes. Stored safely away in a small medicine chest in the pantry, the housewife kept a ready supply of dried plants against the time when someone became sick or injured.

Universal among the traditions of the Polish people was the art of healing with herbs. Doctors almost never came to the very small, rural villages, so everyone depended on their own knowledge about various plants and herbs to treat their aches and pains. The plants could be found growing in the cottage garden but, more often than not, were found growing in the open meadows or along the wayside. In many humble Polish homes, the gathering and preparation of remedies was the *gosposia's* or *gospodyni's* (housewife's) single most important task. Spring, summer, and fall were periods to harvest essential herbs and plants. As she collected and stored them carefully, she knew that life itself depended on her activity. Her knowledge and skill of the healing properties of the different herbs were often passed down from generation to generation. The good Polish housewife knew that the healing properties of all the plants and herbs she collected were more effective, sometimes even miraculous, if blessed. It was said that all blessed herbs and flowers are happy to be helpful to man. When it came time to choose which herb or flower to cut the plants were said to be whispering: *"Święć i mnie! Co mogę to pomogę!"* (Bless me also! I will help as much as I can!) The use of herbs and plants for healing was carefully passed down to the Polish housewife under the supervision of her mother or grandmother, or from a local herbal practitioner. Useful for the health and healing of the Polish peasant were:

Bobkowe Listki (Plantago major), commonly known as plantain. This plant is so abundant, growing in roadsides, pastures, and lawns that it is seen today more as a weed than a helpful herb. For the Poles, it was an invaluable first aid medicine. The mashed, green leaves were applied to cuts and

160

swollen or running sores. This was covered by a clean cloth or bandage. The process was repeated often until the area healed.

Bez Czarny (Sambucus nigra), commonly known as elderberry, or as the Polish people called it, the black, or wild, lilac. The ripened berries were crushed and made into a syrup which was drunk during times of high fever. It also healed whooping cough. The soft, white, inner core of the branch was dug out, and after drying was placed on hot embers. The sick individual was instructed to breathe in the smoky fumes to reduce a cough. Aside from its medicinal properties, however, the elderberry was not favorably looked upon. When the women went into the fields to gather plants, grains, herbs, and flowers to be blessed on the day of Our Lady of Herbs, they gathered all that grew except for the branches of the black lilac, for it was believed that Judas hanged himself on a black lilac tree.

Borówka (Vaccinum myrtillus), always kept on hand in either dried or syrup form. Blueberries were helpful in stopping prolonged diarrhea associated with abdominal pain and blood.

Bylica (Artemisia vulgaris), medicinally, mugwort was very important when it came to treating the special ills and problems of Polish women. Housewives of both the nobility and peasantry used the herb in treating young maidens and wives who were having difficulty beginning their menstrual cycle by encouraging them to drink mugwort in warm wine. It also assisted Polish women through the difficult task of childbearing and childbirth. The drinking of it during pregnancy ensured a safe and strong fetus and sprinkling the herb on either food or drink ensured a shortened labor and speedier delivery. For those women who were unable to conceive, it was believed that if bylica was picked from the borders of nine different fields, it increased fertility. Blessed on August 15th for greater efficacy, mugwort was often added to vodka for the treatment of stomach troubles and pains. Vodka played a large role in the relief of stomach remedies, because the theory behind the stomach illness was that it had developed a "cold" which occurred when the person drank too many cold drinks. The sick person was often given a hot toddy made of vodka or beer, to which was added a generous portion of bylica. He or she was then put under a *pierzyna* (eiderdown) and left there "to sweat." Sometimes, instead of being taken internally, an application of bylica was used externally as a poultice placed on the stomach. Another approach, especially if the chief symptom was shooting pains in the side, the leaves of bylica were fried in butter and eaten, or steeped in water and then drunk. The Poles also believed that *padaczka*, or epilepsy, was the result of a terrible fright or unsuspected scare. Included among a variety of treatment modalities for the illness were burning of flax and hemp, which the afflicted individual was encouraged to inhale, and followed by a dousing of ice cold water. The afflicted individual was immediately given a tea of mugwort to drink. The root of this herb was felt to be so powerful it could even prevent epilepsy.

Dzięgel pospolity (Angelica silvestris), often found in damp and wet places. A tea made of the root, seeds, or leaves of angelica was helpful in calming numerous digestive disturbances, especially excessive gas.

Dziewanna (Verbascum thapsus) A tea made of the mullein flower was used as a gargle for the throat and as a tea for colds and congestion of the chest.

Dziurawiec (Hypericum perforatum) The flowers of St. John's Wort were steeped in alcohol and then cut down to one part alcohol mixture and three parts water for the treatment of fresh or festering wounds. The leaf and flower also made a tea that helped children who wet the bed.

Krawnik (Achillea millefolium), commonly known as yarrow. A strong tea was made of the leaves and drunk repeatedly for all illnesses tied with the loss of blood, such as bloody stools or sputum. It was also one of the best remedies for treating common colds as well as chills and fever since it induced sweating. Womenfolk used yarrow to regulate menstruation.

Lipa (Tilia cordata), commonly known as lime or linden tree. The flower of this tree was steeped in boiling water and the brew drunk during times of high fever, or for a cold and cough.

Łopian (Arctium lappa), commonly known as burdock. Lopian was effective among the country people for treating headaches and loss of hair. The root of the plant was dug out, cleaned, and soaked in *spiritus* (alcohol) for a few days until it released its oils. It was then rubbed into the scalp. It was useful in various facial skin diseases and disruptions.

Macierzanka (Thymus serpyllum) The flowering foliage of thyme was used externally in bathing as an effective remedy for those suffering from rheumatism and paralysis.

Piołun (Artemisia absinthum) Wormwood encouraged a flagging appetite and provided relief during times of abdominal cramps and pain.

Podbiał Pospolity (Tussilago farfara) Commonly known as coltsfoot, this plant blossomed in the early spring and grew wild along fields and lanes. It was prescribed as a tea for various pulmonary complaints. The leaves, steeped in boiling water and made into a tea, were used to treat coughs. The leaves were also dried and smoked as a tobacco for the curing of breathing problems. The tiny leaves were also used to treat boils.

Pokrzywy (Urtica dioica), commonly known as nettle or stinging nettle. Of nettle the Poles used to say, "There is no need to plant bad things — they will surface by themselves." Anyone who has been the victim of a casual walk through a nettle patch certainly understands the merit of this old folk saying. Nevertheless, nettle played a part in Polish folk medicine. The root was boiled and drunk as a tea for those who felt "weak" and without strength. Those who were afflicted with rheumatism were instructed to rub the body part everyday for a few minutes with fresh nettle leaves.

Rozmaryn (Rosmarinus officinalis) A tea of the leaves of rosemary taken every morning and night cleaned and aided in digestion of the stomach. White wine steeped in rosemary was an excellent remedy for heart troubles and any kind of swelling.

Rumianek (Chamaemelum nobile), commonly known as chamomile. Among the Polish peasants it was made into a tea and used extensively to treat any stomach aches or ailments.

Siemię lniane (Linum usitatissimum), commonly known as linseed, the seed from the flax plant. The flax plant was of exceptional economic importance to the Polish people, playing a crucial role in the cottage industry of weaving. The fibers from the stem of the plant were the basis for linen which was then woven into fabric, and cut and sewn into clothing apparel. The flaxseeds from the plant were as important as the fibrous stem. The oil from the seeds of the flax plant was an invaluable aid in the treatment of burns and skin diseases. A spoonful of the seeds was placed in a glass of water, which was allowed to stand and thicken. It was taken every evening by those with a tendency towards constipation.

Świetlik lekarski (Euphrasia officinalis) The dried leaves of eyebright were used to make a tea which was used as an eyewash for those with eye problems. Another method was to soak a cloth with the mixture, and place it over the eyes fastened with another cloth to hold it in place.

Skrzyp (Equisetum arvense) Used for treatment of swollen feet, the tips of horsetail were boiled and then the feet soaked in the resulting mixture.

Szałwia (Salvia Officinalis) Of ancient sage, it was said "*Śmierć tego nie ubodzie u kogo szałwia w ogrodzie* (Death will never sting him who has sage in the garden). Steeped in water and wine, it cleansed the liver and kidney, and a tea made of half sage and half wormwood produced an even greater effect. Old festering wounds healed quickly and surely when washed with a concoction made of sage.

Żywokost (Symphytum officinalae) Commonly named comfrey, this plant was one of the best loved of all healing herbs. This tall, hairy leaved plant was used for all broken bones, and also for the aches of rheumatism and the troubles of tuberculosis. The root was cut into small pieces, and then cooked in a small amount of fat and a spoon of honey. This "pap" was applied to the bad bruise, sore, or broken bones to promote healing. Another method of using the root was to soak it in alcohol for a few weeks. The root was then strained out, and the mixture poured into a bottle. The mixture was then used as a liniment and applied to aching areas afflicted with arthritis.

Herbs of Love and Magic

Bylica (Artemisia Vulgaris), commonly known as mugwort, bylica is one of the oldest, most esteemed and respected herbs in Polish folklore. This member of the wormwood family is a tall plant that grows from three to four feet in height, and has grayish green leaves and masses of grayish yellow flowers. For centuries, it was used in a multitude of ways that ranged from healing to household use to its more widely recognized use as a magic herb that could break spells and deter witches. Its place in Polish life was so significant that even as far back as the sixteenth century, mugwort was deemed by Polish herbologists to be the mother of all herbs.

The principal use of this herb centered around its special properties as an herb of witchcraft and magic, an herb that could break all spells and keep away witches. Of all the nights of the year it played its greatest, most important roles on June 23rd, the night of the summer solstice. The English called it midsummer night or St. John's Eve. The Poles called it *Sobótka*, or *Wigilia Święto Jana*. On this night fraught with magic and superstition, when witches and devils roamed the earth freely, looking to do mischief and harm, mugwort was the chief means of holding those forces at bay. The association of this herb with the Eve St. John stems from two beliefs that have long been part of European and Polish folklore: that St. John wore a girdle of it in the wilderness for protection and that when he was beheaded his head fell among mugwort plants. So closely tied to the activities of this night, the herb was commonly referred to as *bylica świętojańska* or *Świętojańskie ziele,* i.e, St. John's herb. At dawn of that day, girls in the Koziegłow area of Poland went out "to pluck mugwort which can grow as tall as the sunflower." Branches of it were hung under the eaves of the barns and stables to keep the witches from coming in at night and milking the cows dry. Sprigs of it were attached to doorways and windowsills to prevent the entrance of evil forces into the house. After assuring the safety of the house, the women of the villages would weave garlands or wreaths from the herb. Added to the bonfires which were lit on this night, it helped to diffuse the flames and made the smoke spread farther across the fields. It was believed that as far as the smoke from a midsummer fire reached, the fields would be protected from evil witches and the destructive forces of hail.

> *Niech bylicy gałąź pęka,*
> *Czarownica próżno stęka.*
> *Myśma tu przyszły z daleka,*
> *Popalali zioła święte:*
> *Nie zabiorą już nam mleka*
> *Czarownice przeklęte.*

> Let the branches of mugwort burst
> The witches lament for naught
> We have come from far
> To burn the blessed herbs
> They no longer gather our milk
> Those cursed witches.

In imitation of St. John, the girls would weave garlands of the herb and wear it around their waists believing that it would prevent and protect them against back troubles. In the Podlasie area, people strongly believed that the smoke of mugwort, carried up the chimney after being thrown on glowing embers of coal, would disperse thunderclouds.

Nasięźrzał (Ophioglossum vulgatum), commonly known as adder's tongue. Wherever one looks in old Polish herbals, adder's tongue crops up over and over again as a plant of magical powers. According to folklore, "any girl who obtains this herb, boils it, and drinks the brew will have special success with bachelors." The strength of adder's tongue was so enormous that it was enough to simply carry it on one's person in order to achieve success in love. Found growing in meadows but more often in woodlands and forests, it was necessary to overcome a series of obstacles in order to obtain it. Since the plant was protected by the devil, the bold adventuress seeking it as a charm was likely to have her head torn off. For the bold and daring who were not fainthearted, however, there was a definite technique for obtaining the magic plant.

In order to find this herb, it was necessary for the maiden to first scout out ahead of time where it grew. She was then to go into the woods at midnight on the first Thursday after the new moon (in the Tarnów and Rzeszow region, they said the maiden should also be naked) and approach the plant backwards (this tricks the devil who only perceives that it is being picked if someone is looking at it). Getting close to the herb, the young woman was not to turn around, but rather to pluck the herb with her hands behind her back, at the same time saying:

> *Nasięźrał rwę cię śmiele*
> *Pięcoma palcami szóstą dłonią*
> *Niech się za mną chłopcy gonią*
> *Duzi, mali, by mnie się wszyscy zalecali.*

> Adder's tongue I pluck you boldly
> Five fingers, the palm the sixth
> Let the men run after me
> Large, small, let them all pursue me.

Lubczyk (Levisticum officinale), commonly known as lovage, this tall perennial herb with a pleasant aromatic smell can still be found growing in herb gardens in and around centuries-old castles and restored villages. Szymon Syreński, in his herbal published in Krakow in 1613, held that this herb was an aphrodisiac. It is believed by Poles that it had the power to make someone love you. A mother who had a particular husband in mind for her daughter would give him a tea made of the plant. Any boy bathed in lovage easily gained the love of girls. A young girl sings:

> *Czy w lubczyku się kąpałeś*
> *Że tak mi się podobałeś?*

Were you bathed in lovage
That I have taken such a liking to you?

Other Interesting Polish Herbs

Betojnika or *Ziele Anioła Stróża* (Betonica officinalis), commonly called wood betony or the herb of the guardian angel. It was the people of the Kielce area of Poland that called wood betony by this latter name. Polish folklore books tell this tale about betony: There was a man who had a wife who was a real sluggard. Every time she was supposed to fix him a meal she took off to the village, visiting and chatting with her *kumosie* (kin). She gave her husband neither his breakfast nor his dinner on time, but only when she felt like it. The husband worked hard all day, but when he came home in the evenings he had nothing to eat. Once, then twice he asked her, "How come you didn't cook any supper?" The wife responded, "I didn't cook because I didn't have any time." The husband lost all patience and began to beat her.

AUGUST

From heaven a guardian angel saw this, and was greatly
saddened that there was such terrible discord between man and
wife. One day the angel became a toothless old woman and came
to the house. The angel asked the woman, "Where's your man?"
The woman replied, "Mowing the field." Happy once more that
she had someone to talk to, the woman began lamenting about
her husband who was mean and rough and beat her. "If he were
to come home now," she said, "he would probably beat you,
too."

The old woman listened to everything and finally said,
"Maybe I could be of help to you. Let us go find him. I will sit
in the grove while you take his lunch to him, and when he begins
to beat you, call for me and I'll intervene. She then taught the
woman how to call out. But the woman, as was her habit, did not
prepare any food on time and brought her husband's lunch when
others were getting ready to prepare supper. Her husband began
hollering, "Good God, woman, what are you doing bringing me
my lunch so late?" The wife replied, "I didn't have time." The
husband was outraged and began waving his spoon in front of her
face in anger. His wife started shrieking and began calling out as
the old woman had taught her. "Betojinka, betojinka, come out
because my man wants to beat me." The old woman came out of
the woods and said:

> Nie płacz, nie krzycz
> Boś sama winna
> Ino strój śniadanie-kiej śniadanie
> Objad-kiej objad
> wieczerze kiej ma być
> nie będzie cię twój chłop bić.

Don't cry, don't holler
Because it's your fault.
When others prepare breakfast, prepare breakfast
When others prepare dinner, prepare dinner

Supper must be prepared at suppertime, then
Your man will not beat you.

Then the toothless old woman became a beautiful angel and
flew away to heaven. The wife, impressed with this spectacle,
recognized her faults, and from that time on began doing as she
should; consequently, her man stopped beating her. From that
time on wood betony was called the herb of the guardian angel.
It is supposed to be helpful on many occasions, but is most
effective when there is discord in the home.

Dziewanna (Verbascum thapsus), commonly known as
mullein or Great Mullein. This unmistakably large, wooly, white-
leaved plant stands four to five feet tall, and can be found
growing wild on sunny banks and waysides. It looks splendidly
regal in a garden. Flowering in midsummer, it was used by
Polish housewives to treat worms in cattle. The secret was to go
out before sunset to the meadows and look for mullein. Once you
found some, you were to break off the yellow flowering tip,
crumble it in your hand, while saying three times: *Jak tego
srokatego (białego, czarnego i t.d.) bydlaka robak męczy, tak ja
ciebie męczę.* (As the worms torture this spotted [white, black
and so forth] beast, so I torture you.) The crumbled material was
then thrown to the ground and buried under a rock.

Paproć (Polypodium vulgare), commonly known as the male
fern. It is believed by the Krakowians that at the hour of
midnight on St. John's Eve (June 23) the male fern blossoms.
The flower is very small, difficult to see, and unlikely to be
found, because the devil himself observes and watches over it. If
plucked, this male fern flower gives the owner the ability to look
into the interior of the earth, where vast treasures are hidden.

The Krakowians tell this tale: There were two young farm
boys who learned of the power of the male fern flower. They
wanted to be rich and not work any more. Between them they
made a pact that, whatever awaited them, they would go and
pluck the fern flower and with its help find the treasures. On the

Eve of St. John's they went into the forest before midnight, armed in case of a struggle with the devil. When the prescribed hour of midnight arrived, instead of the expected shape of the devil, there arose throughout the forest terrible whirlwinds, roaring, and storming. At the sight of a tree being uprooted and whirling in a circle, the young boys succumbed to their fears and scattered. One of them managed to find a road and returned home. The other, more prone to error, fell among grasses, herbs, and fallen trees and got stuck. When the storm calmed, he was barely able to extricate himself from the thicket and find a footpath. He did not know that he had found that which he sought. During his fall in the overgrown weeds, the male fern flower had broken off and, unbeknownst to him, fallen into his boot.

On the way home, the young farmer felt like a magician. Wherever his eye moved, he saw under the earth gold and silver of untold wealth. He walked into his home and said to his father, "Father, take a pair of horses with a wagon and the trough from scalding the pigs and we will go out into the world gathering money because I know where to find it." He also called to his brother, and taking him and a shovel, went out on the road for treasure. They were riding past the house when the farmer-magician hollered to his father, "Good gracious, father, hold it! Near the well in the garden I see a large cauldron of gold. Let's dig it out now and then we'll go on." The garden was overgrown with plants and herbs and in order to dig deep into the earth all three briskly chopped at the roots with an axe and dug with the shovel. In their haste they tired quickly and it became harder and harder for the farmer-magician to work with his boots on so he threw them off. Unfortunately, the male fern flower, which had fallen accidentally into his boot, fell out again and the young man lost his clairvoyance. The young farmer nearly went crazy with despair and for a long time afterward contemplated his fate, trying to understand what had happened to him. He finally "saw"

171

again. This time, he saw that nothing comes free to any individual on this earth.

Rozmaryn (Rosmarinus officinalis), commonly known as rosemary. A pale evergreen shrub with a spicy fragrance and soft blue flowers, rosemary was another plant that played an important part in Polish weddings. From time immemorial, rosemary has been known as the plant of fidelity, and was linked with weddings and bridal wreaths. This is especially true in the Poznań area of Poland. The groom, dressed in his holiday best, would wear rosemary tied with a white ribbon on his left lapel. The best man, also dressed in his very best, carried a white kerchief and whip, both of which were decorated with branches of rosemary tied with a red ribbon. A sprig of rosemary could also be found decorating his hat. The bride and bridesmaids also wore wreaths of rosemary on their heads. Or, the bridesmaids wore it pinned to their breasts. Long ago, during a Poznań wedding, the priest placed small wreaths of rosemary on the heads of the couple as a symbol of their fidelity to each other. This would be used instead of wedding rings.

Ruta (Ruta Graveolens), commonly known as rue. A perennial with yellow flowers and semi-evergreen foliage, rue has played many roles in the life of our ancient forefathers, but none so much as that for young Polish maidens. In the annals of Polish herbal folklore, rue has been and ever will be the herb of young Polish maidens. The custom of young girls, among both peasants and princesses, of decorating their heads with wreaths was noted by Poland's oldest chroniclers.

Traditionally, the *wianki*, or wreaths, were made of foliage which did not lose its greenery, such as rosemary and myrtle. Such plants were always felt to have mystical and magical meanings and properties. But utilized more than any other plant was rue. It was an herb much cared for and cultivated by the young country girls as well as those of the nobility from time immemorial for their bridal wreaths. It is reflected in the proverb *"podsiała sobie rutki,"* or "she sowed herself some rue."

Throughout Poland, "*siać rutę,* " or to sow some rue, meant the same as announcing to anyone who might be interested, that one was available for marriage. For passers-by, seeing the herb growing in the garden told them that within the house resided a young girl who was of marrying age.

There are literally thousands of Polish folk songs that deal with young girls and rue. The songs of Mazowsze indicate the growing of rue:

> *Nasieję ja ruty, w nowym ogrodzie*
> *Hej, mocny Boże, w nowym ogrodzie.*
> *Uwiję ja trzy wianeczki, puszczę po wodzie*
> *Hej mocny Boże, puszczę po wodzie.*

I will sow rue, in a new garden
Dear Lord, in a new garden.
I will weave three wreaths, and release them on water
Dear Lord, I'll release them on water.

Or, *Na Św. Młodzianki stroić się trzeba w ruciane wianki,* meaning: On St. Innocents Day (December 28), one must dress up in a wreath of rue, which meant it was time to get married. The period immediately following Christmas and before the beginning of Lent was one of the traditional times to get married. The girls carefully covered and protected the plant over the winter in order to have at least a small piece to wear in their hair on Sunday.

Rue played its most important role in the engagement and wedding ceremonies. In the Kaszubian region of Poland, during the three weeks of the engagement period, the girl wore a special headdress when venturing out in public: on a black head band inlaid with brass rested a wreath of rue that was decorated with silver and gold foil and hanging ribbons. In the Mazowsze, Śląsk, and Podlasie areas, this wreath of the bride-to-be had the shape of a crown, and was made from gold paper and trimmed

173

with nine colored ribbons. Not only was a wreath of rue an intrinsic part of the dress of the bride, but it was also in Medieval Poland one of the ways of confirming the marriage agreement. In pre-Christian times, the young girl gave a wreath of rue to the young man, who in turn reciprocated with a gift or payment, the amount of which had been determined earlier in the marriage contract. Later, with the influence of Christianity, the custom arose of the reciprocal exchange of wreaths as the binding act of entering marriage.

The custom of exchanging wreaths between the newly engaged couple after acceptance of a proposal of marriage signified each other's willingness to enter into the marriage. The young couple exchanged the wreaths between themselves, or sometimes had it exchanged by a third party, usually the matchmaker. The matchmaker removed the wreath from the head of the young girl and placed it on the head of the young man, and then placed the wreath of the young man on the head of the girl. Much later, the exchange of wreaths entered the actual marriage ceremony where, instead of rings, the priest blessed and exchanged wreaths between the young couple.

Rue was used to decorate the *kołacz* or wedding cake, the staff of the marshal of the wedding ceremony, the hats and whips of the groomsmen, and even the whip for the horses that pulled the wagon carrying the bride to church for her wedding. The bride was accompanied to the church by the shooting of guns and cracking of whips. As a talisman for young girls, rue had no equal, to the point where, should a young, unmarried girl die, a wreath of rue was added to her coffin.

Słonecznik (Helianthus annuus), commonly known as the sunflower. In the Krakow area of Poland, there is usually a small garden planted with numerous flowers in front of the home. Here any chance passer-by could see carnations, chrysanthemums, peonies, and yellow lillies. Standing tall and mighty above the rest would be the sunflower, which was used to decorate holy pictures of the Blessed Mother and the crucifix. Tales from the

Krakow region state that the sunflower was unchallenged king of the garden for years, until from some foreign country across the ocean came the stuck-up and haughty dahlia. Eventually, the new flower was planted in even the most modest and humble of cottage gardens. It is believed that the sunflower became an even deeper shade of yellow out of jealousy, and turned its face away in anger.

Herbs of the Blessed Virgin

There existed in medieval times the custom of planting "Mary gardens," which were made up of all the flowers and herbs that are ascribed by love and legend as belonging to the Blessed Virgin. This tradition was especially active in Poland, where the Blessed Mother is the Patroness of Poland and where love of her is almost universal. The herbs which were associated with the Blessed Virgin were:

Baranki Najświętszej Panny—Lambs of the Most Blessed Virgin (Sanguisorba officinalis). In English, this herb is commonly known as Great Burnet and was believed by the Polish people to be helpful in inflammatory disorders.

Dzwonki Panny Marji—Bells of the Virgin Mary (Hypericum perforatum). St. John's wort was known to be helpful against magic and evil forces. It eased the pains of childbirth and, present on the midwife, assured that neither the mother nor the new infant would come to harm from evil forces.

Koszyczki Najświętszej Marji Panny—Baskets of the Most Blessed Virgin (Verbena officinalis). Known both as verbena and vervain, this was an herb that, if dug out under the sign of Venus, was helpful in matters of the heart, but was used chiefly in promoting an easy delivery.

Warkoczyki Najświętszej Marji Panny—Braids of the Blessed Virgin (Verbascum thapsus). Used chiefly for incensing cattle during illness, it was also effective in treating coughs and had a calming effect for those who were prone to nervousness.

Panny Marji Drzewko—Virgin Mary's Tree (Artemisia abrotanum). Southernwood was also very often called *Boże drzewko* or God's tree. All parts of this plant have a pleasant lemony fragrance, and were used by Polish women in caring for their hair.

Włosy Panny Marji—Hair of the Blessed Virgin (Trifolium repens). White clover is a perennial herb, whose flower heads were used as treatment for fever and diarrhea.

Legend of the Aspen and Hazel Trees

When the Holy Family was fleeing from the pursuit of the soldiers of King Herod who were rapidly catching up to them, the Blessed Mother caught sight of a large aspen and, riding up to it, explained their predicament and asked if it would shield them with its branches. The aspen began to shake in fear and replied that it was afraid to incur the wrath of the king, who would order it to be cut down; thus, it would only die with them. For being so unhelpful the Blessed Mother decreed, "So continue shaking and be afraid to the end of time," and hurriedly continued on their flight.

They next met a wide-leafed hazel tree of which the Blessed Mother made the same request. The hazel tree covered the Holy Family with its branches and in doing so, saved the Holy Family from the hired assassins. From that time forward, the leaves of the aspen tree have shook even in the absence of a breath of wind while the hazel grows large and strong, bestowing fruit and coolness to all who pass by. It is perpetually safe from storms and lightning. That is why branches of the hazel tree are tucked into the eaves of the house.

Perhaps because of its history of protecting the infant Jesus, the leaves of the hazel were often used in the care of children.

176

AUGUST

Ancient herbal remedies offer this advice: In order for children to grow straight, one should bathe them in water in which were boiled branches of hazel. It was also felt that hazel leaves in the bath water would help the child to grow strong and to walk early. Another suggestion was during the bath of the young child, one had to put on its head leaves from the hazel tree to protect him against boils.

Why do flowers grow so mixed in the fields? The Polish people offered this legend: One spring day the Lord Jesus wanted to sow the fields with flowers. He told two angels to carefully choose and arrange in a basket some seeds of flowers, and to take them to earth for sowing. On the way there, the angels fell into an argument and in the squabble, their orderly arrangement of seeds were jumbled up. What were they to do? They sowed the seeds as they were — all mixed up. From that time on to this, the fields and meadows change like a brightly variegated carpet. You will find campion growing next to water-pepper next to bluebottle, without rhyme or reason.

September

For centuries, most marriages in Poland took place in the beginning of September and continued through the fall and winter months except for the holy weeks of Advent and Lent. This was a time when the all-important harvest and field work was completed; the grains were milled, the poultry and hogs were sufficiently fattened and slaughtered, and the pantry and larder full enough to hold and host a major celebratory party such as a wedding. Numerous proverbs also testify to this time of year as a popular wedding time:

Na Św. Idzi (Sept 1), swaty do mnie przydzi.
On St. Idzi, the matchmaker will come to me.

W dzien Św. Reginy (Sept 7) wabią chłopaków dziewczyny.
On the day of St. Regina, the boys are attracted by the girls.

Other proverbs proclaim:

Na Święto Młodzianki
Stroją sie w ruciane wianki.

On the Feast of Holy Innocents (Dec.28)
They dress in a wreath of rue.

Na Święty Franciszek
ożeni się nasz braciszek.

179

On St. Francis (Jan.29)
our brother will be married.

Girls, who were of age but knew they were not to be married
that year, often sang of the marriage season in a song called *"Nie
moja jeszcze jesień przyszła,"* i.e., "My fall has not yet arrived."
Most marriages in early Poland, like those of all Indo-
European countries, were arranged affairs whose main purpose
was to improve or enlarge fortunes. Whether an individual was
a prince or pauper, love played a very minor role in most
marriage contracts.

Among the nobility, marriages were often contracted while
the children were still young. The marriage of the son of
Bolesław Chrobry (Bolesław the Brave 967-1025) was arranged
in just this manner, as was the son of Bolesław Krzywousty
(1085-1138), whose wife was brought to Poland as a child to
await her marriage. Arranged marriages were not limited to the
noble and wealthy. The common peasant also looked for a wife
who would enlarge his fortune, humble though it may be. If he
was unable to locate someone who would substantially improve
his lot, the peasant at least aimed at finding someone of equal
standing.

Marriages were also often contracted without the consent of
the girl. She was taught from an early age to obey the will of her
father. Males were also under the rule of the father, and marriage
unions in defiance of the will of the family were unusual. If a
couple did manage to marry in this manner and things did not go
well for them, they were viewed by the rest of the village and
family as receiving their just desserts, "for God would never
bless such a pair." Even at times when the young were attracted
to each other, the choice and final decision rested in the hands of
the parents.

Marriage among the Polish people was viewed as a holy
responsibility begun in heaven and blessed by God. The unmarried "cannot be happy and has difficulty obtaining salvation of

his/her soul." Most Polish villages had few unmarried people. Marrying while still young was common, with public censure and mockery the fate of those who postponed marriage too long. A very popular time for marriages was between Christmas and the Feast of Three Kings, and up until the beginning of Lent, especially during *Zapusty*, or Shrovetide. Those who were eligible but avoided marriage or failed to get married during this time were subject to ridicule through a custom called *klocki*. This custom existed both among city and country people. In 1869, an article in the Warsaw newspaper, the *Kurjer Codzienny*, described klocki in which men and women who had not been joined by the end of the carnival season as having blocks of wood or egg shells pinned on their backs, and being objects of much kidding because "they did not want to carry the yoke of marriage, so let them instead carry these wooden blocks."

In other parts of Poland, such as those surrounding Krakow, pieces of wood, various bones, and geese or chicken feet were hung upon the backs of the dresses of unmarried girls. In the Sieradzkie area, the older boys tied a young man down to a large block of wood, placed on his head a wreath of peas (a sign of bachelorhood) and danced circles around him, making fun of him until such time as he bought his way out with a round of drinks and promised to do better next year.

Depending on the locale, there were a variety of ways a Polish peasant with a marriageable daughter could announce his desire to marry her off. One of the most ancient customs was dotting one side of the house with whitewash. It was always the role of the father to paint these dots, for it was he who decided whether his daughter was ready for marriage. Sometimes only the area around the windows was dotted, and sometimes the entire house was done in this manner. In the Mazowsze and Podlasie areas, these dotted houses were called *tarantowate*, or dappled. In the Sandomierz and Krakow areas, they spotted the fence surrounding the house or the gate. The Górale, the mountain folk of the Tatras, used similar marks and signs, but also hung a

181

wreath on the front door of the house. In the Kurpie area, the front yard was sprinkled with sand in the shape of flowers, and on holy days branches of a spruce tree were displayed. In Mnichów, a home in which there was a marriageable girl had the windows painted blue or had some type of circular decoration in that color on the side of the house. In the area of Górna Wisłoka, a sword and pistol made of tin hung in front of the house on a post as a sign that a marriageable young man lived within.

Wywiady—Inquiry and Proposal

The preliminary or initial act of a possible marriage was called the *wywiady* or *zamowiny*, and it was initiated by a young man wishing to marry. Its purpose was to determine whether a family and a particular girl would welcome his suit. In Kujawy this was called *oględy*. In Częstochowa it was called *przeględy* and in Mazowsze it was called *wypytanie*. There were other names also, depending on the region, but their purpose was the same.

It was a universal custom throughout all of Poland that any endeavors for the hand of a girl were to be done through an intermediary, who would be a go-between for the male. The name for the intermediary differed according to the region of Poland. The Mazowsze called him *dziewosłęb*. In the Podlasie area, he was known as *swat, starszy swat, raj, rajek* or *rajko*. In the Bug area, he was called *poseł*, and in the Krakow area was known as *starosta*. In Lithuania, which at one time was under Polish rule, the intermediary was called *marszałek*. This intermediary was usually an older, respected man in the community who could be trusted to act in the man's best interest. Sometimes it was the young man's godfather, but whoever was chosen had the grave responsibility to see to the conclusion of the marriage and that everything took place as it should, right up until the bridal pair was put to bed.

Before the church became involved with the marriage ceremony, it was conducted by the swat or dziewosłęb acting on behalf of parents. Eventually, the role of the swat was taken over by the priest, but as so often happened, many of the primitive customs were incorporated or carried over and intermingled with the newer versions of the event.

Thursdays and Saturdays were the days when a swat generally approached a particular family regarding their marriageable daughter for the zamowiny or wywiady, the making of an inquiry and putting forth a marriage proposal. Sometimes one visit was enough to come to a satisfactory arrangement but often a few visits were needed. Among the landed gentry near the Narew River, the swat went with a young man on Tuesday night, the second time on Thursday night for a definite decision, and a third time on Saturday night for the final decisions regarding the dowry and the official engagement.

Nighttime was a popular time for conducting the zamowiny. Its purpose was to provide some privacy from gossips regarding what was seen as a very delicate matter, but this custom was also rooted in early beliefs that evil spirits had a marked hostility to lovers and prospective brides and grooms. Fearing that some evil person or dead spirit would cast the evil eye or wish them ill, most zamowiny were conducted at night, under cover of darkness, when people were about to retire for the night.

The swat and prospective groom approached the house and knocked on the window, asking to be let in. On entering the house, he and the young man bowed low, praised the Lord, asked after everyone's health, and then made very indirect and discreet inquiries. The swat asks "Don't you have a heifer for sale, for we'd like to buy her," or "we're looking for a particular goose and wondering if you might be willing to part with it." As he talked, he took out a bottle of whiskey or vodka brought specially for this occasion called a *gęsiorka*. The bottle was topped with a small bouquet of flowers, and the neck of the bottle tied with a red ribbon. He put the bottle on the table and asked the young girl about whom the inquiries were being made to bring him a whiskey glass. The refusal of a suitor was always done in an indirect, non-insulting manner but which left no doubt about the decision. If the girl went into the next room to look for a glass and did not return, it was a sign of refusal. Or, if the family had no wish for the match, they denied that they had anything for sale, the swat is not offered a whiskey glass nor do they accept anything to drink. The swat and the young man leave the house.

If the family accepted the proferred vodka, it was an indication of their willingness to consider the match and they then indicated on which day the suitor was to return for their decision, usually within a couple of days. On Thursday, the swat and young man returned for a final decision. Bringing out the gęsiorka again, the swat asked for another whiskey glass. If the young girl produced a glass quickly, it was an indication of her agreement to the match which had been previously discussed and agreed upon by her parents. The swat filled the glass with vodka and said "Let's drink." The father took the filled glass and gave it to the daughter. She took the glass, drank a little of the vodka, and offered the rest to the young man who had come seeking her hand. When the young man drank the rest of the vodka, the agreement was sealed. It was only after this that talk could begin in earnest about dowries and settlements. Without the mutual drink, there was no understanding or agreement.

If, after much deliberation, the answer to his suit was negative, a suitor could be offered *arbuz*, i.e., watermelon (the Polish word for watermelon having two meanings: watermelon and to meet with refusal). The same meaning was attached if he was given dark soup, *czarnina*, or duck's blood soup. In Ostrołęka, in the Kurpie region of Poland, when a young man returned with his intermediary on Thursday, the family immediately sat them down to dinner. If they offered czarnina or, as it's called in this area, *szary barszcz*, it was eaten and the suitor and his intermediary quietly left without further discussion. If something else to eat was offered, then the intermediary knew that he could begin talking about the dowry and the wedding plans.

In some parts of Poland there were variations on the custom of wywiady. In Mazowsze, for instance, the young man, wishing to save himself the embarrassment of a refusal, sent out an older, trusted woman called a *rajka* to conduct this first step. If the rajka received the news that the family would welcome the suitor, the young man and his male intermediary made their visit to the house. If not, the rajka was sent elsewhere to make inquires. This woman was also called different names in different parts of Poland, including *starościna* or *swata*, and she, too, came to play an important part throughout the courtship and wedding ceremonies. The wywiady were as binding as any marriage contract, and breaking off after agreements were reached and drank upon was a rare occurrence. To break off after declaring oneself was seen as a shame and disgrace. The family of the girl had the right to beat the would-be suitor and the girl who broke her promise was subject to having her feather ticks ripped open and allowed to disperse to the four winds.

Zaręczyny or Zrękowiny—Engagement Period

After the Tuesday and Thursday meetings, the official engagement occurred most frequently on Saturday of that same week. The swat and young man dressed in their very best and returned to the house where the young girl's relatives and close friends would have gathered for this happy event. The engagement was most often called *zaręczyny*, the name appearing in the sixteenth century. In more ancient times, when the official engagement took place through an exchange of wreaths, called *wianki*, it was called *wieńczyny*. And because the engagement was as binding as marriage, it was once called *ślubiny*, or marriage. The most ancient name was *zmowa* or *zmowiny*, i.e., talk or agreement, from the times when a man could simply obtain a wife through verbal agreement and purchase. The main event on the night of the engagement was the tying together of the hands of the couple to be married. There were numerous variations on this custom, but in whatever form it appeared, the central elements were an uncut loaf of bread and a white towel or scarf. Because the engagement was as binding as the marriage itself, it was always done as a public act in front of family and friends who acted as witnesses.

In Kozieglow in Mazowsze, a large loaf of rye bread and a cheese decorated with myrtle was covered with a cloth. The starosta or swat joined the right hands of the couple above the bread, tied them together with the cloth, and made the sign of the cross over their joined hands. He then cut two pieces of bread for them to eat, with the larger piece for the girl as the symbol that she have plenty for her children. This tying of the hands, having some magical properties left over from very pagan days, was now to represent "the joint endeavors of the man and woman to prepare the bread," "that they always have bread beneath their hands," or as a symbol of "mutual forfeit of freedom." Chroniclers in the thirteenth century noted that "the swat joined the hands of the young couple." Much, much later in 1838, a writer indicated: "two white scarves, with which the hands of the young couple were tied together were cherished throughout their lives and on their death placed in their coffins beneath their heads." The giving of a scarf by the groom to the bride was the most common of engagement gifts. It was this scarf which was used in the tying of the hands.

In Nowy Sącz, before the starosta joined the hands of the young couple, he asked those present "Do you agree to this joining?" three times and, after receiving the affirmative, he joined their hands together and gave the blessing. In the Łęczyca region, after the dancing and as the guests were about to sit down to something to eat, the swat asked the guests, "Do you agree for Mary (or Elizabeth, etc.) to join herself with another?" The guests replied "We do!" Then he asked her mother the same question, but she remained silent the first two times. On the third questioning she answered "May God bless them." The same was asked of the father. The swat then tied the young couple's hands together and gave a blessing. Everyone present then came forward, placed their hands on the young couples' and stated "may God bless you." Sometimes the bread was cut into small pieces and the groomsmen went out into the village, offering it to the villagers in the name of the newly engaged couple, asking in return for their blessings on the young couple.

The main purpose for the evening concluded, the guests were treated to various refreshments including coffee and milk, bread and butter, cheese, or whatever the household could afford. Gifts were also exchanged. The bride's family usually placed a plate on the table and the young man was expected to place a few coins on it as an engagement gift. The bride-to-be offered a silk kerchief for the groom. Everyone stayed to eat, drink, and celebrate.

The morning after the official engagement, the young couple went to the priest for the placement of the banns. The engagement period lasted for the three weeks of the banns. In the Poznań area, as soon as the first bann was called, the engaged couple pinned rosemary to their lapels as a sign of their engagement. The bride-to-be usually supplied her bethrothed with the plant which she had growing in the garden for just this purpose. During this time, the bride was excused from most of her everyday responsibilities to prepare for the wedding. Her time was taken up with weaving material for her trousseau and preparing necessary wedding gifts.

In the Kaszuby region, the engaged girl would present her betrothed with a shirt, pants, a pair of socks, mittens, and a kerchief for his neck and nose. If the father of the groom was alive, he also received a shirt, a kerchief for his neck and nose, and also a pair of mittens from his future daughter-in-law. His mother received four yards of fabric, his married sisters two yards, and any unmarried sister one yard. All of his relatives also received a pair of mittens, as did the parish priest, so that a young bride sometimes made as many as 30 pairs.

On his side, the groom in the Kaszuby region gave his fiance two yards of fine fabric, a pair of shoes, and a silver coin. If he had a father or brothers, they also gave up to a silver coin in money. He gave his future father-in-law a fur cap and each sister-in-law a yard of dark material with which to make a vest. In this area, the mother of the bride did not receive anything.

Zaprosiny—Invitations

In the second half of the nineteenth century, wedding traditions demanded that guests be invited in a certain obligatory manner. The first invitations were issued to relatives or friends to act as groomsmen or bridesmaids. The bride and groom then went to invite their godparents. The remaining guests were usually invited on a Thursday after the first or second reading of the banns. In the Mazowsze and Podlesie area the *zaprosiny*, the first invitation to come to the wedding, could be done by the bride-to-be along with her maid of honor or mother, all going on foot to issue their invitations directly. In this section of Poland, old customs forbade the exclusion of anyone in the village from being invited to the wedding, even those chance-met on the road, be they a gypsy, beggar, wanderer, or child. Everyone had to be asked for a blessing and invited to the wedding. No house was omitted, even if the house was not a Christian one. They would visit every hut in the village to ask for blessings and attendance at the wedding. It was understood by everyone that this was simply a matter of form. Not everyone invited actually came to the wedding. While issuing her invitations, the bride might receive a small gift from those she has seen and visited. At her relatives' she would receive something to help her establish her household, such as a chicken, piglet, or new lamb.

In the Łęczyca area of Poland near Łódź, inviting the guests was the responsibility of two groomsmen. Guests were usually invited twice — on the Thursday (considered a lucky day) before the wedding day, and the wedding day itself. After entertainment at the home of the bride with music and supper, it was decided who would be invited. The groomsmen, appropriately dressed, carrying whips and with the musicians in tow, would go through the village issuing invitations. Cracking their whips as they went along, they loudly sang short ditties and songs. When they arrived at a home, they did not enter the home at once but stood outside the doors or under a window singing loudly. On entering the house, they doffed their hats and bowed low to the head of the household. "Praise be to Jesus Christ. I greet all of you." The gospodarz usually responded "And we greet you and invite you further." The best man then recited a lively invitation to the wedding to which the gospodarz, or head of the house, usually answered in the affirmative. When these formalities were over, the best man called for a toast. The younger groomsman handed over a small whiskey glass and a bottle of vodka decorated with a red ribbon and a sprig of myrtle. The best man filled the whiskey glass, lifted it to his lips, and drank it down. After shaking off any excess drops, he filled it again and offered it to the gospodarz. The housewife was also offered a drink, as were the rest of the adults in the house. If there were marriageable girls in the home the husband and wife invited the groomsmen and musicians to the table and offered them refreshments of some kind. Oftentimes, the household took advantage of the present musicians and the opportunity to dance with some eligible males, and began dancing and singing in celebration of the upcoming wedding.

Since most marriages took place on Sunday, guests were again invited on the Saturday before the wedding or in some cases, the morning of the wedding itself. This second invitation was very important for only those guests invited a second time were actually invited to the wedding. This was done by two groomsmen, who were sometimes accompanied with music. This invitation did not have the elaborate ceremony as did the Thursday invitation. This was more of a reminder or, if the guests were reluctant to attend because of sudden, unexpected responsibilities, the groomsmen were compelled to pull them away and even went so far as helping them get dressed to make sure they attended.

Dziewczyny wieczór—Maiden Evening

The evening before the wedding was a very important night with respect to Polish wedding customs. On this night before her marriage, the bride-to-be gathered her bridesmaids around her in what the Poles called the *dziewczyny wieczór*, or maiden evening. This getting together served a variety of purposes, including helping to decorate the house and doorway, making boutonnieres for the groomsmen, and cooking for the wedding feast. But the most important reason for the evening was for the girls to officially say goodbye to their friend as a single woman and to perform one last service for her. This was to help her prepare her final *wianek*, or wreath.

In the Podlasie area, the maiden evening began with the covering of the table with a white tablecloth. With all the girls surrounding the table, the bride-to-be brought rue from her garden in her apron and placed it on the table while the girls sang. In Mazowsze the wreath was woven from rue, but rosemary or myrtle (*myrtus communus*) were also popular, while in the Poznań region, rosemary was the herb of choice. While singing special songs for just this special occasion, the girls begin to weave a wreath of rue for the bride, which would be worn the following day and for the very last time in her life.

Besides weaving a wreath, the bridesmaids were also responsible for preparing the *rózga weselna*, or wedding branch or wedding rod. Sometimes it was called *krzak* (bush) or *wieniec*

17 BRIDE-TO-BE WITH WREATH

(wreath). Up until the second half of the nineteenth century, this wedding branch was done the night before the wedding, when the older women and young girls gathered together to make the wedding bread and plait the wreath. The wedding branch was usually made after the *korowaj*, i.e., the wedding bread, was placed in the oven. The preparation of the wedding branch was the responsibility of the bridesmaids. Two of them would go into the woods with a knife or sickle and cut off a branch of spruce or pine about one half to one yard long. In the Kurpie region, the branch had to be juniper. It was stripped of its lower branches so that it could be held easily, but still had at least two additional branches on the center one. The maid of honor, accompanied by the bridesmaids, brought it to the home of the groom. Fastened to this branch was the small wedding wreath woven earlier in the evening with one or two ribbons attached to it. The meaning of the wedding branch is not completely clear, as some Polish folklorists of the nineteenth century advocate that it was a symbol of the consolidation of the marriage contract and had its roots in the Middle Ages when it was customary to hand over a green branch at the time of a business transaction. It was, however, a symbol associated with the male.

Once the wedding branch and the bridesmaids arrived at the home of the groom, where the groom, his groomsmen and family were waiting, it was decorated by the bridesmaids and groomsmen. In more ancient times, the wedding branches were often decorated with natural flowers, herbs, feathers, and apples, but by the nineteenth century, it was adorned with plain and flowered silk ribbons provided by the groom and bride. One of the two side branches was designated as the bride's side, and on this side were hung two blue ribbons with a white pattern embossed on it which were purchased by the groom. The other side was designated as the groom's, and this was also decorated, but with plain red or blue ribbons purchased by the bride. To these branches were also added four small candles, two on each side. Sometimes, depending on the location, to the middle of the wedding branch such items as stockings, shoes, or a scarf were attached as gifts from the groom to the bride.

After decorating the wedding branch, everyone—the groom and his family, the intermediary, bridesmaids and groomsmen—all headed for the home of the bride, where numerous guests gathered to officially open the wedding festivities. The groom and swat were usually on horseback, with the swat holding the wedding branch in his right hand. When the party arrived in the front of the *dom weselny*, the wedding house, the candles on the wedding branch were lit to announce the arrival of the groom, but the group would find that they were unable to enter. The gate leading to the house had been closed against them!

18 DECORATED WEDDING BRANCHES

The custom of locking the gate and barring entry to the groom and his entourage can be traced back to the seventeenth century, when bridestealing was still a fairly common occurrence throughout Poland and all of Europe among both the peasants and nobility. A young man, in love with a particular girl but not favored by the parents, would gather together a few of his cronies. Under cover of night, they furtively approached the house, broke down the door, pulled the girl out of bed in her nightclothes and ran off with her while the braver of the relatives followed in hot pursuit. Such affairs never ended without fighting and bloodshed, so the courts and fathers with marriageable daughters began taking closer precautions against such occurrences by keeping their gates and doors tightly locked. Over time and civilizing influences, bridestealing became less common and then ceased altogether, but remnants of this way of life made their way into marriage customs so that a groom in Poland still had to overcome obstacles before being joined with his one true love.

When the groom was to arrive with his wedding party in Rabka, in the Tatra Mountains, the gate was closed and the relatives of the bride armed themselves with large sticks, pitchforks, and brooms. As the groom arrived at the gate the relatives sang in indignation "Who are these people?" "Where do they come from and what for?" and generally made it difficult for the groom's party. After a long ceremony, the parents and brothers of the bride-to-be opened the gate, saying "These are peaceful guests." In other areas of Poland, the intermediary was forced to haggle with the inhabitants for entry through the gates, while the groom remained seated on his horse, saying nothing. If the intermediary was unsuccessful, the groom showed his ardor and impatience to see his bride by taking matters into his own hands; he jumped over the gate with his horse. Only the door to the house acted then as the final obstacle and, there again, the intermediary was forced to haggle. They were refused entry twice, but on the third request to open the door, the bride would call out to let them enter, and so the groom and his party were allowed in, the swat still carrying the rózga weselna.

As the groom entered, the bride and her bridesmaids were hidden away in another room. The family sat the groom and his entourage at the table which would be covered with a white tablecloth, a loaf of bread at each corner. The family offered the groom a drink and then the whiskey glass made the rounds to the others. The swat then went into the room where the bride was being kept and brought out a girl covered in the fur of an animal. The girl would hunch her back and walk in a crippled fashion. The intermediary would decide that this particular person didn't appeal, and they don't want her. He would then bring out another girl who acted in much the same manner. At long last they brought out the bride who was also covered in fur, but walked straight. The intermediary, holding the wedding branch, would say that this one appealed and that they would keep her. He would then take the fur off the bride and place it on a bench, fur to the outside, in order to begin the *rozpleciny*, the unbraiding, if it is to be done at this time. Before this custom began, the bride had to be given the wedding branch.

For this part of the wedding custom, the groomsmen all lined up in a row, beginning with the best man down the line. Directly across from them stood their female counterparts, the maid of honor across from the best man, etc. The bride and groom stood across from each other with the intermediary facing them. With a steady, solemn speech, practiced and perfected over the years, that deals with the wreath as a symbol of her virtue, the intermediary handed over the wedding branch to the bride. In some areas the intermediary would take the bride into a dance. Holding the branch in his right hand, he grasped her with the left and placed the bottom of the branch so that they were both holding it, dancing around the room slowly as everyone sang. After dancing around the room, the intermediary gave the branch to the bride who then passed it on to her bridesmaids so that they could begin unpinning the ribbons to decorate the bride and groom and to wear in their hair.

The *rozpleciny*, or unbraiding took place at different times in different parts of Poland. In the Podlasie, Mazowsze, and Wielkopolska area, the symbolic unbraiding of the hair took place during the night before the wedding, in the presence of the groom and his attendants, the parents, the matchmakers responsible for the match, and the bridesmaids. Later it began to take place the day of the wedding, either in the morning before leaving for church or in the evening. From the time of the sixteenth century, custom dictated that young women went to their husbands with their hair long and loose. Usually tightly braided as a sign of girlhood and virginity, the appearance in public of long, flowing hair represented the transition from girl to married woman. Songs of the period called first for the brother of the bride to unbraid the hair and then other family members, relatives and bridesmaids as a sign that they agree to the marriage.

Almost universal throughout Poland, as well as Russia and other Slavic countries, was the custom of unbraiding the hair while the young bride sat on a kitchen dough box, or dough bin used for making bread, that was covered with a sheepskin coat with the wooly side out. The reason for this custom was rooted in the belief "that the finances of the young married pair would grow as does dough in a dough box" or "so that their bread always thrives." Sometimes it took place on the morning of the wedding, before leaving for the church ceremony, and the bride would go to church with her wreath over her loose hair.

In some parts of Poland, the unbraiding was done later in the day in the wedding hall. If this were the case, on the morning of her marriage, the young girl would plait her long hair into two braids that hung down her back for the very last time and wear her wreath above the braids.

Pieczenie kołacza i korowaja—
Baking the Wedding Bread

In all of Poland, neither king nor serf was married without a *kołacz*, or wedding bread. In the eastern regions of Poland this bread was called *korowaj*. This specially decorated or "adorned" bread was baked as a symbol of abundance and prosperity for the young couple.

The name kołacz, or korowaj, is derived from the ancient shape of a circle, which as a symbol was attributed to have special, magical powers. It was so important that there were regular established rules regarding the baking of this round wedding bread. In the Rzeszow area, the wedding bread was usually the godmother's responsibility or that of some other blood relative. In the event that there were no such relations, the woman baking it had to be married and somewhat well-to-do in order to sustain the cost of baking it. For any single wedding, more than just a single bread was baked. There was one to be shared with the wedding guests, one for the priest, another for the grand marshal who had conducted the wedding, and one for the bride.

In eastern Poland, in the Białystok and Chełm regions, the wedding bread was baked a little differently. Tradition decreed that the wedding festivities take place equally in both the home of the bride and the groom. A wedding bread had to be prepared for both homes and the baking roles were filled by both godmothers. They invited a few select women well versed in the baking of korowaj who brought flour and eggs or a special bowl for the mixing. Even though this select group often numbered as many as twelve, the actual preparation of the dough was the chief responsibility of the godmothers. This was usually done late in the evening the night before, and accompanied by much singing. The wedding bread was usually made of the finest wheat flour, but if that was too expensive, a better grade rye flour was used

19 WEDDING BREAD

instead. The dough for the wedding bread was very carefully prepared, for it was believed if the bread baked poorly, that is, if the top cracked in the baking, it meant the marriage would not be a success. The oven where the bread was to be baked was very carefully cleaned out and the prepared dough was placed in the oven with great ceremony and prayer. This wedding bread was considered so important that in instances where the bread had risen to such a degree that it would be broken if attempts were made to remove it, the bakers would take the stove apart rather than damage the wedding bread.

In most instances, the wedding bread was round, but in certain parts of the Mazowsze area it was called a *pierog weselny* and was a longer, braided bread. In the Kurpie region, the wedding bread was made in the shape of a large cap. The dough was pressed unto a bowl turned bottom up in order to achieve a hollowed-out effect and was then baked. This cap, or *czepek*, from dough was briefly placed on the head of the bride after the removal of the bridal wreath from her hair, and just before the *oczepiny* ceremony (the capping) began. It was believed that the larger and heavier the bread, the better the future life of the young couple. There is documented evidence that the wedding kołacz baked in Krakow for the wedding of the nephew of King Casimir the Great was so large and heavy, it required two oxen to pull.

Half of the prepared dough was made into a large bread and the other half was used to make the adornments or figures that traditionally rested on top of the bread. Whatever the shape of the bread, small clumps of raw dough were fashioned into figures of birds, roosters, chickens and other farmyard animals indigenous to the area. Sometimes elaborate hearts and flowers were made or figures of people were placed on top. Branches, symbols of fertility, were made of dough and placed upright on top of the bread. Two branches depicted the couple, and a third symbolized future offspring. Apart from the dough, other media were used to decorate the top after baking — the greenery of asparagus or myrtle, paper flowers, or perhaps apples (a sign of love), and nuts (a sign of fertility) were hung from the dough branches. The simplest form of decoration was the sign of the cross on top or the application of poppy seeds in a complicated manner. This specially baked and adorned bread was then removed to a designated, out-of-the way place until the time came for its role in the wedding festivities.

The bread was usually brought forth during the festivites and placed on the wedding table for all to see. It was the responsibility of the intermediary to cut it into pieces and offer it to the guests in exchange for a gift or money for the bride. In some areas, especially in southwest Mazowsze, in Rzeszów and in the adjacent Podgórze regions, there was a dance that took place with the kołacz/korowaj. The intermediary put the bread on his head and very majestically entered into the wedding hall in cadence to musical accompaniment. He executed a short dance in the middle of the room and then began cutting and distributing the bread.

In the Białystok region, the bread was wrapped in an elaborately embroidered and decorated towel that had been specifically made just for this purpose. It was brought into the wedding hall by the mother of the groom and then cut and distributed by the male kinsmen. Universally, however, it was absolutely necessary for every single wedding guest, even the smallest child present, to receive a piece of the wedding bread, as a sign of abundance and goodwill towards the newly married couple. A proverb says it all about the importance of the kołacz: *Bez kołaczy nie wesele* (Without a kołacz, there is no wedding).

Aside from the main wedding bread, there were other breads baked for the wedding. *Szyszki* were small rolls baked in various shapes. In the Białystok region they were called *byczki, huski* or *gąski*. These rolls were distributed to the village children who had gathered to see the bride and groom when the wedding party was leaving for the church, or as the bridal pair left the church. There was the custom in some areas of throwing bits of the wedding bread on the roof, so that even the birds could enjoy the wedding.

The Wedding Day

It was customary to have musicians playing as the wedding guests began arriving at the *dom weselny*, the place where the wedding festivities were to take place, usually the home of the bride. This musical entertainment was called *odgrywanie*. The musicians either stood on the side of the door or sat on a bench along the wall. On seeing a guest approaching they would begin to play, for which they were sometimes rewarded with a small tip. Inside, the invited guests were treated to some bread and coffee and then settled themselves down on chairs and benches to await the beginning of the festivities.

When the groom arrived with his swat or *starosta*, grooms-men and family members, the *staroscina* and maid of honor began dressing the bride. After helping her into her dress, apron and shoes, the bride was seated on a stool or chair so that ribbons could could be pinned in her hair and so that the wreath that had been made the night before could be secured. In the Poznań area, the bride's head was almost entirely covered with green ribbons, the ends of which trailed down to her shoulders. The bridesmaids pinned flowers and ribbons of a different color in their own hair, and both the bride and her maids carried small bouquets of rosemary with blue and red ribbons. The groom wore a green ribbon on his cap. The bridesmaids pinned bows to the left arm of the groomsmen or sprigs of rosemary to their hats.

Very early headdresses for brides in Rzeszow consisted of the dome of a straw hat completely covered with artificial flowers and beads, with eighteen pink and white ribbons sewed to the back. Towards the very end of the nineteenth century, the headdress changed. On a strip of white fabric, pink, white, and sometimes blue ribbons were attached to the center, along with beads and myrtle. The ends of the white fabric were then tied at the back of the neck beneath loose, flowing hair. By the twentieth century, the center of a long white ribbon was covered with flowers, beads, and myrtle along its entire length. The ribbon was tied at the back of the neck with the ends hanging even with the skirt. Bridesmaids wore a curved band across their heads covered with artificial flowers.

One of the oldest headdresses in Kujawy consisted of multicolored ribbons pinned on a regular kerchief which was tied at the back of the neck. The ribbons were attached in rows in a tubular or looped effect with pins, until the entire kerchief was covered, with the ends hanging down the bride's back below the waistline and sometimes in line with the hem of her skirt. The ribbons were usually rose, blue, white, and gold. Red was avoided because "the pair would fight all their lives."

Near Kielce, the most humble headdress consisted of a small wreath of myrtle, with ribbons falling down the back. Very often, the ribbons had to be borrowed from friends invited to the wedding. The bridesmaids simply pinned sprigs of myrtle in their hair.

Everyone would gather at the home of the bride to accompany the bridal couple to the church, but also to witness the blessings and symbolic farewells of the bride with her parents, relatives, and friends. Before those two events could occur, important speeches were made by the intermediary to the gathered individuals. These speeches were generally passed down through the years from father to son and varied according to the person and his powers of oration, but the essence of the message was generally the same:

"Honored guests! We've gathered here today to this home in order to take part in the wedding and to accompany the bridal pair to church so that Almighty God can bless them through the hands of a priest. Holy marriage does not originate with the people of this world but comes from God Almighty. When God made Adam He settled him in paradise so that he could act as the landlord of the earth. But even though Adam had plenty of everything, he was melancholy, for he had no one to talk to. So God put him into a deep sleep and took a rib from his right side and made a woman whom He named Eve and gave her to Adam as his wife. Thus we see, dear guests, that marriage originates from God."

To the groom the intermediary says:

"Here, young man, see before you your future and faithful wife. She leaves her mother and father in order to join you. See her as your faithful and loving wife. Think not of her as a slave of some kind, for as Jesus Christ is the head of the holy church, so is the husband the head of his wife. But as Jesus cherishes his holy church, so should a husband cherish his wife as his companion for life. I join you together so that God will bless you."

After the speeches, it was time to depart for the church. Before leaving, the *pożegnanie*, the saying of farewell by the young bride to her family and home, had to take place as well as the *przeprosiny*, the asking of forgiveness, and the *błogosławienie*, the bestowal of blessings. Since she would be leaving the home of her parents and going to live with her husband and his family after her marriage, the young girl knelt before her parents, kissed their hands, thanked them for her upbringing and "for the bread that you have given me." She asked forgiveness for any troubles she may have caused them and said goodbye to them. The mother kissed her daughter, blessed her with holy water, and threw grains of wheat at her feet.

The blessings by the parents were seen as more important than the church ceremony itself. Children whose parents blessed them would always do well, prosper steadily, and live a long and successful life. Sometimes the bride and groom stood before a table on which there were burning candles, a crucifix, flowers and holy water. The young couple would kneel down. The mother gave her blessing first. Crossing her hands over their heads she stated: "I bless you, dear children. May you be fortunate." She then sprinkled them with holy water and gave them the crucifix to kiss. The father then did the same. The young couple embraced their mother and father by the knees, kissed their hands and face, and then said their farewells. If one of the parents was dead, someone was asked to act in his or her place. In some parts of Poland, the act was even more humbling. Both sets of parents sat down on benches, and the young couple approached their respective parents on their knees, and kissed their feet and hands, asking forgiveness and blessings. The parents said "God forgives and blesses you." After the receiving of the blessing, everyone stood in a circle around the couple and the mother blessed them with holy water and showered them with hops. The blessings were so important that, if a mother or father

203

had died, the wedding party would stop at the cemetery, where the groom or bride asked for blessings from the deceased parent while the bridesmaids or groomsmen sang:

Powstań, powstań z grobu
pobłogosław córkę do ślubu.

Arise, arise from the grave
Bless your daughter on her marriage day.

At the conclusion of the farewell and blessings, and on a signal from the intermediary, whose role it was to continuously oversee everything, the wedding party began to line up to the sound of marching music to exit the house. The bride walked surrounded by two groomsmen. Two groomsmen also followed the bride. The groom was surrounded by bridesmaids, some of who also followed behind him. At the forefront of the procession was the intermediary, who carried the rózga weselna, the wedding branch.

When the young couple was getting into the wagon to go to church, two older women showered them with oats and sprinkled them with holy water. Nearby observers sometimes caught the oats in their caps or aprons, and their catch was given to the bride, who took some with her to the church where it was blessed. She would save these specially blessed oats and mix it with other oats to use in the first sowing of the year. Other grains that were popular for showering the bridal pair were poppy, flax seed, peas, and millet. The other grain in Poland that was a favorite for showering the couple among both the peasants and nobility was hops, or *chmiel*. Writings from 1495 reveal that hops were used at the wedding of the Russian Princess Helena to King Alexander Jagiellończyk, and Polish peasant wedding songs make innumerable references to hops including:

Oj, chmielu, chmielu,

ty bujne ziele
Nie będzie bez ciebie żadne wesele.

Oh hops, hops,
you fertile herb
without you there is no wedding.

In the Białowieża area, a custom that dated back to the twelfth century decreed that the korowaj baked the night before must be walked around the wagon carrying the bridal pair. It was then to be placed for a moment before the horse and wagon that would carry them to the church, as a symbol of their bread on the future road of their life together. In Podlasie, as the young couple was getting into the wagon that would take them to the church, the mother of the bride came out of the house with bread and salt, placed the bread before the horse and sprinkled salt on the bridal pair to protect them against evil. In Podhale, the family stuck a few grains of oats, barley, and flax into the bride's shoe. In Czarny Dunajec, they gave the bride a crumb of bread and a pinch of salt "so that she have plenty in her life," a pinch of sugar, "so that her life flowed sweetly," and money,"so that she have no lack of it."

The trip to the church took place in various ways, with the bride and groom riding together or in separate wagons. The bridal couple may have been tied together with red and white ribbons or a rope made of straw. A witness to a wedding party in the middle of the nineteenth century in the Tarnowskie-Rzeszowskie area described it in this way: "Four young boys outfitted in full Krakowian dress preceded the wedding party. Their four-cornered hats with peacock feathers were decorated with a fresh sprig of myrtle and each had a colored kerchief tied to his arm. Four stately horses, also dressed in their Sunday best with bouquets of flowers pinned to their heads, followed them, pulling a wagon on which stood the driver, cracking his whip for everyone to get out of his way. Behind him were a fiddler and double bass player playing a merry tune. Along both sides of the wagon were eight lovely girls holding bouquets of flowers. In the middle sat the bride, wearing a beautifully woven wreath on her head. Behind the wagon, on horseback, rode the master of ceremonies, the *starosta*, carrying a whip made of braided leather and the best man with a bottle of vodka who alternately offered it to the wagon driver and the starosta. Behind them came four more groomsmen surrounding the groom who was also on horseback. Everyone sang — the bridesmaids, the groomsmen, the musicians and even the wagon driver."

Church Ceremony

In Płock in 1554, it was noted that "the groom gave a wreath to the bride and placed it on her head and she gave him a wreath but he only held it in his hand." In the middle of the nineteenth century marriages in Poznań were still being conducted with wreaths instead of rings, the wreaths being made of rosemary. About the size of a silver dollar, the wreaths were blessed by the priest and placed on the head of the bride and groom. In some sections of Wielkopolska, the couple had wreaths of myrtle decorated with ribbons, and the priest placed these on their heads. Rue was also used for making the marriage wreath. Later, when rings became popular, an exchange of both wreaths and rings was seen and with the passage of time, only rings were used.

During the church marriage ceremony it was expected of the bride to cry. If she didn't, it was believed that she would cry throughout her married life. In the *Kurjer Warszawski*, in 1825, it was noted that "the bride cried until she sobbed, which was approved by all." Crying was also supposed to bring good luck, as attested to in a song from Krakow which asks the bride, *"A czemuś nie płakała kiedyś ślub brała?"* ("Why didn't you cry during your marriage ceremony?").

One of the items that were carefully watched during the church service were the candles on the altar. If one happened to go out on the groom's side, he would die young, and the same would happen to the bride if the candle went out on her side. If the candles failed to burn brightly, it was taken as a sign of an unhappy married life together. In some parts of Poland, the bride and groom took bread to church with them which had been given to them during the blessings. Upon exiting the church, the bride broke off a piece of the bread and offered it to the groom; he did the same. A very common custom was the distribution of *kukiełki*, small buns baked especially for this purpose, to the village children. In Mazowsze, the bread was distributed to the poor and also to beggars who may have gathered outside the church.

Leaving the church ceremony, the bride sometimes threw handfuls of straw on the young boys and girls who followed the wedding party. Whoever it landed on was prophesied to marry before the others. Another belief was that whichever one of the bridesmaids touched the bride or her wreath first after the marriage would marry that year.

Even at the turn of the nineteenth and twentieth centuries, it was a universal custom after the wedding ceremony for the wedding party to stop at a local tavern where the guests ate, drank, and danced until they were called to the *dom weselny*, the home where the wedding feast was to take place. Each housewife brought to the tavern something to eat—bread, cheese, butter, pierogi or sausage.

When the newlyweds, followed by the wedding party and invited guests finally arrived, they found the door closed to them. The starosta sang a song to open up and the door was opened by the mother who stood before the stoop, sprinkling the married couple with holy water. This was done to turn away any evil or bad forces which might be lingering about the threshold. Another variation at the threshold had the mother or matchmaker, holding a loaf of bread, asking the bride: "Which do you prefer—bread or your groom?" If the bride answered "bread," then one of the groomsmen pretended to beat her with his whip until she changed her mind and said "Bread and the groom — so that he might work for it." Kneeling, the bride accepted the bread, kissed it, and entered the house. When she crossed over the threshold, the women within showered her with candy or grains. They did this with the hope that it would assure a pleasant and fruitful life of plenty.

In customs that can be documented back to the sixteenth century, the young couple was most often greeted at the entrance of the house with bread and salt. In the lives of both the nobility and common people, salt had equal footing with bread in all family customs and celebrations from birth to death. It was believed that salt had the power to heal and cleanse, uncover thieves, protect houses against fire, dispel storms and hail, and drive away evil spirits.

In Mazowsze, the mother greeted the young couple, blessed them, and offered them bread and salt. In Ropczyce, the bridal pair were greeted by the parents with two loaves of bread, as well as sugar and salt. Pieces of the bread and salt were saved as a talisman of plenty.

Uczta weselna—The Wedding Feast

If the family was well-to-do, the tables were covered with white linen and decorated with greenery. The young couple always sat at a table which was located along the wall containing holy pictures. On one side sat the female wedding host, the *starościna* or *swata*, and on the male side, the swat. First to be placed on the tables were bottles of vodka and beer, and the wedding banquet began with "zapicie," i.e., to wash down or to drink. This was done with one glass which traveled from hand to hand. The first toast was conducted by the starosta, drinking to the staroscina, who may have had as much to do with bringing about the marriage as he did. The groom toasted his bride and then all down the line. During this drinking, everyone wished one another good health and fortune, kissed one another and if so moved, sang patriotic songs. After this, the food was brought out.

Among the peasants of Poland it was a universal custom and ancient tradition that the first food a married couple ate was *kasza jaglana*, a cereal or porridge made of millet. It was served unsalted and cooked in milk, "so that their married life be sweet." Among the *Kaszubians* the kasza was made of buckwheat and also cooked in milk. The proverb "*Kasza matką naszą*" (Cereal, our mother) voices its antiquity. Chicken was also a ritual food served at Polish weddings, as were peas, a symbol of fertility. Other foods served depended a great deal on the locale, but the meal always included sauerkraut, beet soup with noodles, and then the kołacz, the wedding bread.

The crowd ate, drank and danced. If it became too crowded inside the house, which happened very often, the festivities were moved outdoors where children and interested individuals watched. If a father could afford it, the wedding sometimes lasted another day. Somewhere around dawn, if the guests were tired from all the revelry and started falling asleep, it was the job of the best man to keep everyone awake. And if it was a groomsman who should be happening to fall asleep, "he gets a rude awakening with a stick," and the groomsmen began calling everyone awake. Bread, cheese, butter, and cakes begin making an appearance, along with more liquor. The lagging musicians trotted out their tunes once again and young and old danced and reveled to the point of falling down. If the father was very affluent, the wedding sometimes lasted as long as a week. The wedding of Zygmunt III to his second wife lasted from Christmas Day to Shrovetide.

On the last night of the wedding, the most important wedding custom of all took place.

Oczepiny—the Capping Ceremony

Of all the customs associated with a Polish wedding, there was none more significant for a young Polish girl than the moment when the *czepek*—the cap of the married woman—was placed upon her head at her wedding celebration. This custom, called *oczepiny*, was one of the most important and oldest Polish wedding customs. It was so essential and played such a vital role in wedding activities that where other customs have disappeared altogether, the oczepiny has survived to this day. In old Poland, it was so significant that it was only after the oczepiny, and not the church ceremony, that a man exercised his marriage privileges towards his new wife.

The capping ceremony began very late at night, at the height of the evening's revelry. Sometimes it even took place after the poprawiny, a continuation of the wedding celebration the following day, and if the wedding was a lavish one, even as long as a week afterward. The most significant moment of the oczepiny was, of course, the placing of the cap on the head of the newly married girl, but there were a series of customs, now long forgotten and no longer practiced, that played an integral part of the entire ceremony. These included the symbolic removal of the hair wreath worn by the bride that symbolized her virginity, and the unbraiding of her hair and its cutting.

In the Radom area, it was the best man who signaled to the maid of honor or her attendants that it was time for the oczepiny by placing a bench in the middle of the room for the bride. It was a decisive moment for the newly married girl, a moment from which she could not return. In putting off this inevitable moment, the young brides of ancient Poland would run outside or hide themselves among the women. The best man, assisted by the other groomsmen, literally chased after her, found her and carried her back, often kicking and fighting. If the bride chose to hide among the women, her attendants and young girls formed a tight, protective circle around her against the groomsmen, who would demand her immediate delivery.

When the groomsmen brought the young bride from wherever she was hiding or when they finally broke through the protective circle, they sat her in the middle of the wedding hall on a dough bin which had been turned upside down and covered with a sheepskin coat. Viewed as a sign of fertility and abundance since ancient times, the thick wool of the sheepskin coat was always placed on the outside.

Sitting on the dough box turned upside down on a sheepskin coat turned inside out, the unplaiting then took place if it hadn't already been done. In some parts of Poland, it was the privilege of the brother of the bride to do the unplaiting. In the Czersk region, it was done by the bridesmaids who sang:

Oj warkoczku, warkoczku!
Oj drobnem cię splatała
O jak mi cię ustrzygą
O będę cię płakała.

Oh braids, braids!
I plaited you so fine
When they cut you off
I will cry for you.

As part of putting off the inevitable moment when they will lose their girlhood friend, the bridesmaids, instead of unbraiding her hair, often insert so many hair pins that unbraiding becomes almost impossible. Everybody then takes a feeble try at the unbraiding while singing and helping themselves to generous amounts of vodka. They know that the actual placement of the cap on the bride's head will bring the wedding celebration to a close.

In some parts of Poland (Ostrzeszów), it was the groom that cut off the hair of his bride. In the Poznań region, it was the mother of the bride. In Sandomierz, it was the married women of the village who cut her flowing, unbraided hair. In the Mazowsze and Lublin region, it was the staroscina and the women present who removed her wreath from her head. The bride's oldest brother unbraided and cut a strand of her hair. The rest was cut off by the married women who then placed the czepek or czepiec, the sign of a married woman, upon it.

The marriage cap itself was usually a gift to the bride from her godmother, if the godmother was still alive. Sometimes the bride herself made the special cap, or had someone in the village make it for her. This first cap was always held as special and reserved for wear to church, for special folk festivals, and on her death, for burial. During the course of her married life, the married woman had other caps for everyday use. These were not as finely made or embroidered as her marriage cap, but usually consisted of a plain white fabric, giving rise to the term *białogłowa*, or white head, synonymous with "married woman."

The placing of the cap on her head was an irrevocable moment for the bride, one from which there was no turning back, and it was put off for as long as possible throughout the evening in a variety of ways. The first time the cap was placed on her head she threw it off, saying the cap didn't fit. One of the married women would whip off her own cap, saying "Maybe this one will fit better," but the bride would refuse that cap also. Someone tried her cap on again and the third and last time the bride had to leave it on her head as a sign of her acceptance into the circle of married women. At this moment and this moment only, she was officially a married lady. Immediately following this, the staroscina began to sing: *Hej Nasza!* (One of ours!). With candles in their hands, the womenfolk officially presented her to the wedding guests as a married woman by singing:

Przypatrzcie się wszyscy ludzie
W wianku była, w czepcu idzie.

Everyone take a good look
She was in a wreath and comes in a cap.

All the women took turns dancing with the bride, as a sign of her acceptance into their ranks. In the Poznań region, this was usually done with the women standing together in a circle holding hands, while one of them took the bride into the center and danced with her. Every woman took a turn with the bride in the center of the circle. During this time the men danced outside of the circle with whomever was on hand.

When all the women had danced with the newly capped bride, she was handed over to her husband, who danced with her and then turned her over to the menfolk. The groom danced with his bride one last time and the wedding ended. The groom arrived with a wagon. He gathered up his wife in her new czepek, placed her among the feather ticks, chickens, and geese that were wedding gifts, and started off to his home or his parents' home to begin their married life together.

Przenosiny—Removal to the Husband's Home

The przenosiny was the ceremonial removing or transferring of the bride from her father's house to that of her new husband. The removal was usually done at night, with the entire wedding party — complete with musicians — in tow. The bride usually tried to put off the event, knowing that a very difficult life as wife, housekeeper, and mother awaited her. The bride hid and tried to escape from the clutches of the groomsmen, who sang:

A gdy na wóz siadała
Ojca, matkę wołała
Nie dajcie mnie brać matulu
Nie dajcie mnie brać.

And as she sat down on the wagon
Her father, mother she called
Don't let them take me, mother,
Don't let them take me.

In Kurpie wedding traditions, the groomsmen would grab the bride when she came out of her room and try and drag her to the threshold; she would pull back, saying she wanted to bid her parents goodbye, grabbing hold of the stove or table to keep from being taken. Amidst much hollering and stubbornness, they forcefully took her out of the door and seated her on the wagon.

According to ancient beliefs, the road to their new home was fraught with danger for the married couple. Evil spirits waited to do harm, such as frightening the horses or overturning the wagon. Many precautions were taken to ensure a safe transfer. Fires were lit along the way. The entire wedding party made much noise, ringing bells, playing music, singing and hollering and cracking whips.

When the bride arrived in front of the home of the groom, her husband's family would greet her at the threshold with bread and salt or bread and honey. In the Olkusz area, when the wedding party arrived at the home of the groom with the bride they customarily broke a pot with ashes. In Olsztyn, it was a pot full of grain. This custom of breaking pots, glasses, or dishes was known throughout Poland. Its purpose was to assure good luck to the bridal pair.

As the bride entered the home of her husband for the first time, it was critical that she enter by placing her right foot first across the threshold. Everyone sang:

Stąp prawą nogą na progu
Będzie szczęscie-chwała Bogu.

Place your right foot first
Happiness will follow, praise be to God.

A Polish proverb attests to the importance of this ceremony: *Prawą nogą przez próg, będzie szczęscie dalibog* (Right leg over the threshold, there will be good luck).

The trunk which the bride brought with her full of linens, pillows, feather ticks, and clothes was brought in and placed in a prominent place and not moved for a whole year, otherwise the new bride would soon die.

Pokładziny—The Bedding Down

In ancient times, putting the bridal pair to bed was a normal and expected part of the marriage customs, and was done with much joking and hilarity. The young couple were directed by the entire wedding party to a room that had been specially prepared for them. The swat, still overseeing that all went according to custom, placed himself on the marriage bed "to warm it up." The womenfolk jumped up and down on the bed to make sure it could hold up and not break down. Rocks or sharp straw or thorns might have been placed underneath the sheets. The swat and swata then chased everyone out of the room and took the bride and groom to the bed and left them alone. The door was locked behind them and after serenading the bridal couple with some very warm and bawdy songs, along with vodka toasts and admonitions "not to be lazy," the couple were left alone.

The next morning, musicians woke the couple and gave them kasza cooked in milk and vodka that had been dyed red as a sign of lost virginity. The sheets were inspected for the expected stain that meant the loss of virginity. This made everybody happy and was the cause of more singing and dancing.

Przebabiny—Entering the Woman's Circle

The very last celebration of a wedding was the *przebabiny*. It was generally preceded by the wywód, or churching, of the new wife, which took place a week later. The bride went to church and awaited the priest in the vestibule. When he arrived, he blessed her. Placing her hand on his stole, the new wife followed him into the church. She approached an altar, knelt down, and prayed for the success of her marriage. After the churching, the new wife went to a tavern for *przebaba*, the buying of her way into the circle of women. In Mazowsze, both the bride and groom went for the churching. They touched the stole of the priest, who guided them to the altar, blessed them, and sprinkled them with holy water. Afterwards, people were invited for something to eat. The marriage wreath was safely hidden away in the bride's dower chest, its leaves believed to be helpful in treating illnesses or in the first bathing of an infant.

October

The month of October, or *Październik,* was an especially rich month for the use of proverbs by Polish peasants. Almost every day was linked with a proverb, which usually centered around the weather. For instance:

Gdy październik z wodami
Grudzień z wiatrami.

If it rains in October
December will be windy.

Na Edwarda jesień twarda.
On Edward (October 13) the autumn is hard.

Or,

Gdy Św. Marek
Z mrozem przybywa
Babie Lato
Krótkie bywa.

If on St. Mark's (October 7)
It is freezing
Indian summer will be short.

Most of October's remaining proverbs are linked with the feast day of St. Hedwig, or Św. Jadwiga, on October 15. The days before and after marked the ending of work in the fields and the preparing for the cold winter months ahead. The sowing of winter wheat, for instance, had to be completed before this important date, as attested to by this particular saying:

> *Zbiera się z roli figę*
> *Kto sieje w Świętą Jadwigę.*
> One gathers nothing from the fields
> Who sows on the feast of St. Hedwig.

> *Po Jadwidze—źle idzie.*
> After St. Hedwig's—it goes poorly.

In the vegetable garden it was felt that St. Hedwig sweetened the vegetables; cabbage, beets, carrots, and turnips were usually gathered immediately after this date.

> *Św. Jadwiga—miodem nakrywa.*
> St. Hedwig, covers with honey.

> *W Św. Jadwigę, jeśli deszcz nie pada—*
> *To do kapusty Pan Bóg miodu nada.*
> On St. Hedwig's, if it's not raining
> God grants honey to the cabbage.

By October 18th, the feast of St. Luke, all work in the fields should have been completed: "*Św. Łukasz, co w polu szukasz?* On St. Luke's, what are you looking for in the fields?"

> *Dzień Urszuli jak*
> *Cała zima tak.*

> As it is on St. Ursula's (October 21)
> The whole winter this way.

OCTOBER

Od Św. Urszuli, nie chodź w koszuli.
From St. Ursula's don't walk around in your shirt.

And finally, the last days of October offered this prognostication:

Deszcz na Świętego Szymona i Judy,
To Luty pełen śniegu i grudy.

Rain on Saint Simon and Judy (October 28th)
Then February filled
With snow and frozen ground.

The mild weather often experienced in October before the onset of winter was called *Babie Lato*, or Old Woman's Summer. The English called this mild period of weather before the onset of winter All Hallow's Summer. The Americans named it Indian Summer after the American Indians, who told them that such a time would come.

During Babie Lato, the Polish peasant walked across his fields once more with his sleeves rolled up. As he wandered around, he would see what appeared to be a thin, filmy substance floating lazily through the air, occasionally landing on clods of earth or entangling itself in the dried plants along the hedgerow. Nature claimed that these were the cobwebs of spiders who would spin much more industriously during this mild weather. The Polish people, however, knew that these floating particles took on a different, much holier meaning. For them, they signified that the Blessed Virgin was at that moment busily at work, holding in her hand not her regal scepter, but a distaff from a spinning wheel.

At this time of year, before the snow fell from the clouds in earnest, Mary, as Mother of Mercy, had gone to count the helpless souls who wandered about the gates of Paradise, shivering from the cold and awaiting grace. It was to clothe her

219

children that the Blessed Mother took up her spinning wheel to spin a thread as fine as gossamer. The angels then wove the thread into a soft, fleecy material to cover these sad and forsaken souls.

Looking downward from heaven as she spun, the Blessed Mother saw that, here on earth, hearts had forgotten or become indifferent to the plight of the souls in Purgatory. She then tore small pieces of the white, fleecy material and scattered them across the heavens where they were caught by the soft wind, and slowly brought down to earth. Seeing this soft, white material bouncing around in the wind, the Polish people knew that this was a reminder from the Blessed Virgin to remember to pray for their deceased brethren so that they could enter the gates of Paradise. And lucky was the person to whom this material clung! Once held in the hands of the Mother of God, whomsoever it touched was under her care and protection. Hearts and burdens became lighter with that knowledge.

Everyone took joy in the spring-like weather. All, that is, except the spider. He once had the nerve to boastfully announce to one and all that he could spin a finer thread than the Virgin Mary. For his haughtiness and impertinence God decreed that the spider would henceforth spend his life in corners and neglected places, spinning his web from material that would break with each strong puff of wind.

In Poland, a birthday was not considered to be the most important day of the year for an individual. What was celebrated was a person's "name day" or *imieniny*, the feast day of the saint whose name was received in baptism. It was also called *dzień patrona*, or patron's day. The Poles considered this "baptismal saint" a special and personal patron all through life. Mothers and fathers took great care and consideration in naming their children, often choosing a name they felt would bestow blessings and good fortune on the child. Because the Blessed Mother was the special Patroness of Poland and Queen of all Saints, many girls received not only the name of Mary (September 12th), but other names referring to Mary such as Marion or Marysia. The boys were often named for St. Joseph, one of the Apostles, or for Michael the Archangel (September 29). As the child grew older, they were made familiar with the history and legend of their own saints, and were instructed to be inspired by their lives and examples and to pray to their saints every day. There were certain customs celebrated by the individual on the feast of his or her particular saint. All who bore the name usually attended Mass in the morning. Upon their return from church the whole family usually congratulated them, offering good wishes. In the Tarnów-Rzeszów region of Poland, friends and acquaintances of the person celebrating his/her name day surrounded the individual on their exit from church, playfully tied the celebrant up with a rope or kerchief, and only let the person free after every individual had wished a happy name day in their own particular fashion, either through verse or song.

In the Poznań area, well wishers went to the house of the *solenizant*(male) or *solenizantka*(female), the person celebrating the name day. The group's leader, bowing low to the ground, would tie up the knees of the celebrant with a stout rope, and while doing so would merrily recite:

> *Na stodole ptak, na kościele wrona*
> *winszuję ci Józefie Twojego Patrona!*

> On the barn, a bird; on the church, a crow
> Wishing you, Joseph, your patron's day!

The celebrant was only set free when he offered refreshments to his guests.

In the Łęczyck region of Poland near Łodz, there existed among the young people of the villages another interesting name day custom. Here the male and female celebrants were given a name day wreath, a *wieniec imieninowy*, which was a symbol of their good wishes and appreciation. If the patron's day fell during

221

the time of warm or mild weather, the wreath was woven of branches of fir and spruce, as well as flowers from the fields and gardens. In winter, it was also made of fir and spruce, but decorated with artificial flowers. It was trimmed with a large ribbon, and cards offering well wishes were attached to it.

The wreath for the bachelors was different from that of the young maidens. For the bachelors, the flowers and ribbons were usually red and/or blue colors, and the ribbon was attached at bottom center of the wreath. For the young girls, rose and white colors were used in the flowers and ribbons; and the ribbon was attached to the center of the wreath. Furthermore, in the bachelor's wreath one often found *pokrzywy* (nettles). In the girl's wreath *ruta* (rue) or *barwinek* (periwinkle) was used.

Sometimes an individual paid to have this wreath delivered to the celebrant. It would arrive at first light on the name day, and was hung on the outside wall of the house, where the celebrant could see it before leaving for Mass. Most often, however, the giving of the wreath and the offering of well wishes was executed with much pomp and circumstance and much participation by friends and acquaintances.

At dusk the day before the name day and after the making of the wreath, the group gathered together. With the accompaniment of a fiddler and drummer, they marched to the house of the celebrant. After hanging up the wreath on the house, they threw the celebrant into the air three times, shouting *"Niech Żyje!"*- (Long Life!) or sang *"Sto lat"* (May you live one hundred years). As a group the friends then recited:

Życzymy zdrowia, szczęścia, fortuny
a po śmierci w niebie koruny.

Wishing you health, good luck and fortune
and after death, a crown in heaven.

Following this joint ceremony, individuals would step forth
to recite their own particular well wishes, often setting it to verse
such as:

Gdy rano wstałem
w niebo spojrzałem
usłyszałem głos ptaszyny
że dziś twoje imieniny.
Ile gwiazd na niebie
tyle szczęścia spotka ciebie
Winszuję ci przez kwiatek róży
żebyś żyła jak najdłużej.

When I woke this morning
and looked into the sky
I heard a birdie say
that it was your name day.
As many stars as there are in the heavens
That much luck come to you.
With these rose flowers
I wish you live as long as possible.

When everyone was done offering their wishes for the day,
the group sang songs, often grabbing the celebrant and passing
him/her from individual to individual as they sang. Sometimes
the celebrant was "showered" with candy or nuts for "good
luck." When all the singing, dancing, and camaraderie was
concluded, the wreath was taken down from the outside wall and
taken indoors, where it was hung on the wall or from the rafters.
Everyone was invited in to partake of a merry meal and, if so
inclined, to more dancing.

November

The desire to remember the dead has been part of Polish life and culture for countless generations. In the most ancient of times, celebrations and special ceremonies honoring the dead were celebrated twice a year in the early spring and in late fall. Then, in 1040, St. Odillo, Abbot of Cluny, inaugurated a memorial feast for all the departed souls in a common annual celebration. This practice was formally approved by the Church, and in the fourteenth century the Commemoration of All Souls was prescribed as a liturgical rite for the whole church to be held on November 2. Called All Souls Day, it is known in Polish as *dzien zaduszny* or simply *Zaduszki*.

Preparations for this special day of commemoration of the dead begins on the night of All Saints (November 1). This eve of All Souls Day was solemnly observed, for it was believed that at this time the dead came back to visit the earth and their own homes. At twilight, the family lit wax candles before the holy pictures of the saints that hung on the walls — often newly cleaned and decorated for the occasion — and gathered together to pray. After prayers, they gathered around a table set with extra places for the invisible guests. The head of the house then opened a front door or window and invited the spirits of the dead to participate in the feast:

> Holy sainted ancestors, we beg you
> Come, fly to us
> To eat and drink
> Whatever I can offer you
> Welcome to whatever this hut can afford

225

Sainted ancestors, we beg you
Come, fly to us.

As the food was passed around the table, each individual placed a serving of the food first on the plate designated for the ancestors that have gone before them and then poured them some vodka.

As on many other special holy days, there were special foods and dishes that were prepared for this night. In Europe, it was common on the Eve of All Souls for housewives to bake a special bread that was known as Soul Bread or Bread of the Dead. In Poland the *gospodyni*, or housewife, also baked this bread or wheaten rolls. This specially baked bread, usually made of rye and shaped into a long loaf to represent a dead person, was called *zaduszki*. Even the poorest and most humble families baked on All Souls Eve and if true poverty prevented them from baking bread, smaller pancakes were substituted. Among the other prescribed dishes for this important event were *kutia* or *kasza*, depending on the region of Poland. As food, both these dishes are older than bread and thus would be dishes familiar to long-dead ancestors.

The food was eaten by the members of the household while being led in prayer for the dead by the head of the house. It was hoped by the family that the souls could hear the prayers being said for them and be consoled and encouraged. After praying and eating, the food was gathered together as leftovers. This leftover food was taken along with the specially baked bread to the cemeteries or the churches where *dziady*, or beggars, were gathered to play their part in the ceremony of honoring the dead.

The beggars were an important part of the All Souls Day tradition, so much so that the term dziady is almost synonymous with All Souls Day. Unlike in the West, where being a beggar was considered shameful, Polish beggars were considered an important part of the village population, having certain recognized functions and claims to dignity. It was at all times a holy act to give to the needy, so one of their chief functions was to receive the generosity of householders, which in turn increased the credit of the householder with heaven. On All Souls Day, it was considered obligatory to give to the dziady. These beggars appeared before the village church to receive donations from the whole community. The women often presented them with small loaves of bread, the zaduszki. In return, the beggars prayed for the dead relatives of all their benefactors, their prayers being that much more effective since so many of them made pilgrimages to holy places. Besides their prayers, the beggars obliged the community with songs and stories chiefly about the saints. In the Lublin area, the men gave the beggars not only money and bread, but also took with them a container filled with kasza, and distributed it by the spoonful to the beggars in the name of dead souls.

It was not unusual among the very wealthy in the Poznań region to bring 30-70 loaves of wheat and rye bread in a wagon to the church cemetery. Here, it was distributed among the beggars, so that they would say prayers for the souls of the departed, with instructions to call the departed by name: "For the soul of John or Barnabas." If an individual wished to give succor to the forgotten souls who had no one to pray for them, the beggar was instructed to loudly call "For the souls of the neglected."

In the Kurpie region, the women baked bread from half a bushel of rye and took it, a few pots of kasza, and sometimes a few pounds of bacon, to the cemetery to distribute to the beggars, who accepted the gifts, all the while praying and singing songs about Lazarus. Amidst the songs and prayers, entire families would kneel at the gravesites to light candles and to pray for their departed members and ancestors. On this usually cold and chilly night, when the first winter winds were already blowing, there were so many candles lit in a cemetery that it wasn't unusual for it to grow so warm that an individual had to remove his or her coat to prevent becoming overheated.

The month of November is not as rich in Polish proverbs as the other months of the year. This may be due, perhaps, to the fact that there is little work left in the fields, garden, or apiary. November officially begins the long season of winter, during which time the Polish peasants spent more time at indoor tasks such as stripping feathers for a new *pierzyna* (eiderdown), spinning wool or flax, repairing harnesses, or devoting themselves to making a new broom or basket. Most of the proverbs devoted to November belong to the saints' days of *Św. Andrzej* and *Katarzyna* (St. Andrew and Katherine). St. Martin is another saint, however, that shares some of the proverbs associated with November. The Feast Day of St. Martin is November 11, or as the Poles call it, *Marcina*.

Martin I was elected Pope in 649. According to legend, he was a man of unusual modesty, and when there was talk of elevating him to the position of Pope, it was said that he hid among a flock of geese. Legends continue to say that once he had reached that exalted position, he did something even more eccentric: during a time of extreme famine he ordered the wholesale slaughter of great flocks of geese and decreed that they be distributed among the hungry. Among the people of Rome, this action elevated him to the status of hero. Every year, on the anniversary of his death, everyone who was able would kill and cook a goose in his memory. This feast day also coincided with the approach of what was at one time a six week Advent period, which was observed with a fairly strict fast. Eating meat on this day may have been a preliminary gorging before giving over to fasting.

On the eve of the feast day, there were few backyards in old Poland that weren't filled with the squawking of geese whose long, slender necks were being placed under the hatchet. Those who were unable to afford a genuine goose still celebrated with some other kind of feathered animal, such as a duck or a pheasant. Sometimes a rabbit would be all that a Polish peasant could get his hands on. The fowl or meat of their choice was sacrificed, cleaned, roasted in the oven, and presented to the gathered company on a large platter.

The proverbs on this occasion begin with:

Dzien Świętego Marcina
Dużo gęsi zarzyna.

On Saint Martin's Day
Many geese are slaughtered.

and:

Na Marcina
Gęś do komina.

On St. Martin's
A goose in the oven.

In old Poland, the feast day of St. Martin's was celebrated with music and dance as this proverb testifies: *Wesele Marcina — gęś i dzban wina.* Saint Martin's — a goose and a jug of wine.

The St. Martin's goose was attributed with miraculous properties and abilities. After the goose or fowl was consumed, the Polish housewife would use the breastbone of the goose to make weather predictions.

Na Św. Marcina
Najlepsza gęsina
Patrz na piersi i na kości
Jaka zima nam zagości.

On St. Martin's
To know what kind of winter will be our guest
the goose is best

Look at the bone in her breast.

If the bone was "white," it foretold a winter with much snow. If it was "red" or "dark," it foretold a rainy and muddy winter. The amount of grain found in the gullet of the slaughtered goose was used to foretell whether the grain crop would be abundant in the following year.

Sometimes it was said that the feast of St. Martin "arrives on a white horse" (*na białym koniu przyjeżdża*), showering snow throughout the countryside. If this happened, it predicted the weather for Christmas Day:

> *Święty Marcin po lodzie*
> *Boże Narodzenie po wodzie.*

> Ice on Saint Martin's
> Water on Christmas Day.

And just the opposite was also possible. If St. Martin's day was a wet one, then Christmas Day could be expected to be freezing.

For the young unmarried men and women of early Poland, the last days of November brought two very important dates—the feast days of Św. Katarzyna (St. Katherine, November 25) and Św. Andrzej (St. Andrew, November 30). The eve of both these days were days of augury and fortunetelling, when young maidens could find out who they would have as husbands, and bachelors could discover something about their future wives. The feast of St. Katherine, the patron saint of maidens, was devoted to the bachelors; St. Andrew was specifically for the unmarried girls. On the eve of St. Andrew's, *Święty Andrzej*, also called *Jędrzejki*, the girl's say:

> *Noc Andrzeja Świętego*
> *Przyniesie nam narzeczonego.*

NOVEMBER

The night of St. Andrew
Will bring us our betrothed.

A practice on the eve of St. Andrew that was common among both noble and peasant women was the placing of two mirrors before one's face in a darkened room. A candle was placed between the two mirrors. While looking intensely at the candle flame and nowhere else, the young maiden was to deeply concentrate on seeing her prospective husband. Intense silence was necessary during these particular moments, and while continuing to focus on the candle she had to count backwards from the number 24. When she finished her backwards count, she was to turn to the nearest dark corner and study the shadows within it. Here she would see the standing shape or figure of her future betrothed. Another custom involved writing down the names of unmarried males in the village on individual cards and placing them under her pillow.

On this special evening dreams were critically important, and every unmarried female strove to remember her dreams as best she could. As she lay down to sleep that night with the names on cards under her pillow, she would murmur: *Panie Boże, proszę Ciebie, niech mi się ten przyśni co mi ma być najmilszy.* (Dear Lord, I beg of you, let me dream of the one who is to be my dearest.) When the young maiden woke up the next morning, she reached under her pillow and drew out a card. Whatever name she found on the first card would be the name of her future husband.

In another custom, the young girls took shells of walnuts and stuck small wax candles inside them. With small drops of wax they also attached the name of either a boy or girl from the village. These shells with candles were then released on a pond, stream or river. It was believed that when two shells touched, then these two individuals would get together without fail.

The belief that animals could foretell the future had deep roots in primitive thinking, so that in the Mazowsze and Sandom-

231

ierz regions of Poland the girls used the following method to find out who would be married first: Each of them baked a *placek,* i.e., a loaf cake. They would each mark it in such a way that it could later be recognized. All the cakes were then placed on a bench. From a small distance they then released a very hungry dog. Whichever of these loaf cakes the dog grabbed first, that girl would be married sooner than the others.

Dogs predicted the future in other ways on this night. While throwing the sweepings from the kitchen floor out in front of the house, the girls in the Małopolska area listened for the bark of a dog. From that direction, their husbands were sure to come. The girls in Kujawy stood in a circle holding hands, and released a goose that had been blindfolded into the center of the circle. The first girl approached by the goose would marry before the others.

There were other ways of uncovering the secrets of the future. On St. Andrew's Eve, the table was set with plates. Under these plates, various items were hidden: a leaf from the rue plant, a piece of lace, and a married woman's cap (czepek). The young women were to choose which plate was theirs. Whoever chose the rue plant was destined to forever be a spinster, for the plant was the symbol of virginity. If she chose the lace, her destiny was to spend her life in a convent. Whoever chose the plate with the cap of the married woman was bound to get married very soon.

The most popular of all fortunetelling techniques however, was the melting of wax. In this custom, a piece of wax was melted on a spoon and then dropped into a bowl filled with cold water. The wax would form into various shapes and make predictions for those who poured. In the Poznań region, the unmarried men and women participating would look at the cooled wax in the water for shapes of tools or implements of the various guilds and trades. If the melted wax appeared to look like a weapon, helmet, or banner, then it augured that the male would become a soldier. If it appeared to look like a violin or a trumpet, the individual would become a musician. If a girl were to pour herself some wax that took the shape of a hammer or bellows, then she would surely marry a blacksmith. If it resembled a chest or cabinet, then she was to marry a carpenter. If it looked like a wagon or sheaf of wheat, she would marry a farmer.

Birth Customs

In the Old Testament, Christians are admonished to "Be fruitful, and multiply, and replenish the earth." Early Christians took the word of the Lord seriously, had many children and felt themselves blessed. Not only was this action a fulfillment of the word of the Lord, but numerous children were considered an asset to most agricultural peoples because each birth meant another pair of hands to work the fields and increase production. The Slavs were no exception.

The inability to have children was seen as a great misfortune among the Slavs and among some groups a man had the right to leave his wife if after seven years she was unable to have a child. In Polish wedding customs and traditions, the symbol of fertility is used over and over again to assure that the couple will be fruitful and multiply. The perpetually green leaves of *barwinek* (periwinkle, also called myrtle) were used in the wedding ceremonies to assure fertility. The wedding bread, or *kołacz*, was decorated with roosters (considered a sign of fertility and good fortune), chickens, and other farmyard animals indigenous to the area. Placed upright on top of the bread were branches (symbols of fertility) that were made of dough. Two branches depicted the couple and a third symbolized future offspring.

Other media were also used to decorate the top of the kołacz—the greenery of asparagus or myrtle, apples (a sign of love), and nuts (a sign of fertility). In Krakow, during the time of oczepiny, a small boy was placed on the lap of the bride so "that she would give birth to sons."

Women went to great lengths to have children. Those unable to conceive made pilgrimages to monasteries and holy places to pray for a miracle. They ate the meat of animals who were famous for their fertility, such as rabbits and roosters. And from the oldest of times the Polish women utilized various herbs to try to increase their fertility. *Bylica* (mugwort) was the most well known of these. It was especially helpful if the herb was gathered from at least nine different fields.

Once a woman became pregnant, she had to take precautions to assure the birth of a strong and beautiful offspring. For instance, she was not to look on individuals who were lame or crippled (so that her child would not be similar); she was not to look at mice (to prevent moles in the newborn); and she was to avoid looking into the fire (to prevent red birthmarks). Looking through a keyhole was forbidden for it might make the child crosseyed. Crossing over a rope on the ground or walking under a rope such as a clothesline supposedly caused problems with the umbilical cord during childbirth. If a mother wanted to have a beautiful baby, she was supposed to gaze upon individuals who were strong and handsome, or on beautiful sights such as blossoming fields or the heavens. If she wanted a son very badly, she borrowed something from a woman who had given birth to a son. Returning the item would in some magical way fulfill her wishes. A pregnant woman also tried to sing and talk a lot so that the child would be jolly and talkative.

It was universally believed by Poles that if a pregnant woman had a clear complexion during her pregnancy, she would give birth to a son. If she was an eyesore with yellow blots on her face, she was surely carrying a girl. The people of the Kujawy region translate this as "the daughter takes away all the mother's beauty." The sex of the child was also predicted by the first person entering the house on Christmas Eve. If it was a woman, then a girl child would be born. If a man, it would be a boy. As in many other cultures, boys were preferred over girls. This is demonstrated in one of the speeches or orations of the swat at the wedding ceremonies:

BIRTH CUSTOMS

Jeżeli młoda będzie mieć syna
To nasz młody wystawi baryłeczkę wina.
A jak córka
To inno chleba skórka.

If the bride will have a son
The groom will bring out a cask of wine.
But if a girl
Then only a crust of bread.

In Poland, as in other countries, it was believed that a pregnant woman's food preferences were to be indulged. An appetite for sour food foretold birth to a son, and sweet things, a daughter.

A pregnancy was concealed for as long as possible, and when the condition became obvious, it was not remarked upon or discussed in any detail. Anyone who made too many inquiries was immediately suspect. Even a woman's husband was expected to avoid making any unnecessary references to her condition. The secrecy was necessary to protect both mother and infant against jealousy, witchcraft, and the evil eye.

If anyone was visiting at the time the pains began, or, heaven forbid, some stranger happened to be in the house, they were politely asked to leave, because it was feared that the evil eye might be cast upon the laboring woman and make her pains more intense or hurt the child. Most Polish peasant women made numerous preparations to give birth at home but, like all women thoughout the world and the ages, this was not always possible. If she ignored her pains and continued her work too long, it wasn't unusual to give birth in the fields or along the road. If she was lucky and found herself doing chores in or around the house, her preparations would not be in vain. In order to protect herself and the infant from any chance of being looked upon by someone who wished her and her child ill, the bed was screened with a sheet from the rest of the room. If the room had a window, it

237

would be covered, so that no one should witness what was happening. She would be sure to have her blessed herbs on hand.

As the expected day of confinement approached, a woman from the village was usually asked to help with the delivery of the child. In early Polish and Russian villages, as well as other Slavic countries, trained midwives were an unknown entity. The function of helping a woman deliver her child was performed by an older, respected woman called *babka*, or *baba*. Because of this critical role in helping with the birth and introducing the child to the community, the baba became part of the family circle and could claim the privilege of calling the child and the child's parents her grandchildren. As a result, the word "baba" in early Poland expressed a kinship tie. It wasn't until later that the word in Polish vocabulary came to be a general name for an old woman.

When the baba arrived, she began to help the woman undress if the woman hadn't already done so. It was a universal custom to undo any type of knot that the pregnant woman might have on her person or near her to ease the pangs of childbirth. In certain parts of Poland, during her first night as a married woman, a woman didn't wear anything with knots "in order for her to have light childbirth." Besides removing clothes and undergarments, rings and earrings were removed, and hair unplaited. The unplaiting of the hair was also believed to call upon the Blessed Virgin Mary, for it was thought that she rushed to the side of a woman giving birth if her hair was loose. Any locks in the house such as chests and doors were opened. If the birthing proved difficult, the pregnant woman was sometimes placed on the ground to draw strength from the earth itself. She had her husband sit on her knee or borrowed her husband's pants to place at her lower back. Another remedy was to use garlic and onion. The strong and pungent odors were seen as capable of chasing away the evil spirits which were causing the difficult delivery. The babka would place onions on the umbilical cord to make the pain go away, or give the mother-to-be chopped onions and garlic to chew, rub them under her nose, or give her a broth made of onions and parsley.

In Silesia, and all of Little and Greater Poland, a child was considered lucky and would live a long life if born with a caul. It was considered so lucky that it was necessary to protect it againt theft where it might be used in making medicine and/or witchcraft. The afterbirth and the umbilical cord were also seen as having medical and magical properties. The dried-up umbilical cord, which fell off the infant soon after birth, was saved and thrown behind a church altar as a means of assuring the newborn a healthy childhood. In Krakow and Pomorze, the dried up umbilical cord was saved in a chest and given to the child when it went to school so that the child studied and learned well.

Of critical importance after the birth was the newborn's first bath. It was usually done in a wooden dough bin used for making bread, in the belief that it would help the child grow. The water had to be drawn before sundown and thrown into the bathwater were herbs blessed on the Feast of Our Lady of the Herbs on August 15th. A boy was bathed in hazel leaves to make him grow strong and walk early. A leaf of the hazel tree was placed on his head to protect against skin ulcers. In Lublin, the infant was bathed in a mixture made with mugwort. Mugwort and thyme were used in the Kielce area, while lovage was popular throughout Poland.

Money was also thrown into the first bath, so that the child would be rich. This was later taken by the woman who had helped with the birthing. After this first bath, the babka handed the child to the father. If the father accepted the child from her hands, sometimes giving it a kiss, it was a sign of acceptance of paternity of the child. The father than handed the infant to the mother. The bathwater had to be thrown out in an area where no one was likely to tread, usually the manure pile. As was mentioned in other parts of the book, the Polish people had very fixed ideas about good and bad hours of the day, lucky and unlucky days of the week, and times which were considered either blessed or sinister.

The day on which one was born, for instance, as a day of beginnings, was carefully watched, for it was something that either plagued or blessed the individual throughout his or her lifetime. A Polish proverb *"Piątek—zły początek"* (Friday, bad beginnings) says that a child born on this day will be unlucky. If you happen to have been born on Good Friday, then you could count on burying three husbands (or wives). Wednesday was also considered unfortunate, giving the person bad luck all their lives. A child born on Monday could become a witch, but for a child born on Saturday that was not possible, as Saturday was blessed by the Blessed Mother; evil did not have any power on this day. In the Pomorze districts, a child born on Sunday would have luck and would "see" more than others or have the ability to "see" souls and foresee the future. Tuesdays seemed to be a day the Poles didn't much care about one way or the other, but they did believe, as did Russians and Ukranians, that morning was the best time for a child to be born, and that those born at night did not have any luck.

Besides concerning themselves with the day and hour on which an infant was born, the Poles steadfastly observed many other customs. For example, baby clothes chould not be prepared ahead of time. In the villages surrounding Lublin, neither an undershirt nor pillow was prepared ahead of time, the parents believing that if they did so, the child would fail to thrive. In Sląsk, the cradle was kept hidden. To have it visible before the birth would cause the child to be born dead.

It was a universal belief that all happy occasions, such as births and weddings, caused the individuals involved in those events to be more susceptible to evil forces. To combat these evil forces, the birth was usually kept a secret until appropriate preparations could be made. The infant initially slept with the mother in the same bed, and to protect the newborn, an axe or knife was kept under the bed or sometimes a piece of steel was placed in the infant's diaper. The devil was powerless against steel or items made of steel and thus the child was protected. In Krakow, they placed a lock and keys under the pillow. To prevent convulsions, which were initiated by the devil, a small knife was placed under the pillow. A godmother taking the child outside the home for the first time, usually to be christened, made the sign of the cross over the child three times with a knife.

The child's name was kept a secret until the christening. It was whispered to the godmother just before departing for church, and definitely not told to strangers before that time. Praising a newborn infant was seen as a way of casting a spell. In order to cast the "evil eye," it was merely enough for some old woman to say, "Oh, what a beautiful child." To repel such a comment, it was necessary to say "Oh, it's an ugly child," and to spit to the side. To protect the child against the evil eye, a red ribbon was tied around its wrist or neck. Coral, or *koraliki*, a red stone, was also placed around the child's neck as protection against evil.

Another custom strictly adhered to was the refusal to lend anything from the house until such time as the child was christened and the mother cleansed through churching. It's unknown exactly why this was so, but anthropologists speculate that the practice may have been considered unclean or perhaps the parents feared the returning item may have been hexed, and therefore evil could enter their house indirectly. In Krakow, it was even considered poor form if one lent a light from the fire, even from that of a blessed candle.

The time between the birth of an infant and its baptism was not always held to a very fixed time in Poland. Much depended on the health of the newborn. If the child was weak or sick, it was baptized as soon as possible after birth. Healthy children were commonly baptized after 3 or 4 weeks, and sometimes it happened that the christening was put off for 6 weeks in order to coincide with the mother's *wywód*, or churching (see February). Prolonging the period between birth and christening longer than six weeks, however, was looked upon with disapproval. In these cases, if a child cried a lot and was restless, the extended family members began to criticize the parents, saying that "*dziecko chrztu woła,*" i.e., the child was calling out to be baptized. It was felt that in its prolonged, unbaptized state, the child was seeing the devil and was afraid.

Picking the godparents to the infant was not an act taken lightly. Because it was believed that the child inherited the characteristics of the godparents, the matter was given a great deal of thought. The chosen individuals would become part of the family circle and forever be able to claim kinship ties equal to that of first cousins. It could be a family member, a very dear and close friend, or a neighbor. The individuals generally had to be older, respected, and devout and/or financially secure enough to be of help to the child in later years or be generous in their christening gift. In accepting the invitation of standing godparent, the individual understood all the attending responsibilities. The person had to remember the child during holidays and accept parental responsibility if the child was orphaned. If the infant died, it was the godfather who prepared the coffin and the godmother who sewed the death shirt and prepared the body for the coffin. When the child married, they acted as the all important swat or staroscina. Individuals "who had an inclination towards spending much of their time gazing into the bottom of a vodka glass" were not invited to be a godparent.

In most instances, the individuals invited to be godparents were married, although older, single men and women were also sometimes asked. Universally observed was the custom of never asking a pregnant woman to be godmother. Doing so would either cause the newborn infant or the child in the womb to die. Women who had never given birth themselves or women whose children had a tendency to die were also not asked. Parents whose newborns seemed to die asked individuals who would be more likely to bring luck to the child, such as the church organist or the parish priest. In Kalisz, up until the time between the world wars, parents whose children seemed to die very young practiced the custom of signing up their sickly child with the Third Order of St. Francis after baptism. The parents said special prayers for the child and if the child lived, then it was instructed to say the prayers and wear the Franciscan habit up until the time he or she was seven years old. If the child died before the age of seven, it was buried in the habit.

The name of the infant was usually decided by the parents, the father choosing for a son, the mother for a daughter. The godparents could suggest a name, but could not make any demands in this decision. Sometimes the child was named for the saint's day on which it was born, or if the child was to be given the name of another saint, it was imperative that the saint's day had already passed in the calendar year so that the child immediately would be under some patron's protective wing. If the child was the result of an unmarried union, the priest could refuse to allow the child to carry the name of a saint, and bestow instead the name of Adam or Eve upon the child, or the names Kordula or Kacper. During the time of partitioned Poland, the parents sometimes chose the names of Polish heroes or past monarchs who had ruled Poland. In very early Poland, if it happened that children rarely survived infancy within a family, the parents often went to great lengths to avoid or confuse the evil forces that spirited away their children. Names like Niemoj (not mine) and Nielub (unloved) were not unusual in these instances.

When it was time for the christening, it was the role of the godmother to dress the infant. Throughout all of Poland, it was customary to give new material as a gift to the mother and new infant. The godmother had to have enough homemade cloth on hand to make the child's first *koszulka*, or shirt, and it traditionally had to be sewn by her. She also often provided the all important cap or bonnet as part of the christening outfit; the hat differed in shape depending on whether the child was a boy or girl. The girl wore a bonnet similar to the bonnet of a married woman; it was of lighter hued colors. The boy wore a round cap usually in more vivid colors of red and green. Both were as richly embroidered as finances could allow, and sometimes studded with artificial flowers, coral, or sequins. Sometimes the cap worn by the infant was the cap the mother had received at her own wedding.

In the Siedlce region, the godmother gave the infant a shirt and diaper made from her wedding sheets, and the godfather a *czapeczka*, or cap, usually colored red for protection against the evil eye; he also gave the swaddling bands for wrapping the baby. The dressed-up infant was placed on a pillow and bound with a strip of soft cloth about 30 inches wide and two to three yards long, called a *powijak* or swaddling band. Tucked inside were a variety of items designed to bring the child plenty: a piece of bread, salt, a coin or an herb blessed on the Feast of the Assumption or on Corpus Christi.

Dressed and bound, the infant was ready to be taken to church. The sex of the newborn infant determined the order of importance in the christening party. If it was a boy, the godfather was lead player of importance, holding the infant during baptism. He also sat in the first place at the table during the christening feast with the godmother at his left. If the newborn was a girl, it was the godmother who carried her and had first place in the celebratory activities. The father generally accompanied the godparents to the church.

Up until the turn of the century, there existed in the Krapuzyn (Mińsk area) the ancient custom of blessing the child before it went to church. The babka — the woman who helped bring the child into the world — took the child into her arms, walked around the table three times, and called upon those present to bless the child with the words "*Niech Pan Bóg pobłogosławi*" — May the Lord bless. Once this was done, it was time to leave for the church, but this was also no simple matter. On the threshold of the door through which the christening party was to cross, an axe was placed to protect the child from witches and bad spirits. In Pomorze, if the family had a lot of infants die soon after birth, the threshold was avoided altogether, and the child was passed through a window when leaving for its christening. The Krakowians say this was done "*żeby śmierć lub chorobę oszukać*" (to cheat death or sickness). Since the threshold had always been the resting place of dead souls and spirits, both good and evil, this action was meant to confuse and disorient evil spirits. This same purpose served in wedding customs. In Kielce, if a woman had buried a husband or two and remarried, she entered the house through the window rather than over the threshold.

The christening party looked neither left, right, nor behind them while traveling to the church, believing that doing so would render the infant a *nieudolna gapa*, a clumsy stargazer. A child was likely to die if on the way to church the party encountered a funeral procession, or if during the christening another church rang its bells for a funeral. During the christening, the people of the Mazowsze area, as well as throughout many other Slavic countries, tried not to have boys and girls christened with the same water. If a girl was baptized after a boy, she would grow a beard and a boy baptized after a girl would not grow a beard. Almost universal among Slavs was the belief that if a child cried during baptism, it would grow stong and loud. If the child was quiet and sleepy, it was interpreted as a bad sign regarding its future health and taken as a sign that it would be lazy. In some parts of Poland, such as the Czarny Dunajec in the Tatra mountains, the child was carried three times around the altar by the godparents after the christening while holding candles in their hands. They would then throw some money into the collection basket as an offering. In other areas, the child was placed at the foot of the altar and surrounded by those present. According to folklorists, this custom was a carry-over from pagan traditions of placing the child on the altar. Being surrounded by the group was a symbolic act of accepting the child into the community.

After the birth and christening was recorded in the church records, everyone either walked or rode back home by wagon or sleigh. In some areas of Poland, it was absolute tradition to stop at the local tavern to drink to the health of the newly named and christened child before returning the child to its mother. Others believed in rushing home as quickly as possible after the church ceremony to protect the infant from evil forces which were lurking about waiting to do harm. Everyone, however, returned along the same route they had taken earlier so that the child would not take a wrong turn in life.

In Raba, the godfather used a willow branch to lightly hit the pillow on which the newly christened child lay. The willow was a symbol of budding life. The same branch was also used to lightly hit the other children in the home, a reminder that they ought to be good to their new sibling and remember his/her christening. The branch was then tucked into the fence surrounding the house, so that the child would not be afraid at night.

In Poznań, when the godparents arrived home with the child, the godfather (if a boy) or godmother (if a girl), returned the infant to its mother and gave the following greetings: "*Wzięłam wam niewiernika, oddaje wam katolika.*" (I took it [your child] without faith and bring you a Catholic). In Warsaw, on returning from the church, the godfather placed the infant in the hands of the father if it was a boy, and the godmother placed the infant in the hands of the mother if it was a girl.

A very common practice, done either immediately after birth or after the christening, was placing the child under the main table of the house. If the infant was a boy, his legs were uncovered and he was placed under the table supposedly to assure that he would be a good provider in the future. If it was a girl, she would be placed under a basin so that she would learn well how to wash dishes. Sometimes the procedure varied in that the girl was placed under the table and the boy taken to all four corners of the main room of the house. In Pinczowa, after returning from church, the godfather placed a few coins under the pillow of the newly christened infant while the godmother placed a few at the feet. All were taken by the babka, the woman who helped with the birthing.

After the christening, the newly named infant was welcomed into village society with a festive meal and celebration. The new father sometimes took wheat or rye to the miller to be ground into new flour for the babka to make *pierogi* (dumplings) as part of the christening feast. If the family was well-to-do, a pig was slaughtered, or perhaps a chicken or a goose. A special vodka drink prepared with honey or sugar, called *pępkowa*, i.e., navel, was also prepared. All the invited guests, relatives, extended kinfolk, and neighbors never came empty-handed, but brought a variety of food and gifts to bestow upon the new infant and the mother. The purpose of bringing food was to assist the weakened mother during this difficult time and also to enjoy the food themselves while participating in the celebratory event. Invited for a christening in Mazowsze, kinfolk brought "*około garnca kaszy, parę funtów słoniny, z pół kwarty masła, pół kopy jaj i pół kwarty miodu*" (about a pot of porridge, a few pounds of pork fat, about half a quart of butter, thirty eggs, and half a quart of honey). Other foods that were brought included flour, potatoes, beans, peas, and barley. Bread, always a critical item at every important life event including weddings and funerals, made its appearance at christenings also. The ritual bread baked for christenings were *kukiełki*, a type of braided bread. The ritual breads had the power, as did all bread, to repel evil and any unholy powers that were surrounding the mother and new infant. In some country villages such as Prądnik, the braided bread was four feet long. Common folklore stated that the bigger and better the kukiełka, the more the christened child would grow. In other parts of Poland, the godparents at least brought a loaf of bread each to the christening, otherwise the child, in its lifetime, would have difficulty making ends meet.

The second most important food that was brought was cheese, which was also attributed the power to repel evil. Older than bread and cheese, and also a traditional food at every wedding, funeral, or christening, was kasza. At the end of the wedding feast everyone had a taste of *kasza jaglana*, a porridge of millet sweetened with honey, which was brought forth by the babka and for which she gathered money and hence the name, *babczyna kasza*. In exchange, the guests were offered vodka, or in more prosperous homes, beer. There was no lack of song, dance, or music for a christening. In the Lublin area, a christening celebration lasted three days; and among the very wealthy, the festivities lasted a whole week.

The custom of giving a newly baptized child a gift was called *wiązanie*, i.e., twisting, because the gift was usually twisted into the corner of the diaper. For wiązanie, the country child usually received a *złoty* (copper) or two — depending on the giver's finances — which was twisted into the corner of the diaper or shirt. The godparents also gave the infant small change or a silver coin so that all his life, he/she would be rich and successful.

Other gifts that were brought were symbolic in nature. For instance, in Silesia the boy infant was given seeds of grain and a girl was presented with flax seeds. In Mazowsze, a boy was given a piece of bread and the girl a needle, believing that with these gifts, a boy would become a successful farmer with bountiful crops and the girl a housewife who would have plenty of cloth to dress her entire family.

A practice that was universal among the Poles, as well as among many Indo-European countries, was that of mothers breast feeding their children. Even in ancient times, it was understood that if the mother should happen to be feeling angry, despondent, or generally upset or unhappy, the infant would receive these particular feelings through the mother's milk. So important was the influence of breast feeding in the life of a growing infant among the Poles, that it is not surprising that numerous beliefs came to be associated with mother's milk. For instance, putting the child to breast for the first time the mother was very careful not to give it her left breast first, for fear the child would become a *mańkut*, i.e., left-handed. Breast feeding a child for a long time was seen as beneficial and healthy. In the Lublin area and the surrounding countryside, the boys were known to be fed to three years of age, when they were already running about and eating table food. The village women in the Kujawy region breast fed their children for two years. If, because of unforeseen circumstances, the child was breast fed for three years, however, it was believed that it would develop the evil eye. In the regions surrounding Krakow, it was said that if a child was breast fed through two Good Fridays, it would, when it grew up, be a thief, or, in the case of a girl, a harlot. In Rzeszow, breast feeding too long was seen as a sin, and as a result, a boy would be forgetful and have a weak memory.

The aspect of breast feeding that seemed to draw the most beliefs and superstitions centered around weaning the child from the breast. This act signaled the end of infancy and the beginning of the child's independence and the moment had great implications for both mother and child. The country women had particular times when they thought weaning was to occur. First, it was not done during the time when birds were flying away for the winter, for fear the child would grow up to be wild and take to the forest and woods. If weaning took place during the time when leaves were falling, the child would go bald early on in life. A child was not weaned during harvest time when the grains were being carefully hidden away, or it would become a very secretive individual. In the village of Gdowa, the child was weaned during the period when trees were sprouting and blossoming, so that the child would be like the trees, always be young. In Mazowsze, the child was weaned from the breast during a full moon so that its face would be full and beautiful. The Czechs also weaned the child when the trees were flowering and while the moon was gradually growing larger. In Śląsk, the best time to wean was on the Feast of St. John the Baptist, in June and at midnight. This assured that the child would grow well. In Krakow, the requirements were that the weather be fair but that it not be done on a Friday and not during Ember Days. (In the Roman Catholic Church, Ember Days were a Wednesday, Friday, and Saturday set aside for prayer and fasting in a special week of each of the four seasons of the year.)

Regardless of how many sleepless nights or how difficult the weaning process was, it was strongly believed that once the child was removed from the breast, it should never be put to the breast again. To do so would be to cause the child to become a vampire, or, at the very least, to become a stutterer.

The newborn infant generally slept with its mother up until the time it was christened. After the christening, it was felt that the infant could safely be removed to a cradle. A cradle, or *kołyska*, were of two types in Poland: hung from the ceiling, or on rockers. The hanging cradles were made of plaited straw or wood that was carved or painted and hung from the ceiling on rope, usually over the foot of the mother's bed where she could periodically give it a nudge without having to get up. The cradle was padded with straw and covered with linen sheeting that was woven at home, or received as a gift from the godparent. Because the mother often did not have someone to watch the child when she had work to do in the fields, she usually had the infant with her. She fashioned a hammock by tying a sheet to two trees, and placed the infant inside. The mother had to be careful that she not place this outdoor cradle on a boundary line, for the *boginki* or *mamuny* (evil spirits) would steal the child while she was busy at her work. In some parts of Poland, special sticks were found or whittled to make a portable cradle that could be easily moved from place to place in order to shield the child from the sun or to move along as work was completed. Two Y-shaped sticks were driven into the ground in a suitable place, with a third pole placed into the notches of the Y on which a hammock-type cradle was fashioned from a sheet for the child to sleep in.

In Rzeszow, there existed a belief that a child could not grow properly unless it was rocked and it was a universal belief among

Poles and many other European countries that an empty cradle should never be rocked nor should someone sit in it. To do so would cause the child to have headaches, to lose its sleep, or to die; the perpetrators would never find the peace of heaven. It was also important to place the cradle in a spot where the moonlight would not fall on the child's face, for it could become a *lunatyk*, a lunatic. In Łowicz, the rocker was placed in the middle of the room beneath a *pająk* (literally translated meaning a spider but similar to today's mobile) made of straw and colored paper to entertain and attract the eyes of the child.

Rocking the child was the responsibility of the entire family but it most often fell to a younger child or elderly grandparent who could no longer work around the house or fields. Singing lullabies was an integral part of child rearing in Poland. As with the lullabies of all nations, the simplest forms are merely humming or a repetition of monotonous or soothing sounds. Here are some old Polish lullabies:

A-a kotki dwa.
A-a, A-a kotki dwa
szare, bure obydwa
jeden duży, drugi mały
obydwa mi się podobały.

Oh, two kittens
Oh, Oh two kittens
gray and dark gray
One big, the other small
I like them both.

Lulaj-że mi, lulaj, czarne oczka stulaj
Jak mi stulisz oczka, spij-że do pół nocka
Hushabye, hushabye, let your dark eyes close
And when they close, sleep through half the night.

Others include:

Oj kołys że się kołys
od ściany do ściany
Oj uśnij że mi, uśnij
mój kwiatecku różany.

Oh rock a bye, rock a bye
from wall to wall
Fall asleep for me, fall asleep
my rosy little flower.

This last one, which makes both promises and threats, was probably sung by sisters or brothers who may have mixed feelings about their sibling:

Śpij, braciszku śpij
Dam ci jabłka trzy
A orzeszków sześć
Będziesz miał co jeść.
Śpij, braciszku śpij
Dam ci jabłka trzy
A jak jabłka nie pomogą
To pomoże kij.

Sleep, little brother, sleep
I will give you apples three
And walnuts six.
You will have something to eat.
Sleep, little brother, sleep
I will give you apples three
And if apples don't help
Then a stick will.

It has been the fate of parents from time immemorial to constantly worry about their children and to make sure they grow healthy and strong. One of the precautions taken to make sure that the child developed normally was to see that no one either accidentally or intentionally walked or jumped over the growing child. Doing so would stunt their growth. Siblings, who were given to thoughtless behavior, were especially cautioned against it. All was not lost if this was done accidently, however, for the situation could be undone if the individual, realizing what he or she had done, jumped backwards. Walking backwards was also filled with mystical properties. Women forbade their children this activity, for it would cause their mother either to die or go to hell.

Another belief common among Poles as well as Russians prohibited allowing a child to look in a mirror, and measuring or weighing a child for that, too, could cause stunting of growth. A child was never to look in a mirror. The Kaszubians in northern Poland believed a child under the age of one should not be kissed or it would not grow. The Czechs and Russians also believed that kissing a child before the age of one would delay its speech development.

First teeth and loss of teeth were important issues in the child's development. If a child's bottom teeth grew out first it was predicted that it would successfully grow to adulthood. If the top ones came out first, the child would die before reaching that stage of life. Among the Czechs just the opposite was believed to be true. When a child's first milk tooth fell out, he or she was told to throw it over his/her head behind the stove and talk out loud to the mice:

Hej, myszko, drewniany, a daj mi żelazny.

Here, mouse, the wooden, give me a steel one.

The milk teeth, falling out by themselves, were seen as feeble and weak things, and were thus considered "wooden." Mice, who have been known to bite through the hardest of substances, were invoked to help provide teeth that were as strong as steel. The milk teeth were not thrown away just anywhere, but behind the stove where the house spirits resided. In some areas of Poland, the milk tooth was taken to church and hidden in some crack or crevice in a wooden wall. Sometimes it was hidden in a rotting tree so that it wouldn't be hard to locate it after death.

Another important episode in the development of the child was the moment it uttered its first sensible words. These first words, usually "mama" or "tata (father)," were listened for carefully, for they were seen as predictors of the sex of the next child born in the family. If it was "tata," the next infant would be a boy and if "mama," a girl.

Last on the list of important events of birth and development in ancient Poland was the first haircut. The first cutting of a male child's hair was at one time a major rite of passage in ancient slavic rituals. In pre-Christian times, the first haircut took place in the eleventh year of life, a time of major transition from child to boyhood. In the chronicles of Galla, written in the twelfth century, and this ancient rite of hair clipping was called *postrzyżyny* and was often accompanied by a large celebration. A Prince Popiel of that century invited friends and family from all parts of the country to his court at Gniezno to witness and celebrate the cutting of his son's hair. Cutting a child's hair before the right time was strictly controlled for fear of causing the child to lose its power of speech or to prevent it from going mad or becoming hunchback. Later, the first haircut took place after the child was three years old. Some preferred to do it on Holy Saturday during the time when the bells were ringing in church for the Gloria. If it couldn't be accomplished on this day it was at least to be done on a day when the moon was waxing or when full so that the hair would grow in full.

The cut hair was not simply thrown away and forgotten about. Hair thrown away to the mercy of the winds and for birds to use as nesting material only invited headaches and broken bones. As an essential ingredient in all manner of witchcraft and spells, it was treated very carefully. The first cut was usually given to a trusted individual to place under a rock or in the chinks of the walls of the house.

Death Customs

In Krakow she was called *Jagusia* or *Zośka*. In Mazowsze she was named *Baśka*. She was imagined to be a female, so tall and slender that she was unable to fit beneath the low ceiling of the cottages; thus she would stand outside the front door or before a window. She could take on a variety of shapes, such as a black cat, white crow, goose, a stone figure of the Blessed Mother, and even a priest in his biretta. Everyone knew she generally resided in the cemetery between the graves. This female dressed in a white sheet, carried a scythe, and came three nights in a row, each time knocking on the window or door by way of giving notice. Nothing had the power to stay her since, if she wished, she could change shape and enter through the chimney or through a keyhole. There were certain protections one could take against her—a few mustard seeds bitten on an empty stomach and lily-of-the-valley was supposedly to have miraculous restorative powers—but in the end no one could totally avoid this presence when it was time. No one escaped Death.

There was, however, some warning of her approach. In Sląsk, a death was foretold by the howling of a dog at night or barking with his muzzle towards the earth. It was believed that dogs could see her and that a person could also see her by stepping on the dog's tail and looking between his ears. In Kraków, a howling dog holding his head up presaged a fire; if the dog's head dropped, then a death. If a dog howled in front of a home where someone was sick, it was said that the dog was giving notice of that person's death. Aside from the dog, other domestic animals could foretell death. If a priest came to see a sick person on a horse, everyone watched the activity of the

257

horse. If the horse pawed the ground, the person would die. A mole seen burrowing near the front stoop of a house and heading towards the fields meant that someone from the house would die. If, however, the mole dug from the fields towards the house, it announced that someone or something, a guest or event, perhaps, would arrive.

A bird was perhaps the most important creature regarding imminent death. In western Galicia, the people would say that there will be a death in a house where all the birds have left. A bird flying into a house was an announcement that someone would sicken and die. A owl was a messenger of death and its hoot was the laugh of the devil. The owl would arrive at night and alight on a roof or nearby tree outside a particular home. If it gave its hoot, one of the individuals within the home would be called to the other world. If an owl happened into a barn, a popular belief was that Death would soon be looking in: *Sowa na dachu kwili, ktoś pewnie umrze po chwili.*

In Poronin, in southern Poland, whoever went out to the field to plow without having eaten breakfast and heard the cuckoo would not live to plow the next year. The magpie screeching on a fence was a call of death if someone in a nearby house was sick. If a hen crowed like a rooster, it foretold death or illness. When a hen crowed, it was a signal that the hen was seeing a spirit which was lost and wanting to be near people; thus, the sound foretold much bad luck. Perhaps the chicken was inhabited by the devil. Such a chicken was to be sold or killed immediately. In such a situation, the women of Poznań offered this solution: With the chicken in hand, one was to measure the length of the wall opposite the main entry to the very door, turning the chicken front and back. If, on the last turn the tail of the chicken rested on the threshold, its tail was to be cut off. If it was the head that met the threshold, then one was to chop its head off and make a good chicken soup.

Unclear sounds and noises were the work of spirits. In the regions of Gniezno, they said that a certain individual had a sick child but had to go to town to look for work. Suddenly he heard next to him a loud sound, as if a rock had fallen off a roof. He looked around but saw nothing and thought to himself that the child must have died. And it happened that this was the case.

In Olsztyn, if a carpenter heard the sound of a saw, he understood that he would get notification to make a coffin. A picture falling off a wall, crunching noises beneath a window, a broom falling without cause, a clock ticking where there was none, a table that made cracking noises, a door that opened by itself all foretold death drawing near. By the same token, candles lit at the bedside of a sick individual also told of that individual's end. A candle lit at the bedside when a priest had come to give communion to an ailing individual was watched when it was snuffed out. If the smoke headed towards the door or window, the individual would die. If it headed up, he or she would live. If a candle would not light or extinguished by itself it could be counted on that the sick person would surely die. If a candle went out during a funeral mass, it was a sign that someone from the family would die.

The atmosphere could also be used to predict impending death. Among the Mazowians, if large snowflakes fell between Christmas and New Year's the older people of the village would die; if small, the young. If on Christmas Eve clothes were found hanging on a line after sundown, people would hang themselves in that year. If the night after Christmas was clear, kings and nobles would die. In Lublin, if a large star was seen near the edge of the moon it foretold the death of some great monarch. If someone was hungry right after having eaten, if someone lost the heel of their boot, or if someone threw rocks in a river they would die soon. Even a rusted lock was a bad sign.

In the last moments of death concern centered around a speedy and painless death. Much importance was placed on whether death came gradually as a result of illness, which was preferred, or without warning, which was seen as a punishment for sins or the result of some curse. Anyone who practiced witchcraft could not die peacefully. That individual would grind his teeth, holler out, cry, jump out of bed. The proverb *Jakie życie, taka smierć*, i.e., "as you live, so you will die," told it all. If a sick individual lingered, fell into a coma and then returned to wakefulness, it was also considered the doing of unnatural forces. On the other hand a long, lingering death was also dreaded. Prayers and litanies were said over the dying, so that God would either alter the course of events or grant them a speedy death. A *gromnica*, a candle blessed on the Feast of the Purification, was placed in the hand of the dying individual, and a scapular around the neck. In Sieradz, dying persons were dressed in things that were worn on their wedding days. Oftentimes the dying requested special songs to be sung such as the "*Gorzkie Żale*" (Bitter Sorrows) or "*Żegnam cię mój świecie wesoły*" (I'm saying goodbye to you happy earth).

Another custom was to have the family pay to have bells for the dying rung; these were called *dzwonki za konajacych*. On seeing their loved one undergoing a prolonged struggle with death, a member of the family would go to the parish church, monastery, or convent with the request to ring the bells. These bells were separate from those that hung in the church steeple; they were generally smaller and hung on the outside wall of the church or convent. The piercing sound of the bell called for those listening to pray for the dying individual by calling on the merciful Christ, through Our Lady of Sorrows, to grant the individual a release from their misery as well as a speedy death. Evidence of this custom is found in a song of the people of Wieliczka:

I dzwonili wielki dzwon
Żebym miała letki skon
Żebym miała letki skon.

And they rang the big bell
So that I might have an easy end, easy end

So that I might have an easy end.

Other attempts to ease the agony of the dying included the removal of the pillow from underneath the head, and placing the individual on the ground. In Kaszuby and Śląsk regions, the pillow was removed if it was made of chicken feathers for they prevented a peaceful death. Even if a pillow was made of goose or duck feathers, it was removed on the basis that if even one chicken feather accidently got into the pillow, it would preclude a restful passing.

Universal among Czechs, Serbs, and Poles was the custom of placing the dying individual on the ground. Its purpose was supposedly to assist the soul or spirit to go underground. The custom may have been a carry over from an ancient Christian custom of placing the dying on ashes on the ground in their penitential garb. In many areas of Poland, the dying individual was placed on the ground on a light bed of hay or straw. In some areas this was done even in the dead of winter. The individual would say confession and receive the last sacraments on this straw. In Małopolska, or Little Poland, this was done supposedly because straw was free from knots. Knots tied a soul to the body, making separation difficult. Fur and pea vines were also placed under such an individual.

Two more things were seen as causing a difficult death. One of these was the inability of the soul to find an opening. Windows and doors were opened and sometimes an opening was made in a thatched roof or a board was removed to allow the soul to go up to heaven; otherwise, it would knock about the interior of the house. The other was the belief that the loud crying and lamenting of the family interfered with allowing the person to die; the grieving family were expected to stop their loud wailing.

At the moment of death, there began a whole series of acts and practices whose purpose was to protect the departing soul from evil forces, and also protected the living from the dead. The first was that the deceased was removed from the bed and placed on a thick plank covered with straw which was propped up between two chairs. This plank was the object of much interest to the living since a great many Polish funeral songs referred to it:

> *Maciek zmarł, leży na desce*
> *A piłby jesce.*

> Maciek died and he lies on a plank
> But he'd still like a drink.

> *Umarł Maciek umarł*
> *Oj, leży na desce.*

> Maciek died
> And lies on a plank.

It was very common throughout Poland for the body to remain on the plank throughout the three days before burial; the body was placed in a coffin on the day of burial.

One of the most ancient and most important customs dealt with preparing and dressing the deceased. The body was washed clean so that the departed would be clean in his future travels. In some areas of Poland, assistance with washing the deceased was done by the same designated women who heated water with herbs of rue, myrtle, mugwort, or any of the herbs blessed on Blessed Mother of the Herbs (August 15). For this final washing, the women sang holy songs and called the individual by name, asking for his or her cooperation in dressing the stiffening body. In the case of an infant death, it was the godmother who washed and dressed the body.

In more ancient times, the deceased of Poland were dressed in special grave clothes, or a death shirt made from new cloth called a *koszula śmiertelna*. This death shirt, either white or gray in color, was given many different names, including *żgło*

(Kaszuby), *kitel, kiciel,* or *czeheł* (Poznań). Numerous songs sung by the living at the coffin refer to the seven yards of material lying in a coffin as one's final reward for the accounting of an entire life. The death shirt, reaching down to the ankles, had to be made of new cloth and without tears, for to bury someone with holes was to invite annihilation of the family line. If the deceased was an older male, a black ribbon was wrapped around the waist, neck, and wrists. If it was an unmarried or young man, a green ribbon was used. The women were dressed similarly except that a kerchief covered their heads and they wore stockings instead of socks.

The unmarried or young were dressed in much the same manner using a red ribbon but without any headdress. The same fabric was used to wrap the feet if the person was without boots or shoes; a special tall hat called a *duchna, duchenka,* or *szlafmyca* was also sewn. Among the very poor, in whose case buying even a few lengths of whole cloth was out of the question, the deceased was wrapped in a paper shroud and paper boots that were made especially for the poor and sold at church fairs and bazaars.

During the sewing of the death shirt, one had to be very cautious not to make any knots in the thread. Knots, used in curses and magical practices even in ancient Egypt and Babylonia, were seen as harmful, and not only in situations concerning death. The treatment for a fever that seemed to come and go, for instance, was to tie as many knots on a string or rope as one saw goslings for the first time in spring. While awaiting the return of the fever, the individual should undo the knots and the rope or string thrown into a fire. Knots were also used to conjure up abundance in the garden. One tied as many knots on a string as one wanted of a particular item, such as cucumbers, and then the knotted string was thrown into the cucumber patch. As many cucumbers would come forth as there were knots on the line.

A knot was avoided in the death shirt for fear the departed would return and demand that they be undone, that sins were tied within the knots, or that the deceased would feel the bumps from them and be uncomfortable and restless in the coffin, or that the deceased would have to untie the knots. If the thread wound itself frequently into knots while a shirt was sewn for an ill person, that person would soon die; but if the sewing went smoothly, the person would live. The needle sewing a death shirt was left in the shirt. Any leftovers from sewing the shroud were destroyed to prevent bringing anyone harm.

Over time, the death shirt fell out of use and the deceased began to be buried in their best Sunday clothes. Many individuals prepared for the moment of death by buying or preparing their burial clothes while still hale and hearty, never touching them throughout their lifetime. In Białystok, every good housewife prepared an entire outfit for herself and her husband while still in the height of health. One woman from Kielce ordered the making of her burial clothes — shirt, blouse, vest, kerchief and stockings — entirely in white. On two corners of the scarf the names Jesus and Mary were embroidered in black, and in the center was a cross. In Mazowsze, it was customary for a man to be buried in his boots. If it was impossible to put the boots on, they were placed at his side. The man was buried in his hat, the woman in her *czepek*, or cap. In the transition period between using the death shirt and that of using regular clothes, the deceased was often buried in both items. For instance, in Poznan the wife asked the women of the village to help her sew a death shirt that covered the deceased as far as the ankles. Under the death shirt the body was clothed in white pants, shirt, socks, and sometimes boots. The deceased wife was dressed in blouse, skirt, apron, stockings, and shoes and if the wife died young, a scarf was also wrapped around her neck. A young girl was dressed in a red or blue skirt, then the death shirt, with a wreath of rosemary on her head.

In many instances, young adults were dressed first in their wedding clothes and then covered with the death shirt. The girls were buried in their aprons, so that in the hereafter they could carry flowers to the Blessed Mother. Young girls were also covered with herbs and flowers. In Przemyśl, a young girl wore a wreath of myrtle and ribbons in her head, a rose ribbon around her waist, and a wax ring on the finger of her right hand. Sometimes the women were buried in two or three skirts; in case one wore out she would have another.

Death in the home called for a change in the running of the household. All work was suspended. No one spun wool or flax. Sweeping the floor or grinding grain was forbidden. All mirrors were covered — someone looking into a mirror at such a time might see the dead person there, and it would mean another death. Clocks were stopped, so that the soul could leave comfortably and because it disturbed the rest of the dead person. In some villages, it was believed that in a house where a dead person lay, no food or water should be left standing around, for the water would be contaminated and the bread would mold. In Kielce, it was believed that the dead souls washed themselves before leaving. Thus, all water was thrown out so the living would not use it. In Częstochowa, as a person lay dying in the home, the rest of the family often removed holy water, blessed herbs, and chalk from the Feast of Three Kings out of the house. In the event of death within the house all blessed things would lose their potency.

A home in which someone had died was considered unclean and had to be marked or identified in a special way in order to warn those entering or passing by. In Poland, as well as throughout Europe, this was usually done by nailing a black cloth to the front of the house. In some areas of Poland, a picture of the suffering souls in purgatory was attached to the black cloth in order to move those passing by to say a prayer. In Kujawy, a mourning banner obtained from the church was placed before the house. This banner was black if the deceased was an older married man or woman, green if a young man, and white if it was a young girl.

In Rzeszów, wooden shavings from planing the boards to make the coffin were thrown down before the house so that on seeing it the people would say an Eternal Rest. Among the Kaszuby, a young boy was sent from house to house, hitting the door with a stick or cane, calling out loudly "you're invited to view the body." In Puck, in this same area, a woman was chosen for the job of going from house to house, hitting each door with a hazel stick. In Śląsk, it was also done with a long stick against the door; the announcer would not enter the house in order to avoid bringing in death. In Radom, a board with skull and crossbones was sent from house to house with the name of the deceased passed along with it. In Lublin, a wooden cross, painted black, with Christ worked on a white metal plate nailed to the center of cross, was owned by the villagers. In the event of death, the closest relative notified the *sołtys*, the village administrator and, receiving the cross from him, would go to the first house saying, "Take the cross, so and so has died," and also mention when the funeral would take place. Those who accepted the news and the cross would go on to the next house and so forth, so that within an hour everyone knew all the particulars. In Krynice, one of the closest relatives gathered herbs called *ziele zimowe,* or winter herbs, and threw them on the doorstep of a house, calling out the name of the person who died. The neighbor was expected to move the herbs along to the rest of the community, which would eventually arrive back at the home of the deceased.

There were occasions when an elderly man might prepare his own coffin, keeping it in the attic. It was often filled with grain to remind him of the emptiness of this life. However, coffins were usually made on an as-needed basis by the local carpenter. Pay was not taken for the labor, as the carpenter saw this as the *ostatnia przysługa,* last favor, but the boards were either paid for or an exchange was made for some other item, such as goods from the field or orchard. Whatever method of payment was agreed upon, it behooved the family not to argue the cost of the coffin, for doing so would weigh heavily on the departed, who could still see and hear all that was going on.

The wood of choice throughout most of Poland was that from some type of "needle" or evergreen tree, such as in Poznań, where the coffin was made of pine. In picking out the boards for the coffin, it was important for them to be clean and without knots, for as many knots as are found, that many children would die. If a knot fell out, the deceased could look out through it and take someone with him to the hereafter, or the deceased could wiggle his finger through such a knothole at someone he wanted to take with him. The board used for a coffin was seen as having great powers. If someone wanted to see a vampire arise from the grave, one had to knock out a knothole from a plank taken from a coffin and look through it. A witch could be spotted in this same manner on the night of a new moon. Whoever looked through a knothole from a coffin on dancing couples during carnival time could see that behind every couple the devil was dancing.

The earliest coffins were made of plain wood, with a cross on the surface. Later on, they were painted different colors. Among the Kaszuby, the coffin for an adult was painted black; for children it was yellow. In Mazowsze and Krakow, coffins were left unpainted, with a black cross in the middle. On the top corners was written "in the name of Jesus." The bottom corners contained "Heart of Mary."

The washed and dressed body was placed between two chairs in the middle of the main room of the house, either remaining on a plank or, if it was customary, placed directly into the coffin. The pillow for the deceased, called *zagłówek*, was made of wood shavings or hay, to which was added wormwood, tansy, southernwood, mugwort, or thyme. In Białystok in the wintertime, wreaths made of the branches of a fir tree were placed under the head. A few coins were placed in the hand after being washed and told, "There, you have received payment. You have no reason to return." Money was also placed in the deceased's mouth in the left cheek, or wrapped in a cloth and placed under the left armpit. Besides placing a hymn book or rosary in the hands of the deceased, favorite articles enjoyed by the deceased were also included in the coffin; a favorite pipe filled with tobacco, a comb, a beautiful brooch or pin, an apple, or in the case of a drunkard, a bottle of vodka. Because friends saw each other in the hereafter, objects could be placed in the coffin for the express purpose of the deceased passsing it on to someone else. In Kielce, a mother distraught over her son's death had forgotten to put a favorite cross in the coffin. When his friend was being buried, she begged that she be able to include the forgotten cross and her request was granted. Very often children were buried with a toy and a picture of their patron saint, a woman with scissors and needle and thread. Along with any favorite objects, at least a few pinches of grain such as rye, barley, oats, and millet were included in the coffins of those being buried in the Rzeszów area.

Candles were lit and kept burning, especially during the first night. The people of the Kaszuby region felt that the burning candle helped the person find his way to heaven. In Radom, up to six candles burned continuously until such time as the body was removed from the house. In Rzeszów, the gromnica was used only during the day. In some areas, oil lamps obtained from the priest were burnt continuously.

Since it was believed that the soul stayed around the body for some unknown time both before and after the funeral, food and drink were left out in the open, as were a chair and a towel. This was especially true for the male head of a house. In Mazowsze, on the evening after the funeral, a chair was placed next to the door with the towel hung on the door. The deceased would return that night, sit on the chair, cry a lot, and use the towel to wipe his eyes. Having done this, the deceased would depart forever. In Poznań, where this was done immediately, a holy picture of one of the saints was pinned to the towel, so that the deceased would have someone to protect and defend him until such time as the body was removed. It was also in Poznań that a small table was placed beside the coffin on which a shot glass of vodka and a piece of bread and butter were placed, so that the deceased could have a bite to eat on the long road to eternity. Sometimes meat, cheese, and beer were left out, as was a boiled wheat called *kutia*, served with poppy and honey. The Górale left out vodka and bread for an older person and honey and bread for a child.

The leaving of food out for the dead gradually evolved into a repast for relatives and friends; feeding them would be the same as feeding the dead person. As villagers came to view the deceased, they first knelt at the side or foot of the coffin to say a prayer. Upon rising, they greeted the family, who then offered a shot of vodka to each person. While partaking of this liquid refreshment, there was often talk of the circumstances around the death, mutual lamentations over the loss, etc. In Białystok, people coming to visit the deceased would help themselves to the food from the table standing next to the deceased as well as a shot of vodka. If there was kutia on the table eveyone was expected to take a taste. This food partaken at the coffin was called stypa.

Those who came to visit the deceased often stayed for the wake either on all three nights that the body was laid out, or on the last night. The wake was called *pusty wieczór*, or pusta noc, the empty night, supposedly making reference to the house being empty without the individual. It was also called straż nocna or opłakanka. Chroniclers from the fifteenth century note that on the day of death, family, friends, and beggars gathered at the house to cry and sing over the deceased. Some areas upheld the ancient custom of continuous singing, from the time the body was dressed until burial. Singing had the magical power to prevent bad spirits from snatching up the soul of the departed. It was the role of the beggars to initiate and maintain the bulk of lamenting, praying, and singing, with others present taking up the refrains or providing background humming. The importance of the dziady or beggars in death and funeral customs is highlighted in the proverb: *na każdym weselu swat, na każdym pogrzebie dziad.* (At every wedding an intermediary, at every funeral a beggar.) Popular songs during the wake were *"Do Ciebie Panie,"* (To you, Oh Lord)" *Kto się w opiekę,"* (He who seeks your protection) and after every song an eternal rest was recited.

Sitting together all night required strengthening with coffee and bread. Vodka was also imbibed; the women took it with a spoon from a bowl while the men used a bottle and shot glasses. As a result, the night often became boisterous, with the living trying to drag the deceased into the drinking and merriment by pouring vodka on his or her lips. To keep awake, the group told riddles and/or engaged in card playing. In the villages of the Kaszuby region, the wake was done in shifts. At 9 P.M., a group gathered around the deceased, either kneeling or sitting, singing songs and saying prayers. At 1 A.M., they were fed and continued on until 3 A.M., when another group arrived. If the deceased had an enemy with whom he never reconciled during his life, the arrival of this enemy for the wake was regarded as a pardon. The wake had more to its purpose than simply keeping the deceased company. One had to watch whether the face of the deceased changed or took on a reddish hue. If this happened, the deceased was a *wieszczym,* or vampire, and his head had to be cut off.

When it came time for the funeral and the removal of the departed one, all the neighbors and friends filed by to say their final goodbye. The traditional signal of farewell by the women was the placing of their hand on the coffin. The men reached out and lightly placed their cap on it. Prayers were led by the beggars, as well as a song, which began with *"Zmarły człowiecze z tobą się żegnamy"* (Departed person, we are saying goodbye to you), with the rest of the group chiming in.

The body was moved out of the house, with the coffin still open if local custom dictated that it be closed at the cemetery, or it was nailed closed before it left the house. Whichever custom

DEATH CUSTOMS

prevailed, metal nails were never used to close the coffin. Wooden pegs were fashioned by the carpenter and used instead. The coffin was taken out feet first. Similar to the customs of the Russians, Czechs, and Germans, those carrying out the coffin would hit it against the doorway three times as a way of the deceased saying goodbye to the house for the last time. Once over the threshold, the coffin was placed on the ground temporarily and water was poured behind it. This was done in case the soul wanted to return. It would find crossing a body of water more difficult, for everyone knew that death eschewed water. The people of Mazowsze placed an ax at the doorsills and if the coffin was being carried on a gate, an ax and lock was placed on it.

The doors and windows to the house were left open, as were trunks and chests of drawers. Anything that locked or closed was opened in case the soul was still lingering about and to prevent it from being locked in by mistake. Sometimes the stables and barn doors were also opened. On the other hand, in some villages everything was closed up tight, so that the soul could not return.

If it was the *gospodarz*, the head of the house, that was being buried, it was imperative that the cattle and bees be notified of the demise of the owner. The Kaszuby drove the cattle out of the barn and shook the beehives, or else it was believed both would fall into a deep sleep called the death sleep. If the weather didn't allow for this, someone at least went forth and announced to them that their master died and was being removed from the house. In Greater Poland, when the coffin was removed from the house, the carriers — usually anyone except family members who should not get too close to the deceased — would stop before the barn, the cow shed and pigsty, hitting the doorways as a way for the owner to say goodbye to all the living things he was leaving behind. If this was not done, the animals could sicken and die. Someone would run out and knock on a fruit tree or a beehive saying, "your master is leaving now." If by some oversight the cow had been out to pasture and didn't get a chance to say goodbye, the cow was be sold as quickly as possible because it would soon sicken.

How the funeral was conducted depended on how much money the family wished or could afford to spend. It was an expensive venture to bury someone with all the proper marks of respect. The cost was a matter that often caused such bitter quarrels between the clergy and parish that in 1740, the bishop of Kraków, "heeding the great quarrels between parish and priest" issued a circular standardizing the cost of a funeral which included:

Funeral procession beyond the church—10 pennies
Accompanying the deceased from the home—20 pennies
Mass sung—3 pennies
Altar boys in dalmatics—15 pennies
Each candle burnt during the funeral mass—6 pennies

Instructions for the family were sometimes left by the deceased, either verbally or in their last will and testament. One Krzysztof Szczedrowski, a fairly well-to-do nobleman of the sixteenth century, left these instructions: "The funeral should be conducted in a modest manner, without pomp and without a funeral feast, summoning as many beggars as possible and the parish priest for the procession for which both are to receive alms for my soul. Do not carry my body in a wagon but by six beggars for which each is to receive a pair of hard dollars. At my funeral, I beg of you, no sermon."

The funeral also depended on whether the village could boast a church and cemetery. If both were nearby, the coffin was often carried on a gate or the shoulders of friends or neighbors. If not, the coffin was placed on a wagon (also an extra cost if the family was so poor as to not own their own) with straw, and slowly taken directly to the cemetery or, if it could be afforded, to the church. Oftentimes, the funeral procession had to travel some distance to reach this neighboring village. Nine kilometers was not an unusual distance. A whip was not allowed to be used to move the animal along. A long stick, with willow being the preferred wood, was used instead.

In Poznań, in the event of the death of a young man or girl, a wreath was carried in front of the funeral procession. In some villages, four girls carried a wreath made of flowers and white or blue ribbon on a silk scarf. In winter, the wreath was made of evergreen branches or myrtle. If it was a small boy that died, the coffin was carried by four girls dressed in white, each wearing a green wreath on their heads; a girl was carried by boys dressed in their finest clothes. Sometimes a white sheet was placed over the coffin, with a loaf of bread placed on top of the sheet. This bread was usually given to a beggar. Family and friends walked ahead singing "*Witaj Królowo Nieba*" (Hail, Holy Queen) or "*Najśw. Panna Maryja, tyś śliczniejsza niż lelija.*"(Most Holy Mary, you're more beautiful than a lily). The funeral procession was sometimes accompanied by a choir and musical instruments if any were to be had.

As the funeral procession arrived at the crossroads leading out of the village, or at one of the roadside shrines that dot the Polish countryside, everyone stopped. If it was the norm, the top was lifted off the coffin so that everyone could see the deceased for the last and final time. The other, more important reason for stopping at this juncture, was for the *odpraszanie* or *przemowa pożegalna*, the goodbye or forgiveness speech. This speech was usually conducted by the eldest of the family, the village administrator, or some respected individual who knew the appropriate words. The individual bowed to those present and, speaking for the deceased, asked forgiveness of any transgressions the deceased may have committed against them. With slight variations, the text ran something like this:

"If there is among the gathered here someone who feels resentment towards our departed, I ask you in his or her name to listen to my words and grant forgiveness for any offenses: I ask my wife to forgive me if during my life I offended her. Dear children and friends, I am a sinful fellow and if I have offended you please pardon me as I overlook your hurts and offenses."

In other speeches, the deceased also went on to thank the earth that held him, the sun that warmed him, and the water which refreshed and invigorated him. It's overall true purpose, however, was to come to some amicable terms with his fellow man. The people generally responded with, "there is nothing to forgive" or "may he rest in peace." Sometimes vodka was passed around during the speech as a goodwill gesture. In some villages, the funeral procession stopped at each shrine along the way. Prayers were said not only for the currently deceased but also for whoever it was that had commissioned or erected the shrine.

Transporting the dead body to another village was not without its problems and concerns. According to beliefs, the dead body should not cross over a body of water such as a river, or else the area would be visited by hunger or some other misfortune. If the deceased was taken from one village through many others, then it was believed that hail would fall in all those villages through which it crossed. After a funeral, if there were floods, the deceased was believed to be a vampire.

In larger villages containing a church and cemetery, a mass was said, if it could be afforded, and the forgiveness speech done at any wayside shrine between the church and cemetery, or sometimes at the gate leading into the cemetery. At its conclusion, most of the funeral procession turned back home, admonished by the speaker to go home and not to look around, for whoever looked around would meet up with the dead person in the night. Only the immediate family and sometimes the priest accompanied the body to its final resting place. Others believed that the family was not to attend the cemetery, with the burial left to others. For instance, a mother who lost her firstborn child was not to go to the cemetery, or else no other child of hers would live.

At the gravesite, there were more prayers and songs, such as "*Salve Regina*" (Save, Oh Queen) and " *Zesłał ci Pan Jesus dwóch aniołów z nieba"*(Jesus sent you two angels from the heavens). Once the coffin was lowered into the grave those present—with the exception of the family members—were expected to throw dirt on the grave. At this critical moment, the deceased could take family members to the grave if they took part in this ceremony. The people of Kaszuby claimed that after death the soul went to its judgment, then returned to the body and stayed there until such time as the priest threw a handful of dirt on the grave. In Zabnie, as long as the body remained in the house, the doors were not locked because before the soul could go to the Creator, it first had to spend a night with St. Barbara. Those who never prayed to St. Barbara, however, would not be let in, so the soul had to sleep on her doorstep and then go to the Creator. If the Creator had judged already, the soul returned to his body until such a time as the priest showered dirt on the coffin. The soul would then go to St. Peter to find out its fate: this side or that (heaven or hell). In Krynica, the soul spent the first night with St. Barbara, the second with St. Tekla, and the third with St. Catherine. Before receiving final judgment it had to visit all the holy saints it had never called upon during its lifetime.

Tombstones marked the graves of those of some standing in the community, such as a priest, church organist, teacher, or doctor. The most common grave marker was a wooden cross made of birch containing the name of the deceased, date of death, and requests for prayers, if the family could pay to have the inscription engraved in the wood. Even more common than a wooden cross was the planting of a particular shrub or plant. Southernwood, periwinkle, daisies, roses, peonies, rue, or a favorite flower enjoyed by the deceased was used to mark the grave. Those who were murdered or committed suicide, women who died in childbirth, and children who died without benefit of baptism were buried separately off to the side of the cemetery. Boxthorn was planted for those who were murdered. In Mazowsze, the custom for those passing the grave of someone who was murdered was to throw down a loose branch, a handful of straw, or twigs upon the grave. When there were enough branches, a fire was lit, helping to cleanse the soul of the murdered.

On the return trip from the cemetery, in those instances where a body was transported to another village for burial, straw was placed at the borders, so that in case the deceased returned, he had some place to take a rest. This straw was called *słoma zmartych*. On returning home, the wagon was turned upside down so that the soul could not cling to it in any way. The room where the deceased lay was swept out, and the sweepings discarded in an out-of-the-way spot not tread upon by man.

The last custom associated with the funeral day was the funeral feast. After the grave was filled, everyone returned home, put away their hymnals, took off their best clothes, put on something less showy but respectable, and then returned to the home of the deceased. In the fifteenth century, the funeral feast was called *uczta pogrzebowa*, and in the sixteenth century it was called *stypa*. It was also called *boży obiadek*, god's dinner and *konsolacja*, consolation.

The most ancient food associated with funerals was *kasza*, or porridge, made of millet or some other grain, such as rye or barley. With honey poured over it, the dish was seen as holy food, the best of all possible foods. At a funeral, it was served only to the dziad or beggar who was eating for the deceased. The rest of the assembled mourners received a meal that was as generous and filling as finances allowed. Vodka with honey was passed around with a "may he rest in peace" uttered at every hoist of the shot glass. In this situation, the people of Kaszuby said: *na te smutki, napijemy się wódki.* (For these sorrows, we will drink vodka.)

If the funeral was for a young bachelor or maiden, the funeral feast was called *bal* or ball, *ostatnie wesele*, last wedding, or *wesele nieboszczyka*, wedding for the deceased. In Śląsk, the funeral feast for the young and unmarried was simply wesele or wedding. The house was decorated with wreaths and green branches because it was seen as a wedding day, and friends, relatives, and those carrying the coffin were invited to eat, drink, and dance.

In the Kraków and Kurpie regions, the mourners retired to the local tavern for tea, vodka, or, if the family was well off, wine. Food was brought in by the family and shared by everyone present. Under the influence of alcohol, the somber mood lightened and the event quickly became a merry repast extolling the fine virtues of the deceased. From the Tarnóow-Rzeszow region of Poland, a funeral song done in 2/4 time eulogized poor deceased Maciek:

Umar Maciek umar
juz go nie staje
odpuść jemu grzechy
miłościwy Panie!
Umiał nas uciesyć
Umiał pięknie śpiewać
lubił cęsto także
w karcmie przesiadywać
Piwa cęsto kupił
Każdy się z nim upił
Już teraz do karczmy
niema poco śpiesyć
Maciek już nie przyjdzie
Kto nas będzie ciesyć?
Już nam nie kupi piwa
Oto pożałujmy wszyscy,
mili bracia karczmarz i karczmarka
Już wszystko ustało
Gdy Maćka nie stało.

Maciek died
he is no longer with us
forgive him his sins

Merciful Lord!
He knew how to cheer us up
he knew how to sing beautifully
he also frequently liked
to sit around the tavern
often buying us beers
everybody got drunk with him
Now to the tavern there is no need to hurry
Maciek will no longer come
Who will make us merry?
He will no longer sing for us
no longer buy us a beer.
We ought to feel sad
every one of us
dear brothers, tavern keeper, and tavern keepers wife
everything has ceased
since Maciek is deceased.

The color of mourning in the Poland of old was white. If the deceased was unmarried, the family followed the corpse dressed in red. White flowers were mourning flowers. The women of Kaszuby wore a white mourning coat over their clothes. In Poznań, a white sheet or cloth was thrown over their heads and back. In Krynica, women wore white beads as a sign of mourning. Red was forbidden in some areas for a whole year and six Sundays. Sometimes families held very rigid mourning periods, avoiding public houses and dancing. If a wedding had been planned, it was conducted without dance or music. Women could not marry for a year, while men were not tied to a mourning period and could take a wife soon after the funeral. In some villages, mourning for a father took place for a year; a mother demanded a year and six Sundays, and none was required for a husband or wife. Red was avoided during mourning. Black was chosen for a head scarf with blue, lavender, and gray as indicative of half mourning.

DEATH CUSTOMS

Masses for the dead were often said on the 3rd, 7th, 9th, and 40th day after death. On the first anniversary of the death, a large meal was sometimes held, with a cow or pig being slaughtered for the occasion, a portion of which was given to the priest and organist for saying a Mass. Relatives and beggars were invited to the Mass and to the house afterwards to eat and sing until noon. In the afternoon, friends were invited to also eat and drink.

Bibliography

Biegelsen Henryk. *Wesele.* [Wedding]; Lwów: Nakładem Instytutu Stauropigjanskiego, 1929.

Biegelsen, Henryk. *U kolebki, przed ołtarzem, nad mogiłą.* [At the Cradle, Before the Altar, Over the Grave]; Lwów: Nakładem Instytutu Stauropigjańskiego, 1929.

Biegelsen, Henryk. *Śmierc.* [Death]; Lwów: Dom Kziążki Polskiej S-KA AKC, 193-.

Biegelsen, Henryk. *Matka i Dziecko.* [Mother and Child]; Lwów: Nakładem Towarzystwa Wydawniczego Ateneum, 1927.

Brückner, Aleksander. *Dzieje Kultury Polskiej. Tom I* Warszawa: Książka i Wiedza, 1958.

Bystroń, Jan S. *Słowiańskie Obrzędy Rodzinne.* [Slavic Family Customs]; Krakow: Akademia Umiejętnosci, 1916.

Bystroń, Jan S. *Dzieje Obyczajów w Dawnej Polsce. Wiek XVI-XVIII Tom II.* [History of the Customs in Old Poland. 16th to 18th Century. Vol.II]; Warszawa: Państwowy Instytut Wydawniczy, 1976.

Bystroń, Jan S. *Zwyczaje Żniwiarskie w Polsce.* [Harvest Customs of Poland]; Krakow: Skład Główny w Księgarni G. Gebethnera, 1916.

Chętnikowa, Jadwiga. *"Wielkanocne Palmy Kurpiowskie i Konkursy w Łysem"* [Kurpie Easter Palms and Competitions in Łysem]. Polska Sztuka Ludowa NR 1. 1980 p.15-20.

POLISH CUSTOMS, TRADITIONS AND FOLKLORE

Ciszewski, Stanisław. *Prace Etnologiczne. Tom I-IV.* [Ethnographic Studies. Volumes 1-4]; Warszawa: Wydawnictwo Kasy Im. Mianowskiego, 1925.

Czaja, Stanisław. "Zapusty."[Carnival]; *Lud* Tom 12 1906 p.35-56.

Dekowski, Jan. *Folklor Ziemi Łęczyckiej.* [Folkore of the Łęczyce Area]; Warszawa: Wydawnictwa Centralnego Ośrodka Metodyki Upowszechniania Kultury, 1981.

Domańska-Kubiak, I. "Wegetacyjny Sens Kolendowania." [Going Caroling]; *Polska Sztuka Ludowa,* NR 1 1979, p.17-32

Fischer, Adam. *Lud Polski* [The Polish People]. Lwów: Wydawnictwo Zakładu Narodowego Im. Ossolinskich, 1926.

Fischer, Adam. *Etnografia Słowianska. T.III-Polacy.* [Ethnography of the Slavs]; Lwów-Warszawa: Książnica-Atlas, 1934.

Fischer, Adam. *Zwyczaje Pogrzebowe.* [Burial Customs]; Lwów: Nakładem Zakładu Narodowego Im. Ossolinskich, 1921.

Ginalska, Maria. *Polskie Boże Narodzenie.* [Polish Christmas]; Londyn: B.Swiderski, 1961.

Gloger, Zygmunt. *Badacz Przeszłości Ziemi Ojczystej.* [Researching the Past of the Native Land]; Warszawa: Panstwowe Wydawnictwo Naukowe, 1978.

Gloger, Zygmunt. *Encyklopedia Staropolska Tom I-IV.*[Encyclopedia of Old Poland]; Warszawa: Wiedza Powszechna, 1985.

Gloger, Zygmunt. *Rok Polski.* [The Polish Year]; Warszawa: Jan Fiszer, 1900.

Gołębiowski, Łukasz. *Lud Polski; jego zwyczaje, zabobony.*- [The Polish People: Their Customs and Superstitions]. Warszawa: w drukarni A. Gałęzowski i Spolki, 1830.

Janicka-Krzywda, U. *Rok Karpacki-obrzędy doroczne w Karpatach Polskich.* [The Carpathian Year-Yearly

BIBLIOGRAPHY

Traditions in the Polish Carpathians]; Warszawa-Kraków:
Wydawnictwo PTTK "Kraj," 1988.
Kamocki, Franciszek. *Atlas Polskich Strojów Ludowych: Strój
Świętokrzyski*. [Atlas of Polish Folk Dress: The Holy
Cross Mountain Area]; Wrocław: Polskie Towarzystwo
Ludoznawcze, 1961.
Kamykowski, Zbigniew. "Kilka Słów o Kolędach Polskich,"
[A few words about Polish Carols]; *Polska Sztuka
Ludowa*, N.1-2, 1949, p.44-50.
Karwicka, Teresa. "Rózgi Weselne z Lubelszczyzny," [The
Wedding Rod in Lublin Area]; *Polska Sztuka Ludowa*,
N.3 1958, p.175-177.
Kolberg, Oskar. *LUD. Jego zwyczaje, sposób życia, mowa,
podania, przysłowia, obrzędy, gusła, zabawy, pieśni,
muzyka i tance. Tom 1-48* [The People. Their traditions,
Manner of Living, Speech, Proverbs, Customs,
Witchcraft, Entertainment, Songs, Music and Dance.
Volumes 1-48]; Krakow: Polskie Towarzystwo
Ludoznawcze, w drukarni Universytetu Jagiellonskiego,
1871-1890.
Kotula, Franciszek. *Atlas Polskich Strojów Ludowych:Strój
Rzeszowski*. [Atlas of Polish Folk Dress: Rzeszów];
Lublin: Polskie Towarzystwo Ludoznawcze, 1951.
Krzyżanowski, J. *Słownik Folkloru Polskiego.* [Dictionary of
Polish Folklore]; Warszawa; Wiedza Powszechna, 1965.
Kurek, J. "Mikołaje-obrzęd doroczny we wsiach Beskidu
Śląskiego," [St. Nicholas Day-an Annual Custom in
Villages of the Silesian Beskids]; *Polska Sztuka Ludowa*
N.4 1973, p. 199-206.
Kwaśniewicz, K. "Zwyczaje i obrzędy doroczne," [Yearly
Customs and Traditions]; *Etnografia Polska* T. XXVIII
z.I 1984 p.157-199.
Łuczkowski, Jan. "Primitywne Instrumenty Muzyczne i
Zabawki Dźwiękowe na terenie Opoczyńskiego,"
[Primitive Musical Instruments and Ringing Toys in the

POLISH CUSTOMS, TRADITIONS AND FOLKLORE

Opoczno region]; *Łódzkie Studia Etnograficzne,* Tom XXVI 1984 p.83-89.

Marlewski, Franciszek, Redaktor. *Rok Boży.* [God's Year]; Katowice: Wydawnictwo Św. Stanisława, 1932.

Mikułowska, Halina. *Atlas Polskich Strojów Ludowych: Strój Kujawski.* [Atlas of Polish Folk Dress; the Kujawy]; Poznań: Polskie Towarzystwo Ludoznawcze, 1953.

Muzynski, Jan. *Roslinne Leki Ludowe.* [Plants in Folk Medicine]; Warszawa: Ludowa Spółdzielna Wydawnicza, 1958.

Olędzki, Jacek. "Doroczne pieczywo obrzędowe północno-wschodniej Polski," [The Annual Baking of Ritual Cakes in South-East Poland]; *Polska Sztuka Ludowa,* N.1, 1961 p.3-23

Reinfuss, Roman. "Architektura Szopki Krakowskiej," [Architecture of Cracow cribs]; *Polska Sztuka Ludowa,* N.11-12, 1948 p.8-24.

Seweryn, Tadeusz. *Tradycje i Zwyczaje Krakowskie.* [Traditions and customs of Cracow]; Kraków; Wydawnictwo Artystyczno Graficzne, 1961.

Seweryn, Tadeusz. *Podłaźniki.* Krakow; Nakładem Muzeum Etnograficznego w Krakowie, 1932.

Stelmachowska, Bożena. *Rok Obrzędowy Na Pomorzu.* [Yearly Customs in the Pomorze Area]; Toruń; Zakład Główny: Kasa Im. Mianowskiego-Instytut Popierania, 1933.

Szewczyk, Hanna. "Rózga Weselna:Poszukiwanie Formuły Interpretacyjnej," [The Wedding Rod: the Search for a manner of interpretation]; *Polska Sztuka Ludowa,* N.1-2, 1983 p.89-94.

Udziela, Marjan. *Medycyna i Przesądy Lecznicze Ludu Polskiego.* [Medicine and Superstitions Healing of the Polish People]; Warszawa: Skład Główny w Księgarni M. Arcta, 1891.

BIBLIOGRAPHY

Zadrożyńska, Anna. *Powtarzać czas początku*. [Repeating the Time of the Past]; Warszawa: Wydawnictwo Spółdzielcze, 1985.

Ethnographic Regions

I. Pomorze/Kaszuby (Pomerania)—located along the shore of the Baltic Sea

II. Wielkopolska (Great Poland)—western Poland bordering on Germany. Includes Poznań and areas of Odra and Warta Rivers

    a. Kujawy
    b. Łęczyce

III. Małopolska (Little Poland) — southeastern Poland

    a. Kielce
    b. Łódz
    c. Radom
    d. Kraków
    e. Podhale
    f. Biłgoraj
    g. Podlasie
    h. Lublin
    i. Sandomierz
    j. Rzeszów

IV. Mazowsze (Mazovia)—central Poland

    a. Kurpie—northeastern Poland at the meeting of Narew and Bug rivers.
    b. Łowicz

c. Podlasie

V. Śląsk (Silesia) — area bordering on northwestern Czecho-slovakia and Germany

Pronunciation Guide

a as in father
ą as in the French word "bon"
e as in whey
i as the e in jeep
o as in oh
ó as the two o's in loop
u as in suit
y as the i in kid
c followed by any vowel except for i is pronounced ts
c followed by i or accented as ć is pronounced like the
    ch in church with the i sound stressed
ch is like the ch in loch as pronounced by a Scot
cz is pronounced like the ch in cho-choo
dz is pronounced like the J in John
dż like g as in hinge or j in jam
l as in ale
ł as like the wl in howl with a pronounced w sound
ś or s followed by an i is pronounced ssh
sz as in the sh in sheep
w as a v
z as in zebra

There is no q, v, or x in the Polish language

Brief Glossary of Terms

bocian (boh-tchan), stork

boże ciało, feast of Corpus Christi

boże narodzenie (boh-zhe nahrrhod-zenya), birth of Christ; Christmas Day

dożynki (doh-shyn-kee), harvest celebration

dyngus (din-goose), custom of dousing someone with water or striking with a green branch on Easter Monday

dziad (jhad), beggar; also a type of ancient Christmas decoration made of straw

gaik (guy-eek), any green branch used in the celebration of spring

góral (goo-rral), the people living in the south of Poland along the Tatra mountains

gregorjanek (greg-or-yan-ek), celebration of the feast of St. Gregory by school children

gromnica (grom-knee-tsa), a candle blessed on the Feast of the Purification (Feb.2) used to ward of lightning, sickness

herody (herr-odeh), live, theatrical production depicting the last day of King Herod

jasełka, Christmas caroling with a portable manger scene and/or live performances depicting Herod ordering the slaughter of innocent children

koleda (koh-lend-a), a Christmas song; it can also mean a Christmas gift

kołacz (co-watch), special bread baked for a wedding

kutia (koot-ja), ancient cereal dish traditionally eaten on Christmas Eve

gospodarz (god-spud-ahsh), master of the house

gospodyni (goh-spud-inni), housewife, lady of the house

oczepiny (oh-chep-eeny), capping ceremony held at a wedding

opłatek (oh-pwa-tek), blessed wafer traditionally shared on Christmas Eve

Pasterka (pas-tear-ka), the Shepherd's Mass; midnight Mass on Christmas Eve

pierniki (pierre-neekee), honey and spice cookies usually baked for Christmas season

pisanki (pee-san-kee), decorated Easter eggs

podkradania (pud-kra-don-ya), custom of good natured stealing that took place on New Year's Day

podłażnik (pud-waz-neek), ancient Christmas bough

nowe latki (nove lotkee), specially baked bread in the shape of barnyard animals usually made for the New Year

ostatki (oh-stat-kee), name given to the three days before Ash Wednesday

sobótka (soo-boot-kah), midsummer solstice celebration

święconka (shvyen-tson-ka), basket filled with bread, butter and some type of pork that was taken to church on Holy Saturday to be blessed and then eaten on Easter morning

szczodraki (schtzod-ra-kee), special cookie made for the Feast of Three Kings

wigilia (vee-gee-leeah), Christmas Eve supper

wywód (vi-vood), ritual cleansing following a six week isolation period after the birth of a baby

zapusty (zah-poost-eh), carnival period before Lent

zielone świątki (ze-lon-eh sh-fee-yunt-kee), Pentecost or Green Holidays

Index

INDEX

POLISH CUSTOMS, TRADITIONS AND FOLKLORE

INDEX

INDEX

INDEX

POLISH CUSTOMS, TRADITIONS AND FOLKLORE

INDEX

INDEX